STRAVINSKY

Roman Vlad

Translated from the Italian by Frederick Fuller

THIRD EDITION

Oxford University Press

Oxford University Press, Walton Street, Oxford OX2 6DP

London New York Toronto
Delhi Bombay Calcutta Madras Karachi
Kuala Lumpur Singapore Hong Kong Tokyo
Nairobi Dar es Salaam Cape Town
Melbourne Auckland
and associated companies in
Beirut Berlin Ibadan Mexico City Nicosia

Oxford is a trade mark of Oxford University Press

Published in the United States
by Oxford University Press, New York

Italian edition © Giulio Einaudi 1974
English edition © Oxford University Press 1978

First English edition 1960
Second English edition 1967
Third English edition 1978
Third English edition first published in paperback 1985

Acknowledgements are due to Boosey and Hawkes Ltd
for permission to quote numerous musical examples; to
Faber & Faber Ltd for permission to quote from
Conversations with Stravinsky by Robert Craft; to Victor
Gollancz Ltd for permission to quote from Chronicle
of My Life by Igor Stravinsky; and to Harvard
University Press and Oxford University Press for
permission to quote from The Poetics of Music by
Igor Stravinsky.

British Library Cataloguing in Publication Data
Vlad, Roman
Stravinsky.—3rd ed.
1. Stravinsky, Igor 2. Composers—United
States—Biography
I. Title II. Stravinsky, English
780'.92'4   ML410.S932
ISBN 0-19-315445-5

Library of Congress Cataloging in Publication Data
Vlad, Roman, 1919–
Stravinsky.
Translation of: Stravinsky.
Bibliography: p.
Includes indexes.
1. Stravinsky, Igor, 1882–1971. 2. Composers—
Biography. I. Title.
ML410.S932V52 1985 . 780'.92'4 [B] 84-27171
ISBN 0-19-315445-5 (pbk.)

Printed in Great Britain by
J. W. Arrowsmith Ltd, Bristol

Foreword

In 1955 the Radiotelevisione Italiana invited me to present the complete works of Igor Stravinsky on its 'Third Programme' in a series of nineteen broadcasts running from December 1955 to April 1956. To anyone unacquainted with the economics of programme building, nineteen broadcasts devoted to the works of a single contemporary composer may seem an enormous number; as it turned out, the series was hardly long enough to provide a comprehensive picture of Stravinsky's vast output. The material collected for the broadcasts was supplemented and enlarged in scope, and substantially revised, and the outcome was the first Italian edition of this book, published in 1958.

For the first English edition, published in 1960, the book was revised and brought up to date, and a new chapter, on *Threni*, was added. The second English edition appeared in 1967. This was again revised where necessary, with new introductory material and a new long chapter on the works written by Stravinsky between 1959 and 1966.

For this new edition, the second Italian and the third English, the entire text has been further revised and in many points supplemented and expanded. Particular account has been taken of the six volumes published by Stravinsky in collaboration with Robert Craft, the last interviews with Stravinsky, and what Craft has written on the subject since Stravinsky's death. A new chapter has been added which deals, I hope satisfactorily, with this great composer's latest works and his thinking during the last years of his life.

It is my profound belief that the relationship between the compositions of Stravinsky and Schoenberg is one of the most important aspects of music during the first part of the twentieth century. In previous editions of the book I started with a brief discussion of the question before commencing my account of Stravinsky's early works. In the present edition I have handled the matter somewhat differently. Firstly, the gradual stages by which Stravinsky took up a serialist position are described at length in their chronological place in the book. This means that, work for work, more pages are devoted to the late compositions than to earlier ones – and this, as I say, reflects my view of the importance of the change which was taking place. Secondly, I have added an appendix in which some of the general features of the relationship between Stravinsky and Schoenberg are discussed. In this way I have, it is hoped, been able to set out my views without obtruding on the general narrative of my account.

Roman Vlad

Florence, October 1975

Contents

Contents

I The Early Years

The beginnings of contemporary music were marked by the necessity to go beyond the traditional tonal harmonic system based on the major and minor scales of seven notes. None of the innovators achieved this aim immediately, not even Stravinsky. Masterpieces like *Petrushka* or *The Rite of Spring* may give all the appearance of a spontaneous iconoclastic outburst of a kind never known before; but actually these works were the sequel to a whole series of what might be called preliminary essays, whose main characteristic is that they enabled Stravinsky to assimilate the basic elements of tradition while at the same time gradually bringing to maturity those particular qualities from which his own personal style ultimately evolved. In Schoenberg the gradual maturing of formal devices, the steady acquisition of mastery over his personal musical idiom, is everywhere evident. But with Stravinsky the process is rather one of slow incubation, until all of a sudden the personality of the artist bursts forth with dazzling splendour. Signs of this process of assimilation and unconscious growth can be discerned as far back as the work which Stravinsky called his opus 1 : the Symphony in E flat, written in 1906-7, while he was studying with Rimsky-Korsakov. Prior to the Symphony, between 1903 and 1904, Stravinsky composed a piano sonata in four movements : Allegro, Andante, Scherzo, Finale. It is dedicated to the pianist Nicola Richter, and it was performed by him for the first time in Rimsky-Korsakov's private circle (9 February 1905) and subsequently at a public concert of contemporary music in St. Petersburg. The manuscript, which was given to Richter, was never published and appears to have been lost. The composer must have felt that the work was not sufficiently mature to warrant publication. In fact, in *Memories and Commentaries*, he refers to this youthful composition, which he hardly remembered, as 'fortunately lost', and as 'I suppose, an inept imitation of late Beethoven'. It is probably of no great intrinsic interest as a piano sonata; however, if only because of the orthodoxy of its formal structure, it does perhaps give us a first glimpse of a classical

bent which in Stravinsky lay dormant for many years until it came
very much to the fore in the compositions of the period immediately
following the First World War. It is also highly significant that late
Beethoven was to be the ultimate spiritual solace of Stravinsky's
declining years.

Stravinsky was born at Oranienbaum in 1882. There is some con-
fusion over the actual date of his birth as given by his biographers.
Casella gives the date as 18 June 1882[1] whereas the symposium
Stravinsky in the Theatre[2] published in the same year states that
Stravinsky was born on 17 June 1882. This date is also given by
Strobel.[3] In the *Dizionario di Musica* of A. Della Corte and G. M.
Gatti the date is given as 5 June 1882. De' Paoli gives both dates,
5 and 18 June 1882.[4] The explanation of the discrepancy is the
difference of thirteen days (fourteen in the last century) between
the dates as reckoned according to the Julian calendar used until
recently in certain countries of the Orthodox Eastern Church, and
the same dates reckoned according to the western calendar. 5 June
'Old Style' is of course the date according to the Julian calendar. In
Russia, this was St. Igor's day.

As regards Stravinsky's ethnic origin, too, there is some discrepancy
among the various biographers. Many of them more or less explicitly
state that the family was of Russian origin. Others, like Lindlar,
hold the view that 'on both sides Stravinsky's ancestors were landed
gentry of unmixed blood from Little Russia', i.e. the Ukraine.[5]
The statement that Stravinsky's ancestry on his father's side was
Polish is made *inter alia* by Malipiero and Tansman.[6]

This is the truth of the matter, as I learned personally from the
composer himself. In fact Stravinsky mentioned his Polish origin as
a possible reason for his spiritual leaning towards Catholicism, since
the Poles are of course fervent adherents to the Roman Catholic
Church. In the chapter on Stravinsky's sacred music I shall have
occasion to discuss this leaning towards Catholicism on Stravinsky's
part – though unlike his sons, who became Catholics, he never gave
up the Russian Orthodox faith. In 1960 he settled, once and for all,
the question both of the date of his birth and of his ethnic origins

[1] Alfredo Casella, *Strawinsky* (La Scuola: Brescia, 1947), p. 28.
[2] Ed. Minna Lederman, *Dance Index* (New York), vol. vi, nos. 10–12, p. 305.
[3] Heinrich Strobel, *Igor Strawinsky* (Atlantis Verlag: Zurich, 1956), p. 30.
[4] De' Paoli, *Igor Strawinsky* (Paravia: Turin, 1934), p. 12.
[5] Heinrich Lindlar, *Igor Strawinsky's Sakraler Gesang* (Gustav Bosse Verlag: Regensburg, 1957), p. 81, note 16.
[6] G. F. Malipiero, *Strawinsky* (Edizioni del Cavallino: Venice, 1956), p. 79.
Alexander Tansman, *Igor Strawinsky* (Putnam: New York, 1949), p. 143.

by publishing his family tree at the beginning of *Memories and Commentaries*. Other particualrs relating to his Polish ancestry are to be found on p. 49 of the subsequent volume of his conversations with Robert Craft entitled *Expositions and Developments*.

Stravinsky's forebears were a noble Polish family, of the same name, from the province of Soulima. The family emigrated to Russia after the partition of Poland. His father was a cultured bass-baritone singer at the Imperial Opera in St. Petersburg. Although he insisted that his son should study law (Stravinsky took his degree in jurisprudence at the University of St. Petersburg in 1905) he encouraged in him a love of music. Igor began to learn the piano at the age of nine; he also had harmony lessons, though he derived very little benefit from them. At eighteen he decided of his own accord to study counterpoint, and in 1902 he sought the advice of Rimsky-Korsakov, by then an old man. Rimsky-Korsakov advised him against entering the Conservatoire, but agreed to give him private lessons in orchestration and musical form. Since he says himself that the study of harmony went against the grain, it was all the more important that he should take full advantage of Rimsky-Korsakov's fabulous knowledge of the subtleties of orchestration and his mastery of form. Rimsky-Korsakov's method of teaching consisted in the study of instrumentation along with musical form, 'because in his view the more highly developed musical forms found their fullest expression in the complexity of the orchestra'.[7] Rimsky-Korsakov died in 1908, and Stravinsky never studied with anyone else afterwards.

The Symphony in E flat, composed while he was studying with Rimsky-Korsakov, and incidentally dedicated to him, shows obvious signs of the master's influence, but this influence is not really of paramount importance. In conception and general plan, the work shows a closer kinship with Glazunov, and Stravinsky himself states definitely that at the time he was writing the Symphony, he admired Glazunov quite as much as Rimsky-Korsakov. He particularly appreciated Glazunov's 'feeling for symphonic form'.[8] For many of Stravinsky's contemporaries in Russia, Glazunov's academic style represented at the time a kind of antidote to the sensuous tendencies of the 'Five', the group to which Rimsky-Korsakov belonged. What Stravinsky sought to acquire from Rimsky-Korsakov was clearly his prodigious mastery of the *métier* of composition, not his taste or outlook. Stravinsky's youthful preferences and predilections are no

[7] *Chronicle of My Life* (Gollancz: London, 1936), p. 39.
[8] ibid., p. 25.

doubt of great significance for his future development, and though
in his instrumental technique we recognize Rimsky-Korsakov's teaching, and other external features of his music bear the hallmark of
Glazunov, the substance of the music which clothes the formal
structure of his Symphony shows evidence of other influences of a
most unexpected kind. The listener hearing Stravinsky's maiden
effort for the first time may be astonished to find that for his
opening theme he has borrowed from Richard Strauss. This theme
is then developed in accordance with the orthodox technique which
has remained unchanged since Beethoven. Gradually it takes on a
more and more chromatic look until it is woven into a polyphonic
fabric which betrays an acquaintance with Wagner's style. At its
most expressive, the musical discourse has all the earmarks of
Wagnerism, of a type not unlike that we find in Schoenberg's
brilliant early works *Transfigured Night* and the Chamber Symphony.
At the time when Schoenberg and Stravinsky began composing, their
point of contact with musical tradition was of course bound to be
the same – chromaticism as carried to its extreme limit by Wagner
in *Tristan*.

Stravinsky admits that while learning his craft he studied Wagner's
scores 'fervently' and that although he took Glazunov's symphonies
as his model he was also influenced by Tchaikovsky, Wagner, and
Rimsky-Korsakov. He had to try to understand the Wagnerian approach and assimilate it before there could be any question of
developing it as far as it would go, and then either going beyond it
as did Schoenberg, or reacting against it, as in fact he did in due
course. It must be said, however, that even in this work Stravinsky
does not make systematic use of Wagnerian chromaticism, but writes
chromatic passages alternating freely with others which suggest a
variety of origins. The second movement is completely in the spirit
of the Russian school; the theme of the Scherzo is reminiscent of
Rimsky-Korsakov's *Flight of the Bumble Bee*, and the Trio smacks
of Mussorgsky; in other passages we find echoes of Borodin and
Tchaikovsky; while the return to chromaticism in the Adagio, in
A flat minor, and the crescendo which brings to a climax the final
section of the movement with descending chromatic chords and the
strings playing tremolo, again suggest the atmosphere of *Tristan* and
Transfigured Night. The Finale, on the other hand, bears the stamp
of Tchaikovsky's academic romanticism. There are indications of the
direction in which Stravinsky's personality was likely to develop in
the rhythmic changes at the end of the first movement, in his

tendency to avoid clotted masses of sound, to give individuality to the different parts of the orchestra and to make every line and every tone as plastic as possible. This is no great achievement, but it is enough to give this eclectic youthful work a documentary interest if nothing more. Incidentally, Stravinsky himself never despised the Symphony. After the first performance in 1907 at the Belaieff Symphony Concerts in St. Petersburg he revised the work slightly, and Ernest Ansermet performed it in 1914. In 1928 he himself conducted a performance in Paris.

The years 1906-7 also saw the birth of *Faun and Shepherdess*, op. 2, a setting of words by Pushkin for mezzo-soprano and orchestra. Here, as well as the influences already mentioned, we find the first hint of an acquaintance with the new French school of Dukas, Debussy, and Ravel.

It may be worth mentioning in this connection that as early as 1902-3 Stravinsky had got to know the chamber music, if not all the major symphonic works, of the French school of composers – César Franck, Vincent d'Indy, Chabrier, Fauré, Dukas, and Debussy. His favourites were Chabrier and Debussy. This new influence is particularly evident in passages like the following:

with their implication of hexatonal structure, or in bars such as these:

where the thematic figure is alternately placed on two distinct harmonic planes defined by two chords of the seventh differing in pitch by a tritone. Harmonic combinations like these have an unmistakable

Debussy-like flavour, although Stravinsky's use of them could theoretically be ascribed to the influence of certain compositions of
Mussorgsky, e.g. the remarkable song 'Night' with its pre-echo of
Pelléas. The influence of French impressionism on Stravinsky becomes
more specific and more marked in the *Scherzo fantastique*, op. 3,
written in 1907-8. This work was composed under Rimsky-Korsakov's
supervision and with his encouragement, although he never actually
heard it, since it was not given its first performance until 1909. The
following preliminary programme note appears at the top of the
score :

This piece was inspired by an episode in Maeterlinck's *Vie des Abeilles*. The
first part describes the busy life of the hive. The slow middle piece, Trio,
suggests the rising of the sun and the mystical flight of the Queen bee, her
mating struggle and the death of the drone. The last part which repeats the
first with some variation returns to the peaceful routine of the hive. Thus
the whole work presents the eternal cycle as a fantastic spectacle, with man
as the spectator.

This reference to the *Vie des Abeilles* has naturally enough led
writers on Stravinsky (including the present writer) to assume that
the *Scherzo fantastique* was actually inspired by the literary subject-
matter of Maeterlinck's work. In one of his interviews with Robert
Craft[9] Stravinsky denies this. When Craft asked him : 'Did you have
Maeterlinck's *La Vie des Abeilles* in mind as a programme for your
Scherzo fantastique?' Stravinsky replied : 'No, I wrote the *Scherzo*
as a piece of "pure" symphonic music. The bees were a choreogra-
pher's idea as, later, the bee-like creatures of the ballet (to my String
Concerto in D), *The Cage*, were Mr. Robbins's. I have always been
fascinated by bees . . . but I have never attempted to evoke them in
my work (as, indeed, what pupil of the composer of the *Flight of
the Bumble Bee* would?) . . . Maeterlinck's bees nearly gave me
serious trouble, however. One morning in Morges I received a
startling letter from him, accusing me of intent to cheat and fraud.
My *Scherzo* had been entitled *Les Abeilles* – anyone's title, after
all – and made the subject of a ballet then performing at the Paris
Grand Opera (1917). *Les Abeilles* was unauthorized by me and, of
course, I had not seen it; but Maeterlinck's name was mentioned in
the programme. The affair was settled, and, finally, some bad literature about bees was published on the fly-leaf of the score, to satisfy
my publisher, who thought a "story" would help to sell the music.'
However this may be, the *Scherzo fantastique* is regarded by some

[9] *Conversations with Igor Stravinsky*, p. 40.

critics as Stravinsky's first important work. His handling of the orchestra is already masterly, and the work has an impressive richness of harmonies and tone-colours. As to the actual writing, it is worth mentioning that alongside the seven-note scale Stravinsky uses scales of eight different notes – the same ones that we find later defining the limits within which superimposed polytonalities are employed in *Petrushka*. Thus in the bars:

the subject matter can be referred to the three different transpositions feasible in what Olivier Messiaen calls the 'second mode of limited transpositions'. The modality

to be inferred from the third bar is precisely that implied – as will be seen in Chapter II – by the famous passage in *Petrushka* for two clarinets quoted on p. 16. The formal characteristics found in the *Scherzo fantastique* are even more strongly marked in the orchestral fantasy *Fireworks*, op. 4, written in 1908 for the wedding of Rimsky-Korsakov's daughter and the composer Maximilian Steinberg. Here, in spite of the influence of Debussy and Ravel, and in spite of direct borrowings from Paul Dukas's *Apprenti Sorcier*, Stravinsky's personality emerges for the first time clearly and distinctively. The clean, sculptured quality of the motifs; the dry, etched lines of the interjections by the brass; the explosive incisiveness of the rhythm; the asymmetrical arrangements of the barring and the frequent displacement of accent; the terse musical utterance; the harsh contrast of timbres; and the overwhelming dynamic power of the whole short piece, with sounds springing to life, clashing, bursting into splendour, and dying away – all these features are part of the real Stravinsky; and they all point the way towards the 'Danse infernale du roi Katschei' in *The Firebird*, and even more towards *Petrushka*.

But if the external configuration of *Fireworks* foreshadows the brilliant period of Stravinsky's first maturity, the work's inner structure anticipates with a surprising directness his serial period of half a century later. Analysis shows, indeed, that the work is not just an impressionistic improvisation, or something moulded for the sake of its pictorial effect. On the contrary: the fantastic liberty which it seems to embody really conceals a complex yet solid structure governing the musical figures in every detail. These figures can all be referred to the single theme of four bars on the dominant which the horns, imitated in canon by the trumpets, state from the seventeenth bar on:

This theme introduces, bar by bar, the various differential motives, which appear successively in different mirror forms until the entire, exact retrograde form of the theme on the dominant:

leads to the final restatement of the original form on the tonic. Stravinsky cast this contrapuntal and structural firework display in

the form of a festive divertimento, three years before Schoenberg began to use similar methods on a large scale for the hallucinatory expressionism of *Pierrot Lunaire*. This same period 1907-8 also produced four other works: *Chant funèbre*, op. 5, on the death of Rimsky-Korsakov; *Two Songs*, op. 6, for mezzo-soprano and piano; *Four Studies*, op. 7, for piano, and *Pastorale* for voice and piano. *Chant funèbre*[10] was never published and the manuscript was lost, so that we cannot discuss it from first-hand knowledge. In the *Chronicle of My Life* (p. 45) Stravinsky has the following note on the work:

. . . wishing to pay some tribute to the memory of my master, I composed a *Chant Funèbre* which was performed in the Autumn, Felix Blumenfeld conducting, at the first Belaieff concert, which was dedicated to the memory of the great musician. The score of this work unfortunately disappeared in Russia during the Revolution, along with many other things which I had left there. I can no longer remember the music, but I can remember the idea at the root of its conception, which was that all the solo instruments of the orchestra filed past the tomb of the master in succession, each laying down its own melody as its wreath against a deep background of tremolo hummings simulating the vibrations of bass voices singing in chorus. The impression made on the public, as well as on myself was marked, but how far it was due to the atmosphere of mourning and how far to the merit of the composition itself, I am no longer able to judge.

The *Two Songs*, op. 6: 'Spring' (The Cloister) and the 'A song of the Dew' (Mystic Song of the Ancient Russian Flagellants), both settings of words by the Russian poet Gorodetsky, are pleasing works akin in style to Mussorgsky's vocal music, with a suggestion of the

[10] In *Memories and Commentaries* (p. 57) Stravinsky refers to this work as 'the best of my works before *The Firebird* and the most advanced in chromatic harmony'. He also says that the orchestral parts must still be in some orchestra library in Leningrad and that he wishes someone would look for them. He was curious to see exactly how he had approached composition just before *The Firebird*. Lindlar (op. cit., p. 18) cites the *Chant funèbre* as containing the earliest evidence in Stravinsky's music of a cult of the dead which on the literary side 'takes up much space and is given great emphasis in his *Chronicle of My Life*', and Lindlar finds its way into his compositions on many occasions, e.g. Symphonies of Wind Instruments, *in memoriam Claude-Achille Debussy* (1920); *Ode, elegiacal chant in three parts*, ('Eulogy', 'Eclogue' and 'Epitaph') for orchestra 'Dedicated to the memory of Natalia Kussevitzky' (1943); *Elegy* for solo viola, 'written for Germain Prévost, to be played in memory of Alphonse Onnou, founder of the Pro Arte Quartet' (1944); *In Memoriam Dylan Thomas*, *Dirge-Canons and Song*, for tenor, string quartet, and four trombones (1954).
The list could be expanded to include many of the works written by Stravinsky during the succeeding period. There are also the works in which the idea of death is expressed without any pesonal reference, e.g. in the 'Lyke-Wake Dirge' of the Cantata for soprano, tenor, female chorus, and a small instrumental ensemble (1952). Lindlar also mentions in this connection the way in which Stravinsky handles the pagan idea of human sacrifice in *The Rite of Spring* and the idea of past and future in *Persephone*.

elegance of manner of Tchaikovsky. Viewed in the light of Stravinsky's output as a whole, the *Two Songs*, op. 6, have a somewhat special significance if we regard them as leading up to the sheaf of vocal compositions directly based on Russian models which occupied his attention about the time of the First World War. Lindlar maintains that these songs, together with several other monastic songs, Christmas carols or 'bell-songs' such as 'Tilim-bom' (1915), 'On Saints' Day in Chigisakh' (1916), and the 'Chant dissident' (1919) 'prepare the way for the ritualism and organic composition of *The Wedding*'.

The accompaniment, built up on a gentle bell-like tinkle, over which the Novice's vocalize in the first of the *Two Songs* delicately unfolds, is one of the earliest examples of Stravinsky's fondness for musical figurations based on the sound of bells, which in the Russian Orthodox Church have a ritual all of their own. Evidence of this predilection is to be found in the most varied forms through the whole range of Stravinsky's works, from 'Tilim-bom' to the finale of *The Wedding*, from the finale of the *Symphony of Psalms* to the Hosanna of the *Mass*, to 'Ariel's Song', the second of the *Three Songs from William Shakespeare* (1953), and to the transfigured conclusion of *Requiem Canticles* (1966). The *Four Studies* for piano, op. 7, reveal a curious influence – that of Chopin's pianoforte writing as handed on through Liadov and Skriabin. The chromatic technique of Skriabin, with its tendency to break away from traditional tonality, is evident here in a very marked degree; and once again, Stravinsky's personal stamp is discernible in the closely-knit interplay of rhythms with metric values set against one another in irrational relationships – 5 against 3; 7 against 3; 5 against 2; 5 against 3 against 2; 9 against 4, etc.

But the most significant work of this whole series is the little vocalize for voice and piano entitled *Pastorale*. Here all of a sudden Stravinsky foreshadows the rustic atmosphere of the neo-classical latterday Arcadia which enjoyed a vogue in Paris in the years following the First World War. The outstanding features of the work are the lucid diatonic purity of its vocal line; the spare linear quality of the instrumental texture; the contrasting effect of dry, staccato notes and sinuous melodic curves; the unobtrusive dissonances, which instead of raising the emotional temperature seem to relax the tension of the harmonies and give the work a novel freshness. All these characteristics point forwards to pieces like that most typical example of Stravinsky's so-called 'neo-classical' style, the Adagietto from the Piano Sonata written in 1924. Stravinsky's liking for the *Pastorale* is evident from the many transcriptions he made of the work. In 1923 he re-scored it for oboe, cor anglais, clarinet, and bassoon; and in 1933 he transcribed it for violin and piano, and again for violin, oboe, cor anglais, clarinet, and bassoon.

Appendix: Stravinsky and Schoenberg

In contemporary music circles Stravinsky was for a long time regarded as the antithesis of all that Arnold Schoenberg stood for. Until quite recently critics have tended to identify these two outstanding figures with one or other of the main currents in contemporary music. Whether this is justified is debatable; nor perhaps is it correct to regard Schoenberg and Stravinsky as marking the extreme limits of earlier twentieth-century music. Webern applied the twelve-note method in a far more thorough-going manner than did Schoenberg, and both Milhaud and Hindemith at times used polyharmony and polytonality much more boldly and consequentially than ever Stravinsky did. Schoenberg and Stravinsky thus mark neither the outer boundaries of modern music nor its only lines of development. What they represent, rather, are two poles around and in relation to which all other musical trends and movements of the twentieth century fall into place. For a long time these two composers seemed to be the embodiment of two irreconcilable tendencies that had destroyed the unity of musical language. But since 1952 there have been many signs to suggest that their paths were ultimately convergent, and that the things they stood for will turn out to be complementary rather than antagonistic.

If we look back from the vantage-point of today, it becomes clear that the true creators of modern music contributed, although in different ways and degrees, to a common historical task. Their achievement was to break through the barriers of the traditional, overworked diatonic system based on the major and minor scales of seven notes, and to give musical composition the free and organic use of all the remaining sound material available within the range of the tempered scale system, in other words the use of all the chromatic possibilities of the twelve separate elements into which the octave had been equally divided since the time of Bach.

Schoenberg and the other composers who followed his example achieved this goal by carrying on the process of sensitizing and chromatically altering the diatonic functions already taken a long

turned to stone, sends everyone to sleep with the enchanted lullaby and gives the Czarevitch the chance to seize and destroy the egg-shell containing the soul and with it the pledge of Katschei's immortality. The parts of the ballet relating to the supernatural world (the Introduction, the Enchanted Garden of Katschei, the Appearance, the Dance, the Capture and Torments of the Firebird, the Magic Peal of Bells and the Appearance of the Guardian Monsters, the Arrival of Katschei and his Dialogue with Ivan, the Appearance of the Firebird, the Dance of the Followers of Katschei Enchanted by the Firebird, the Infernal Dance of All Katschei's Subjects, the Lullaby, and finally the Death of Katschei) all give evidence of the masterly coherence with which Stravinsky follows up and develops the experience gained in works like *Faun and Shepherdess* and particularly the *Scherzo Fantastique*, from the point of view of the more and more general use of modes (other than the traditional major-minor), while at the same time the experience of the mirror symmetry structures of *Fireworks* is likewise deepened. Predominant here is the unrestricted use of the tritone interval which in the modes of limited transpositions takes the place of the dominant. Beginning at the eleventh bar of the *Introduction* the mode shown on page 7 produces chords literally anticipating the harmonic shape of the germ cell of *Petrushka* (cf. page 16). In other passages (see No. 116 in the score) the effects of polytonality seem to be suggested by the arrangement of the white and black keys of the piano – here again heralding certain peculiarities of Stravinsky's manner of composing which I shall try to clarify further in the part of this chapter devoted to *Petrushka*. The way in which the magical subject-matter of the pieces is reflected in the capillary mirror structure of the musical images on which they are based would warrant a thorough and exhaustive analysis. They are based essentially on the succession of intervals established by the first four notes of the work (A flat, F flat, E flat, D – a major third and two minor seconds reckoned downwards, and on the retrograde form of this succession and the relative inverse and inverse retrograde forms. The way in which Stravinsky combines similar modules in an intrinsically highly coherent musical discourse (though giving every appearance of complete liberty of invention) foreshadows his future serial technique in a way which is bound to surprise those who have come to regard *The Firebird* as Stravinsky's most conventional work merely because it is the most popular. When all is said and done, universal acceptance does not necessarily imply shunning exuberant complexity and intrinsic quali-

tative excellence. The music of the parts of *The Firebird* relating to
humans, to the Czarevitch, the princesses and the knights turned to
stone who are restored to life in the finale of the ballet is different.
The diatonic motifs used by Stravinsky here do not fit into the pre-
neo-classical scheme outlined in the *Pastorale*, but for the last time
in Stravinsky's works they exploit nineteenth-century taste as represented by 'The Five' and in a lesser degree by Tchaikovsky. In fact
Stravinsky even uses three Russian popular tunes in these pieces :
two are used in the 'Khorovod' of the princesses, while the third, a
popular ballad from the district of Smolensk, leads into the finale.
Both the first, a tune from the government of Novgorod, and the
third, were published in Rimsky-Korsakov's collection. Incidentally,
in *Petrushka* also, Stravinsky uses a Russian popular song taken from
Tchaikovsky ('Down St. Peter's Road'), but in a rather more modern
manner. It should be said, however, that even the parts of *The Firebird* discussed above, in spite of the sophisticated writing and the instrumental invention (e.g. the glissandi on the harmonics of the strings
in the *Introduction* which at the time amazed Richard Strauss) are
not so much a revelation of the future as stamped with a certain
post-Wagnerian harmonic flavour that links them with the sensuous-
ness of Skriabin and the decorative chromaticism of Dukas, Debussy,
and Ravel. The orchestral writing still tends towards lush or osten-
tatious masses of tone-colour. In general the music attempts not so
much to sum up the scenic action as to describe it with evident
pictorial intent. The one exception is the 'Danse infernale' of King
Katschei, where Stravinsky's personal style comes through very
clearly. The themes are laconic, the musical argument falls into
massive squared sections, rough-hewn and powerful. The scintillating
diatonic tonal planes conflict and clash. The rhythm is already beginning to achieve a discursive quality in its own right. Synthetic
blending of tone-colours is replaced by the unpolished effect of pure
timbres. We get the feeling that the orchestra is being taken to pieces
and analysed. Here it might be truly said that Stravinsky lit the first
fuse beneath the instrumental make-up of the nineteenth-century
orchestra.

The first performance of *The Firebird* was given by Diaghilev's
ballet company at the Opéra in Paris on 25 June 1910. Its success
was overwhelming, and Stravinsky's name was made; he found himself overnight enjoying an enviable position in western musical life.
From now on his work brought him into close contact, in all
branches of art, with every experimental movement of significance

that came to the surface in the seething cauldron of Parisian culture. A highly fruitful relationship gradually grew up between Stravinsky and various aspects of western culture. But the success of *The Firebird* did more than mark an important stage in his personal career; it changed the very nature of the Russian Ballet. Instead of merely exporting Russian art, from now on Diaghilev was encouraged by this success to try to stimulate the creation of new works of art on an international scale, promoting real collaboration among leading musicians, painters, and writers, with results which will go down as landmarks in the history of modern art in general.

While he was composing *The Firebird*, Stravinsky had what he describes as 'a fleeting vision' of a pagan rite enacted in the context of the old Slavonic mythology, and it gave him the idea of a prehistoric ballet. He sought the advice of his friend Nicholas Roerich, a painter and a student of ancient Slav rites, and between them they worked out a plot for *The Rite of Spring*. Stravinsky submitted the project to Diaghilev, who accepted it with enthusiasm. But the production of a work like *The Rite of Spring* demanded time for unhurried reflection, so that while waiting until he felt equal to tackling this exacting task he applied himself to the composition of two songs with words by Verlaine, and also sketched out a 'sort of *Konzertstueck*' for piano and orchestra. In the *Chronicle of My Life*, he describes how he had in his mind in composing the music 'a distinct picture of a puppet, suddenly endowed with life, exasperating the patience of the orchestra with diabolical cascades of arpeggios. The orchestra in turn retaliates with menacing trumpet-blasts. The outcome is a terrific noise which reaches its climax and ends in the sorrowful and querulous collapse of the poor puppet.' Once again Diaghilev's intuition proved right. When he heard the sketch of the dialogue between the piano and the orchestra, he urged Stravinsky to expand it and turn it into a new ballet. The puppet will be recognized as Petrushka, the 'Pierrot' of the Slav countries, 'the immortal and unhappy hero of every fair in all countries'. The orchestra's rhythms accompany the dancing throng at a Russian Easter fair. The *Konzertstueck* for piano becomes the third tableau of the ballet. The musical idea on which it is built :

becomes the germ-cell of the whole work. It consists of two super-imposed arpeggios belonging to different tonal orbits: a C major chord in root position, and the first inversion of an F sharp chord. This novel device may have been suggested by the black and white keys of the piano keyboard, the chord of C major being all on the white keys and that of F sharp on the black keys.[1] A whole literature has been written about this idea. It has repeatedly been maintained that it was the beginning of polytonality. In point of fact it is by no means the first polytonal passage in musical history. Examples of what was virtually polytonality are to be found in Bach's Brandenburg Concertos, and in Mozart's *Musikalischer Spass* (Divertimento in F Major, K. 522). But here for the first time we find a polytonal passage not used casually, as an oddity, but having a structural significance. Attempt after attempt has been made to give theoretical sanction to this superimposing of elements which according to orthodox musical 'theory' are heterogeneous.[2] Aesthetically, Stravinsky's use of the device hardly needs any such justification. His innate sense of its complete appropriateness to its expressive and artistic purpose amply justifies it. The dissonant friction of major and minor seconds produces a musical effect at once burlesque

[1] This is not the only passage in Stravinsky where his creative imagination appears to have been stimulated by the idea of the fingers running up and down the keyboard – quite apart from the fact that he invariably composed at the piano and explicitly stated as his opinion (*Chronicle of My Life*, p. 15) that it is a thousand times better to compose in direct contact with the physical medium of sound than to work in the abstract medium produced by one's own imagination. Thus while as a rule he used the piano to translate his thoughts immediately into music, there were also occasions when these very thoughts arose and took shape as a result of the mechanical potentialities of the instrument. In addition to the passage from *Petrushka* already quoted, there is another particularly clear instance which the composer mentions himself in the *Chronicle*, namely the *Piano-Rag Music*, written in 1919. 'What fascinated me most of all in the work,' he writes (p. 137), 'was that the different rhythmic episodes were dictated by the fingers themselves. . . . Fingers are not to be despised: they are great inspirers, and in contact with a musical instrument, often give birth to subconscious ideas which might otherwise never come to life.'

[2] Some writers on Stravinsky, including Schaeffner – who is by no means dull-witted – find the superimposition in question inexplicable. See André Schaeffner, *Strawinsky* (Rieder: Paris, 1931), p. 23

and harrowing which admirably expresses the 'musical soul' of *Petrushka* and at the same time arouses a sympathetic reaction in the listener. On the other hand, from the formal point of view, it must be pointed out that while no traditional tonality contains all the different notes of the two arpeggios in question, there is nevertheless a mode which includes them, the one in fact referred to on page 7. This consists of eight different notes instead of the seven we find in the usual diatonic scales, and as already explained, it admits of only three modulations; hence the name 'mode of limited transpositions' given to it by Olivier Messiaen.[3] Examples of the use of a similar mode are found occasionally in Rimsky-Korsakov, Skriabin, and Ravel. They are also to be found in nineteenth-century compositions, especially where the intervals of a diminished seventh chord are filled melodically. Examples are to be found in the works of Verdi, Chopin, Liszt, and others. One of the earliest and most surprising is to be found in the score of C. M. von Weber's Concerto No. 2, op. 32 (Ed. Robert Lienau, Berlin-Lichtenfeld, p. 32), where the soloist plays passages made up of the notes of the scale, or the mode B C sharp D E F G A flat B flat.

As we saw in Chapter I, Stravinsky used it liberally in the *Scherzo fantastique*, op. 3, and *Fireworks*, op. 4. All he does now is use and develop in a bolder and more radical way the procedure already alluded to in *The Firebird* of taking a harmonic projection grouping all or some (in this instance six) of the eight different notes of the mode of limited transpositions into simultaneous chords. These may not be homogeneous from the tonal point of view, but the fact that they are common to this mode makes them modally homogeneous. Clearly the novelty of this astonishing device of superimposing scales to give a polytonal effect in *Petrushka* did not come about on the spur of the moment, but emerged gradually out of the sensibility to mode shown by Stravinsky from his very earliest works. Thus we have here a further example of the slow and unobtrusive way in which his innovations matured. Many of the polytonal passages in Stravinsky's work, though not all, admit of a similar modal interpretation. At times, he superimposes melodic lines or harmonic clusters in which different tonalities are placed in a contrapuntal relationship. In such cases the tonal discrepancies are not neutralized modally,

---

[3] Olivier Messiaen, *Technique de mon langage musical* (Leduc: Paris, 1944), p. 52. On the use made of the modes of limited transpositions by other composers, see also Roman Vlad, 'Petrassi', in *L'Immagine* (Rome), no. 13, year II, May–June 1949, p. 247, and *Modernità e tradizione nella musica contemporanea* (Einaudi: Turin, 1955), Chapter XVII.

and we get real polytonality. But it would be more correct to speak simply of 'polyharmony' where there is superimposition of harmonic elements which have different functions within the framework of one and the same tonality. Thus Stravinsky developed a partiality for superimposing tonic and dominant chords, the alternating use of which forms the basis of the whole system of classical harmony.

The innovations in *Petrushka*, however, concern not only the intrinsic structure of the music, but also its instrumentation, its architecture, and above all the aesthetic outlook which this implies. In 1911, the vogue ran from impressionist haziness to the boisterousness of the post-Wagnerian symphony á la Strauss. Against this background, the unleashing of the crude, spiky, and incisive sonorities we find in *Petrushka* was bound to appear startlingly revolutionary, the more so since Stravinsky in *The Firebird* had helped to develop the technique of atmospheric harmonic effects to an unprecedented pitch of refinement. Here in fact we see the first evidence of one of the most salient qualities of Stravinsky's personality – his power of renunciation. Another composer might well have gone on indefinitely making capital out of *The Firebird* by continuing to write along the same lines, and exploiting the ingenious discoveries embodied in the work. Stravinsky left this to his imitators. Even today, *The Firebird* provides an inexhaustible fund of 'recipes' for the magical and mysterious effects needed by Hollywood film producers. Stravinsky was moving on. This in itself would not, of course, prove that in *Petrushka* he had suddenly abandoned the use of instrumental sonorities for their own sake; nor indeed would the fact that, whereas Debussy's orchestra tends to sound like a harp, the orchestra in *Petrushka* conjures up the picture of a gigantic accordion,[4] or a wheezy barrel-organ. The difference is mainly one of quality, the result of a definitely new aesthetic outlook in which the reaction

---

[4] Adorno calls 'the gigantic accordion of the *tutti*' in *Petrushka* 'the antithesis of the gigantic neo-romantic harp'. In my opinion, the way in which the orchestra imitates the accordion or barrel-organ in *Petrushka* does not belie the basically pianistic nature of the work nor invalidate the contention that this music has its origin in the essential spirit of the pianoforte. The Three Movements from *Petrushka*, i.e. the well-known concert suite for solo pianoforte which Stravinsky took from the ballet in 1921 at the request of Artur Rubinstein, transcribing three pieces and arranging them as 'Danse russe', 'Chez Pétrouchka' and 'The Shrovetide Fair', are not so much a 'transcription' as a real 'restitution'. This suite proves conclusively that the key to all the sound effects in *Petrushka* is the desire to show off the peculiar mechanical and musical qualities of piano tone. The re-casting of the few pages of the orchestral score of *Petrushka* so as to restore them fully to the instrument from which they were derived seems to lay bare Petrushka's mechanical yet all too human heart.

against Romanticism is carried to its extreme limits. A great deal has been written about the impersonal quality which Stravinsky is said to have given to music as a counter to the romantic cult of personality, about the purity of his music as compared with the psychological padding of that of his predecessors,[5] about the music's independence of the scenic action to which it refers,[6] etc. I personally see no reason for considering the music of *Petrushka* as either purer or more independent than many nineteenth-century works, whatever the poetic or pictorial subject which inspired them. If it is to have life, musical composition must always follow music's own laws; the non-musical subject must be no more than a pretext or a starting-point. Only then can the music have an independent life of its own. This is the case with all the Stravinsky ballets which have gone into the symphonic repertoire; but it is equally true of masterpieces of the Romantic period, including a good deal of Wagner's music. It is not that the music is divorced from the action any more than it would be, say, in a piece by Tchaikovsky. Indeed, at times its relationship to the characters in the action is very much closer, tending to represent structurally the characteristics of the protagonist. This is what happens when the music apes the accordion or suggests the bars of a cage by means of a parallel row of pizzicato chords behind which three bassoons stalk to and fro like the caged Moor on the stage.[7] The really new feature is the relationship between the stage *persona* and the music. Here for the first time perhaps, the *persona* avoids the direct expression of his individuality and of his spiritual aspirations. The relationship between *persona* and work of art here incorporates a critical element. When the character is debarred from expressing himself freely, he shouts at the top of his voice the opposite of what he really feels. Instead of reflecting the tragic situation of *Petrushka*, the music portrays the wild abandon of carnival. But the unspoken contrast between the implied emotional situation and that actually expressed gives the former great tragic power. Judged from the orthodox aesthetic point of view, the use of devices such as the inclusion of the French café song 'Elle avait un' jamb' de bois' in *Petrushka* or the hackneyed Tyrolese Waltz by

---

[5] The most uncompromising statements on this subject are those made by Charles Albert Cingria in his article 'Le musical pur', *La Nouvelle Revue Française* (Paris), year XXVIII, No. 320, 1 May 1940. They are discussed along with other similar assertions in Vlad: *Modernità e tradizione*, Chapter VIII.

[6] See, for example, Tansman, op. cit., pp. 167-76.

[7] This translation of objective phenomena into pure musical forms was commented upon for the first time by Ernest Ansermet in his essay 'L'Œuvre d'Igor Strawinsky' in the July 1921 number of *La Revue Musicale*.

Lanner might seem an outrage to the dignity of music, particularly
'highbrow music', yet *Petrushka* is definitely 'highbrow' music. Its
extraordinarily moving quality is due to the ambivalence of its
expressive power. First there is the obvious effect exerted by the
tremendous rhythmic vitality pulsating within it, the catchiness of
its tunes, and the opulence of the instrumentation. The other significant aspect of its power is on a deeper level. The phenomenon of the
sublime so easily turning into the ridiculous is here reversed – the
drama of a straw-stuffed puppet takes on a human quality. There are
critics who go so far as to find a symbolic meaning in the resulting
poetic values. Adorno sees *Petrushka* as a premonition of the coming
drama of the individual in an age of mass production and mechaniza-
tion in which personality tends to be submerged.[8] Such an interpretation probably goes beyond the composer's intention. But there are
always fundamental links between a great masterpiece and its
historical context, even though they may be forged without any
conscious intent and may be discernible only in retrospect.

[8] Wiesengrund-Adorno, op. cit., pp. 89-94.

III The King of the Stars

As we have seen, the idea of composing a prehistoric ballet based upon pagan propitiation rites for the coming of spring found Stravinsky momentarily unequal to the prodigious task involved. While he waited for his imagination to suggest musical ideas for *The Rite of Spring*, he wrote a series of other works – *Petrushka*, *Two Poems of Verlaine*, the cantata *The King of the Stars*, and *Two Poems by Balmont* for voice and piano.

The two settings of poems by Verlaine were composed in France at La Baule during the summer of 1910. They are very short songs based on the well-known poems 'La lune blanche' and 'Un grand sommeil noir'. Their interest is chiefly documentary. The choice of words and the obvious influence of Debussy in the musical setting point to the most patent attempt ever made by Stravinsky to identify himself with the spirit of French art, and it is the last work in which Stravinsky took stylistic and spiritual features from elsewhere without succeeding fully in breaking down their elements and transmuting them in the fire of his own personality. Incidentally, Stravinsky acknowledges his debt to Debussy in so many words. Craft discusses it at some length in *Conversations with Igor Stravinsky* (p. 48).

The other set of two songs was written in 1911 in Russia, Stravinsky having returned there temporarily on a visit after the triumph of *Petrushka*. They are two lyrical songs based on love poems by Balmont – 'The Flower' and 'The Dove'. The tenderness and delicacy of the settings of these two lyrics foreshadow some of the more moving lyrical passages in *The Rite of Spring* and the later acts of *The Nightingale*.

The last composition in this group immediately preceding *The Rite of Spring* is the cantata *Zvesdoliki* (literally 'The Starry One' or 'The Starfaced One', usually known in English as *The King of the Stars*). It is a short piece of forty-eight bars plus the title, which is sung, and it lasts only six and a half minutes. The words are again by Balmont, and it is dedicated to Debussy. *The King of the Stars* is perhaps the most problematical of all Stravinsky's works, and one in which he reaches an extreme degree of harmonic complexity. As André Schaeffner[1] remarks, if Stravinsky had continued along the path he seemed to be following in *The King of the Stars*, it would soon have crossed that of Skriabin and Schoenberg. On the other hand Alexander Tansman maintains that in the evolution of Stravinsky *The King of the Stars* marks 'a negative point . . . an exhaustive expression of a general conception to be eliminated, and it is toward that of the *Rite* anticipated by *Petrushka*, that the composer was definitely to direct himself. Certain technical devices in the harmonic superposition, in the use of the ambiguous third and that of modal opposition, were to become a part of the composer's stylistic tools, but it is evident that the judgement passed upon a work that has not been completely realized by its contact with the perceiving agent, the actual performance, can only be approximate, and has no determining or even subjective value.'[2] In fact *The King of the Stars* is an exception to the rule that the works of Stravinsky have immediately become widely known, making a deep impression and exercising a decisive influence upon the course of contemporary music.

Even Debussy was taken aback, and prophesied that the work would remain a closed book. In a letter thanking Stravinsky for sending him the score,[3] he writes as follows: '. . . The music from *The King of the Stars* is still extraordinary. . . . It is probably Plato's "harmony of the eternal spheres" (but don't ask me which page of his!); and except on Sirius or Aldebaran, I do not foresee performances of this "cantata for planets". As for our more modest Earth, a performance would be lost in the abyss.' This half-serious, half-facetious statement sums up the actual situation very neatly. In point of fact, for more than forty years *The King of the Stars* has remained practically a dead letter. Stravinsky's own explanation of this is that owing to 'inherent difficulties involved in the execution

---

[1] Quoted by D. De' Paoli (op. cit., p. 53). Casella (op. cit., p. 52) holds the same view. Actually, it has been pointed out that there are points of virtual contact with the art of Schoenberg also in other works of Stravinsky dating from the years leading up to the First World War. Further reference to this point will be made in connection with the *Japanese Lyrics*. Adorno maintains that Schoenbergian influences are also to be found 'in many details of *The Rite of Spring*, especially in the Introduction', and even in *Petrushka*, where he says that 'the look of the score in the final bars of the well-known "Russian Dance" of the first tableau, immediately after No. 32, especially from the fourth bar on, is hardly conceivable except in the light of Schoenberg's orchestral pieces, op. 16' (op. cit., p. 93, note 1).
[2] Tansman, op. cit., pp. 172-3.
[3] Quoted in *Conversations with Igor Stravinsky*, p. 51.

of this very short piece, with its important orchestral contingent and the complexity of its choral writing as regards intonation, it has never [until 1935] been performed'.[4] Tansman, on the other hand, speaks of 'a single rendition at Brussels' (though he may be referring to a radio performance on 19 June 1939), while Lindlar mentions that Milhaud told him personally that, to the best of his recollection, there was a performance in Brussels before 1914. There seems to me to be some doubt about this performance, however; otherwise we can only suppose that it took place without the composer's knowledge.[5] The manuscript of *The King of the Stars* was in the possession of Debussy, but when he died his heirs sold it to an unknown person, and it disappeared. Moreover, the edition published by Jurgenson in Moscow in 1911 very quickly went out of print, though fortunately Stravinsy himself still had a copy on his shelves at Beverly Hills, California. All these things have conspired to prevent *The King of the Stars* from becoming known even to students of the composer's work, let alone the public generally.[6] Incidentally, in the series of broadcasts on the Italian radio from which this book originated, *The King of the Stars* was the only Stravinsky work of any consequence which could not be given a performance. However, a performance given in 1949 in Carnegie Hall, New York, under the direction of Robert Craft,[7] and still more the performance given on 8 February 1957 by the Cologne Radio, aroused a great deal of interest in the cantata and showed it to be a work 'no less significant in crystallizing Stravinsky's spiritual outlook than in establishing his personal musical idiom'.[8] On the spiritual side, the importance of *The King of the Stars* can be gauged in the light of the religious background of Stravinsky's art (see Chapter XVIII). This comes through for the first time quite unmistakably in the cantata.

Whether like Debussy we regard *The King of the Stars* as the 'harmony of the spheres', or consider it as 'a uranian pendant to the tellurian *Rite of Spring* composed about the same time',[9] or see in it a manifestation of 'the pentecostal mystique', the 'medieval austerity

[4] *Chronicle of My Life*, p. 63.
[5] Lindlar, op. cit., p. 82, note 19. The whole mystery is solved, however, if we assume that Lindlar's 1914 was a misprint for 1941. I at any rate am satisfied that the first performance of *The King of the Stars* was indeed that given in Brussels in 1939, conducted by Franz André.
[6] ibid.
[7] See Craft, Robert: 'A Personal Preface', *The Score* (London), 1957, June issue, No. 20, dedicated to Stravinsky on the occasion of his 75th birthday.
[8] Lindlar, op. cit., p. 16.
[9] ibid.

of the Church Fathers',[10] or link it with the symbolism of Russian
writers like Alexander Blok and Konstantin Balmont, who wrote the
words, or compare it to 'the cubist Orphism coming to the fore in
the early paintings of Chagall',[11] at any rate there is no mistaking
the spiritual impulse which generates in this apocalyptic cantata an
expressionist intensity of the kind postulated by Kandinsky in his
famous essay on the spirituality of art in *Der blaue Reiter*. It may
provide a clue to the spiritual background of the cantata if we give
a translation of the Balmont poem[12] on which it is based:

> His countenance was like the sun
> At midday when the sun rides high.
> His eyes were like the falling stars
> Before they break loose from the sky.
> The colours of the rainbow served
> As warp and woof, design and thread
> For raiment rich and sumptuous
> In which He rose up from the dead.
>
> About His head the thunder roared
> Amid the dense, torn banks of cloud,
> And like seven golden candlesticks
> The stars burned round Him in a crowd.
> The blazing sheafs of lightning burst
> Like mountain flowers of vivid hue.
> 'Keep ye the Word?' He asked, and we
> In anguished awe murmured: 'We do'.
>
> 'I am the First and Last': His words
> The thunder echoed back again.
> ' 'Tis harvest time: sharpen the scythe!'
> The star-eyed Reaper cried, 'Amen'.
> We stood in fear, a faithful flock.
> The sky's last dying embers glowed,
> And seven star-clusters showed the way
> Towards His boundless, dread abode.

The King of the Stars shows us in a nutshell Stravinsky's conception of art as 'an ontological reality'. This is the conception which
Stravinsky later set forth in a more explicit manner, as the main
principle of his *Poetics of Music*,[13] the principle which explains many

---

[10] Lindlar contrasts the spiritual quality of Stravinsky with the 'sensual
mystification of Rosicrucianism' which, he says, influenced Debussy in the
Martyrdom of St. Sebastian. In spite of the spiritual dissimilarity, Lindlar
maintains that this work, produced shortly before Stravinsky composed his
cantata, had a 'catalytic effect' in regard to the composition of *The King of the
Stars* (op. cit., p. 17).
[11] Lindlar, op. cit., p. 16.
[12] Translated from the Russian original by Frederick Fuller.
[13] *Poetics of Music, in the form of six lessons* (Harvard University Press:
Cambridge, Mass., 1947). The work is based on a series of lectures given at
Harvard in 1940. In an essay on 'Stravinsky and Prokofiev' published in 1925

of his apparently paradoxical, provocative, and controversial statements. What we have in mind particularly is the statement concerning the powerlessness of music 'to *express* anything at all'. Stravinsky uttered this dictum in the *Chronicle of My Life* apropos of the fact that what fascinated him in the Russian poems he used during the years of the First World War for the composition of the vocal works of the period (see Chapter V) was not the semantic value of the words but merely the cadence they created which, he said, produced 'an effect very closely akin to that of music'. It was this interest in sounds as abstract values that prompted Stravinsky's statement :[14]

For I consider that music is, by its very nature, essentially powerless to *express* anything at all, whether a feeling, an attitude of mind, a psychological mood, a phenomenon of nature, etc. . . . *Expression* has never been an inherent property of music. That is by no means the purpose of its existence. If, as is nearly always the case, music appears to express something, this is only an illusion and not a reality. It is simply an additional attribute which, by tacit and inveterate agreement, we have lent it, thrust upon it, as a label, a convention – in short, an aspect which, unconsciously or by force of habit, we have come to confuse with its essential being. Music is the sole domain in which man realizes the present. By the imperfection of his nature, man is doomed to submit to the passage of time – to its categories of past and future – without ever being able to give substance, and therefore stability, to the category of the present. The phenomenon of music is given to us with the sole purpose of establishing an order in things, including, and particularly, the co-ordination between *man* and *time*. To be put into practice, its indispensable and single requirement is construction. Construction once completed, this order has been attained, and there is nothing more to be said. It would be futile to look for, or expect anything else from it. It is precisely this construction, this achieved order, which produces in us a unique emotion having nothing in common with our ordinary sensations and our responses to the impressions of daily life.

Later in his *Poetics of Music* Stravinsky corrected and clarified this statement, making use of a theory concerning the specific problem of musical time, of the *chronos* of music, formulated by a friend of his, the Russian philosopher Pierre Souvtchinsky, who was in Paris at the time. Taking his cue from an article by the latter entitled 'La notion du temps et de la musique', Stravinsky expounds and endorses the thesis that musical creation appears as[15] 'an innate complex of

---

in the Berlin periodical *Melos*, Vol. IV, No. 10, Boris de Schloezer states apropos of the compositions of Stravinsky's Russian period that 'between the two states of mind – that which gives rise to the work and that to which the work gives rise – the work itself remains free from any affective (psychological) bond and possesses musical (ontological) reality alone'.

[14] *Chronicle of My Life*, pp. 91-93.
[15] *Poetics of Music*, pp. 30-32.

intuitions and possibilities based primarily upon an exclusively musical experiencing of time – *chronos,* of which the musical work merely gives us the functional realization'.

Everyone knows that time passes at a rate which varies according to the inner dispositions of the subject and to the events that come to affect his consciousness. Expectation, boredom, anguish, pleasure and pain, contemplation – all of these thus come to appear as different categories in the midst of which our life unfolds, and each of these determines a special psychological process, a particular tempo. These variations in psychological time are perceptible only as they are related to the primary sensation – whether conscious or unconscious – of real time, ontological time.

What gives the concept of musical time its special stamp is that this concept is born and develops as well outside the categories of psychological time as it does simultaneously with them. All music, whether it submits to the normal flow of time, or whether it disassociates itself therefrom, establishes a particular relationship, a sort of counterpoint between the passing of time, the music's own duration, and the material and technical means through which the music is made manifest.

Mr. Souvtchinsky thus presents us with two kinds of music: one which evolves parallel to the process of ontological time, embracing and penetrating it, inducing in the mind of the listener a feeling of euphoria and, so to speak, of 'dynamic calm'. The other kind runs ahead of, or counter to, this process. It is not self-contained in each momentary tonal unit. It dislocates the centres of attraction and gravity and sets itself up in the unstable; and this fact makes it particularly adaptable to the translation of the composer's emotive impulses. All music in which the will to expression is dominant belongs to the second type . . . Music that is based on ontological time is generally dominated by the principle of similarity. The music that adheres to psychological time likes to proceed by contrast. To these two principles which dominate the creative process correspond the fundamental concepts of variety and unity . . . For myself, I have always considered that in general it is more satisfactory to proceed by similarity rather than by contrast.

This passage is of the utmost importance, not for its intrinsic value, which might indeed be challenged, but because in my opinion it is the key to the understanding of some of the most deep-seated and fundamental impulses of Stravinsky's creative mind. That is why it is quoted at this particular point, well ahead of its place in the chronology of Stravinsky's activities, since it was written in 1939. The categorical anti-expressive and anti-psychological statements quoted above from the *Chronicle of My Life* are corrected by the more recent assertions in the *Poetics of Music,* in the sense that the absolute denial of the expressive power and the psychological implications of music is retracted (Stravinsky in fact recognizes that music 'which adheres to psychological time is particularly adaptable to the translation of the composer's emotive impulses', under the control of his 'will to expression') and is replaced by the composer's statement of his preference for the type of music which he considers to be bound up with 'ontological time'. Furthermore, the negation of the expressive content of this latter type of music is based on the contention that it partakes of the absolute reality of Being, as in Eduard Hanslick's aesthetic theory, which denies that music has any 'sentimental content' but at the same time maintains that it is only by means of this denial that we can 'preserve its spiritual content'.

In spite of Stravinsky's statement as to his preference for the kind of music which rejects contrast in order to attain a sublime 'dynamic calm', I would not by any means agree that this preference is altogether borne out in his works, or that, taking his works as a whole, the majority could be said to belong to this category. In fact, precisely in the most outstanding works of his early years of maturity – *The Rite of Spring* in particular – the irrational Dionysus seems to triumph over Apollo, whose rule Stravinsky identifies elsewhere in the *Poetics of Music* with the triumph of lucid order, substituting the symbolism of Greek mythology for that of Christianity. He even admits that 'if I proceed by the juxtaposition of strongly clashing tones, I can produce an immediate and violent sensation'.[16] No doubt in the works he wrote from his neo-classical conversion onwards, 'dynamic calm' became more and more evident in his work, reaching its peak, as we shall see, in a ballet whose title is particularly significant in this connection – *Apollo Musagetes*. But the first work in which this 'calm' prevails is *The King of the Stars*, the work coming immediately before *The Rite of Spring*, where volcanic forces are unleashed with a violence unparalleled in the history of music; so violent, indeed, as to relegate *The King of the Stars* for a long time to the limbo of forgotten things.

The poetic and spiritual nature of the theme was of course what suggested the peculiarities of the choral writing, which rightly or wrongly are regarded as the main obstacle to the performance of this work. Two groups of tenors and basses, twelve in each group, further subdivided into two or three parts, following each syllable of the text in accordance with the strict tonic accent of the Russian language, set up vertical columns of chords which fall into polymodal, polytonal, and absolutely chromatic clusters. The uniform syllabic scansion, and an insistent, regular metrical pulse create what Lindlar describes as the 'hymn-like, other-worldly grandeur of choral tone', From the first chord, which combines harmonic features of both C major and C minor, it is clear that the effect of these superimposed

[16] ibid., p. 69.

harmonies is not to create tonal tension of a dynamic kind, but rather to dissipate it and to neutralize its harmonic impact. Here again the intention is not to produce an inert mass which will embody the rhythm, as discussed below in connection with *The Rite of Spring*, but to do the very opposite, namely, to strip the musical fabric naked and invest it with a sense of the sublime, the transcendental, the hieratic. Even the sound of the orchestra, based on the frequent use of extremely subtle combinations of fluttering woodwind, muted horns, whispering harps, rumbling percussion and strings playing harmonics high up on the finger-board, seems disembodied, hovering round the solid choral tone, iridescent and halo-like. The contrast between these ethereal sonorities and the pregnant earthiness of those in *The Rite of Spring* is immense. Indeed, from this as from every other point of view, the two works exactly complement each other. Their dialectical relationship is the key to the principal values, not only of Stravinsky's world but of the whole ideal world which modern music has created – a spiritual outlook of detachment from all the contingencies of mere existence is counterbalanced by the most bitter experience and utter involvement in the tragic reality of existence. In this connection it is highly significant that immediately after a work heralding the advent of the time when all earthly contingencies are transcended, Stravinsky gave expression to the infernal dance of that same earth, convulsed by the dark, tumultuous forces unleashed within it. As far as the relative value of the two as works of art is concerned, no definite conclusion is possible; for the former, spiritual and visionary in theme, was destined to be hidden from the world for years and thus robbed of any historical immediacy, so that it has remained the composer's least known work, whereas *The Rite of Spring*, barbaric and earthy, broke out of the circle with a vengeance, exerting a decisive influence on the course of musical history and establishing itself as the most famous of all Stravinsky's works. The result is that although *The King of the Stars* was a dead letter at the time as far as Stravinsky's future development was concerned, it was by no means a 'negative point' or a gesture 'to be eliminated' as Tansman mistakenly called it; it was a hidden landmark for Stravinsky's future creative activity, a pregnant seed which decades later yielded an abundant harvest. The seclusion of *The King of the Stars*, though long, was not to be permanent; at the same time, the path which seemed to lead through this work towards the future twelve-note music led nowhere. The journey by which Stravinsky reached that goal forty years later first took him almost to the opposite extreme; but in the course of his Odyssey, he enriched the musical scene, endowing twentieth-century music with some of its most characteristic features.

IV The Rite of Spring

As soon as *The King of the Stars* was finished, Stravinsky set to work at once composing *The Rite of Spring*. The first performance, given in Paris on 29 May 1913 at the Théâtre des Champs-Elysées, with choreography by Vaclav Nijinsky, caused one of the most notorious scandals in musical history. Apparently the whistling and booing from the audience was so loud that it completely drowned the orchestra – although the volume of sound produced was greater than any composer had ever wrung from an orchestra! Yet *The Rite of Spring* ultimately became one of the most famous compositions in the whole of modern musical literature. As a result of the scandal of the first performance in Paris, Stravinsky was made out to be the arch-revolutionary, an iconoclast out to destroy all the most sacred canons of musical aesthetics and grammar. And this was the man who before very long was being referred to – sometimes in praise, sometimes disparagingly – as a 'classical' and even 'reactionary' composer rather than a 'revolutionary'! Stravinsky himself strongly denied the validity of the epithet 'revolutionary' as applied to him. In the *Poetics of Music* he writes:

In the tumult of contradictory opinions my friend Maurice Ravel intervened practically alone to set matters right. He was able to see, and he said, that the novelty of the *Rite* consisted, not in the 'writing', not in the orchestration, not in the technical apparatus of the work, but in the musical entity. I was made a revolutionary in spite of myself.[1]

[1] *Poetics of Music*, p. 10. See also Mario Labroca's article 'Strawinsky musicista classico', *Pegaso* (Florence), Vol. I, Jan. 1929. Casella too speaks of Stravinsky's art as 'reactionary', using the term in an entirely positive sense synonymous with 'revolutionary' (op. cit., p. 50). Tansman again refers to the 'revolutionary reaction' accomplished by Stravinsky in regard to modern music (op. cit., p. 168). The term 'reactionary' in the pejorative sense is applied to Stravinsky by many of the more intransigent and dogmatic champions of twelve-note orthodoxy, especially René Leibowitz (see his article 'Igor Strawinsky ou le choix de la misère musicale', *Les Temps Modernes* (Paris), No. 7, April 1946, and the introductory chapter 'Prolégomènes' to his book *Schoenberg et son école* (Janin, Paris, 1947). This view is, however, not shared by some of the younger composers of the Webern school (see Pierre Boulez's article 'Trajectoires: Ravel, Strawinsky, Schoenberg' in *Contrepoints*, no. 6, Paris, 1949). Adorno divides his *Philosophie der neuen*

Looking back at that first performance of 1913, however, one must admit that the reaction of the public, caught off its guard, is not altogether surprising.[2] No one had ever heard music like it before; it seemed to violate all the most hallowed concepts of beauty, harmony, tone, and expression. Never had an audience heard music so brutal, savage, aggressive, and apparently chaotic; it hit the public like a hurricane, like some uncontrolled primeval force. *The Rite of Spring* is the very antithesis of all those saccharine 'Springs' one had come to expect from every musician, painter, and writer under the sun. Here is spring seen from within, from the very bowels of the pregnant earth, which writhes in the pangs of labour and gives birth to dark tellurian forces. 'What I was trying to convey,' says Stravinsky, 'was the surge of spring, the magnificent upsurge of nature reborn.'

To carry out this vivid concept in music; to depict the barbaric cruelty of the rites performed by the Russian peasants to celebrate the advent of spring, reaching a climax with the sacrifice of a virgin; to suggest the sense of awe which these primitive folk feel in the face of the mysteries of nature; to bring all these exotic designs to fruition, Stravinsky assembled a colossal body of orchestral resources – large flutes, flute in G, four oboes, cor anglais, piccolo clarinet in E and D, three clarinets in B flat, bass clarinet, four bassoons, two double bassoons, eight horns, little trumpet in D, four trumpets, bass trumpet in E flat, three trombones, four tubas (two tenor and two bass), bass drum, guero (rape), cymbals, cymbale antique, gong, tambourine, triangle, timpano piccolo, four large timpani, first and second violins, violas, cellos and double basses. Using this ensemble Stravinsky composes a work in which all the formal characteristics sketched out in *Petrushka* are enhanced and intensified : the emancipation of dissonance, the extension, and at times even suppression of the boundaries of traditional tonality by such means as polyharmony, polymodality, and polytonality; and the unleashing of primeval rhythmic forces. As regards their outward structure, these *Pictures of Pagan Russia*, as the sub-title calls them, are divided into

Musik into two parts: *Schoenberg und der Fortschritt* (Schoenberg and Progress), and *Strawinsky und die Restauration* (Stravinsky and Reaction). He accuses Stravinsky of identifying himself with all that is retrograde in the contemporary world (see pp. 108 et seq.: *Permanente Regression und musikalische Gestalt*).

[2] Jean Cocteau, one of the main sources of inspiration of the *avant-garde* of the time, likewise wrote: 'All in all, the *Rite of Spring* is still a savage work, an organized savage work (*œuvre fauve*).' *Le Coq de l'Arlequin*, Editions de la Sirène: Paris, 1918, p. 64.

two parts, and these in turn are further divided into seven and six sections respectively. The work as a whole is thus in the form of a vast suite of thirteen movements.

The Rite of Spring opens with a solo bassoon playing a theme originally from Lithuania, though it is reminiscent of some of the rhapsodic themes of the Carpathian shepherds, or of a Tibetan tune. Just as the first three notes in Weber's *Oberon* seemed to open a door on to the Romantic world, so these astringent sounds take us back suddenly to the atavistic remoteness of a prehistoric world. Arpeggios, trills, and tremolos from the woodwind suggest the gurgle of the rising sap and the shudder that runs through nature as it bursts out and germinates. In the second section man comes on the scene; a crowd of youths dance the 'Augures printaniers'. Here, perhaps for the first time in musical history, rhythm plays a major rôle in the musical discourse, sweeping all the melodic and harmonic elements wholesale into the vortex. This happens in the very opening phrase of the 'Cercles mystérieux des adolescentes', where a complex, vigorous chord

Dominant seventh on E flat

Chord of F flat major

is insistently repeated with a violent asymmetrical rhythmic accent, first for eight bars, then for nine, and finally for a solid thirty-five bars. The persistent hammering of this chord was in fact Stravinsky's original inspiration for *The Rite of Spring*. If we analyse it, we find that it breaks down into an F flat major chord and a dominant seventh on E flat, and the effect of juxtaposing two heterogeneous harmonic poles in this way is like the effect of short circuiting or combustion, melting the musical fabric and welding it into a solid plastic mass. The forces of harmonic, melodic, and tonal propulsion are cancelled out, and the opaque, inert material thus created serves merely to give body to the rhythm. The incredible dynamic intensity of the rhythm swallows up every other element of the musical discourse. On its first appearance, the 'Augures printaniers chord', as it is often called, appears in its synthetic compactness to be nothing more than a kind of harmonic 'aggregate', but immediately afterwards there is a virtual analysis of the differential elements of which it is made up. The cellos first of all spread the lower chord of F flat (written out enharmonically as E major) in pizzicato arpeggios, alternating it with a C major triad derived from the 'aggregate' chord by a shift from C flat to C natural. At the same time the bassoons make a juxtaposition between this triad and the E minor triad (likewise implicit in the general harmonic scheme), while the cor anglais fashions out of the upper chord, the dominant seventh on E flat, a figure which is repeated in a regular pendulum motion. A careful analysis of the whole piece leads to the conclusion that the chord in question serves as a sort of germ cell in exactly the same way as the polytonal clarinet arpeggios in *Petrushka*. Thus Tansman[3] would appear to be right in saying that this chord 'constitutes a pole for the entire work', and that 'this rhythmic harmony gives birth to melodic patterns, all of which correspond by the tones that compose them to some inner tone of these harmonic aggregates, while contrasting by their particular rhythmic movements with the persistence of the unifying rhythm. Obviously, in spite of the percussive aspect of the strings, these pulsations, with their asymmetrical accents, also serve the purpose of harmonic poles and melodic sources, owing to the detail of their composition.'[4] It is interesting to note that this method by which Stravinsky establishes a mutual relationship between the vertical, spatial simultaneity of harmony and the horizontal, temporal succession of melody is analogous to some of the typical rules of serial technique. Next comes the 'Jeu du rapt', in which the orchestra is let loose in a madcap gallop. In the 'Rondes printanières' the pace slows to a solemn procession. The melodic flow of the 'Augures printaniers'

[3] op. cit., pp. 73-74.
[4] In 1969 Boosey and Hawkes published facsimile reproductions of the autograph sketches for *The Rite of Spring* made by Stravinsky between 1911 and 1913. The sketchbook (which also contains pages of sketches for *The Nightingale*, *Cat's Cradle Songs*, *Souvenirs de mon Enfance*, and *Three Japanese Lyrics*) is a document of inestimable interest and importance in assessing the way in which one of the basic masterpieces of twentieth-century music was conceived and moulded into shape. The development of the musical organism, starting from the original cell referred to on page 32 ('the persistent hammering of this chord . . .'), can be followed with an impressive clarity which fully confirms the genetic, polarizing function just mentioned. The persistent polytonal cluster appears in the centre of the first page, preceded by various more open forms – arpeggios and other melodic figures. This leads Craft (see his *Commentary to the Sketches* included in an Appendix to the volume) to the conclusion that, contrary to Stravinsky's own recollection and contention, the initial idea noted down for *The Rite of Spring* had come to him in melodic and not harmonic form. Be this as it may, it is interesting to note that the polytonal arpeggios reflect, as earlier in *Petrushka*, a pianistic origin – the basic division of the keys into black and white.

theme returns. Ten years later Puccini took this motif bodily and incorporated it into the aria 'Tu che di gel sei cinta' in *Turandot* – needless to say first removing the harshness of its harmonies. The giddy theme of the 'Jeu du rapt' now reappears in a madder and more compact form in the 'Jeux des cités rivales'. The 'Cortège du sage' (who 'adores the earth' so as to propitiate its dark forces) goes on its way with a deafening clamour of tubas, timpani, bass drums, and tamtams. In the 'Danse de la terre' which comes next, the very earth seems shaken with frenzied convulsions. Here again it is rhythm that reigns supreme.

The second part of *The Rite of Spring* begins with an Introduction whose icy sonorities conjure up the polar night. From the cold harmonics of the strings and the echoes of the horns comes a theme of weird astral lyricism, which is developed in the 'Cercles mystérieux des adolescentes'. The extremely subtle ruggedness of the accompaniment gives it a harsh quality which makes it still more restless and harrowing. This moment of lyric tenderness is followed by three dances which work up to a delirious climax: 'La glorifica- tion de l'élue', which Stravinsky originally conceived as a wild cavalcade of Amazons; 'Evocation'; and 'Action rituelle des ancêtres'. The work ends with the 'Danse sacrale' – which the elected virgin must dance till she dies of exhaustion, in order to ensure the return of spring. Here the rhythmic fury reaches its height in an orgiastic paroxysmal climax, the rhythmic pattern of each bar differing from that which precedes and folows it: $9/8—5/8—3/8—2/4—7/4—$ $3/4—7/4—3/8—2/4—7/8—3/8—5/8$, etc., though the metric unit of the crotchet remains unchanged. Many critics have expressed views similar to that of Casella, that in the finale of *The Rite of Spring* 'for the first time in the history of music, rhythm is given a structural value and replaces in a certain sense the older thematic development'. This is not altogether true, since as far back as the Ars Nova in France in the fourteenth century the technique of the isorhythmic motet based on the so-called *talea* and *dragma* devices implied specific structural relationships between rhythmic and mel- odic values. In the *talea*, especially, the rhythm took on a thematic aspect, the invariable character of the metrical motives being offset by the variability of the melodic intervals, whereas in the *dragma* the relationship was the reverse, different rhythmic values being assigned to melodies with fixed intervals. It is true, however, with exceptions which are too few to disprove the argument, that for over 500 years rhythm had become petrified in formulas of a stereotyped squareness, and had been relegated to a subordinate position in relation to the other elements of musical discourse. Thus, while in an absolute sense *The Rite of Spring* was not the first work in which rhythm was a structural factor, it was certainly the first time for six centuries that rhythm had been so used on a really large scale. Incidentally, the importance of Stravinsky's innovations in this sphere is recognized even by the *avant-garde* composers of today whose ultimate goal is to serialize all the elements of form, and especially rhythm.[5]

In view of the character of the work, it is hardly surprising that the public did not grasp its meaning at the first performance and revolted against its ferocity and violence, which was taken as a deliberate, outrageous challenge to musical common sense. It is also said that Nijinsky's choreography was inappropriate and contributed to the exasperation of the audience. Stravinsky himself says as much :

> . . . what struck me then, and still strikes me most, about the choreography, was, and is, Nijinsky's lack of consciousness of what he was doing in creating it. . . . How far it all was from what I had desired ! In composing the *Sacre* I had imagined the spectacular part of the performance as a series of rhythmic mass movements of the greatest simplicity which would have had an instantaneous effect on the audience, with no superfluous details or complications such as would suggest effort. The only solo was to be the sacrificial dance at the end of the piece. The music of that dance, clear and well-defined, demanded a corresponding choreography – simple and easy to understand. But there again, although he had grasped the dramatic significance of the dance, Nijinsky was incapable of giving intelligible form to its essence, and complicated it either by clumsiness or lack of understanding.[6]

The fact is that this music is so powerful that no stage representation can ever hope to do it justice and will always seem inadequate. The music of *The Rite of Spring* goes far beyond the visual subject on which it is based and beyond the metaphorical theme, namely the terror and panic which man feels in the face of the unknown forces of nature arrayed about him. Although the setting is a remote corner of the ancient world, the music seems to presage the tragic future that was in store. In 1913, no prophet of doom could have foreseen how successfully forces of evil to all appearance extinct for centuries were to be loosed on the world. But in *The Rite of Spring* we seem to sense the impending catastrophe. Even more than

[5] See Pierre Boulez, 'Propositions', in *Polyphonie* (Paris), No. 2, 1948, for an analysis of the principles of rhythmic variation applied by Stravinsky in *The Rite of Spring*.
[6] *Chronicle of My Life*, p. 82.

Petrushka, this masterpiece testifies to the mysterious prophetic quality possessed by great works of art. In *Petrushka* the tragic symbol of the destruction of individual values in the rule of the masses had the edge taken off it by being treated in a jocular way. Here the symbol is presented with utter directness, with bloodthirsty cruelty. The theme of voluntary self-annihilation and self-extinction highlights the tragedy of the surrender of the individual to the community at first sight, the method employed by Stravinsky to tighten the bonds between the fundamental, intrinsic meaning of his music and individual existence, to anchor the music to the present and still more to project it into a near future which he presaged with prophetic clarity, may seem strange. Instead of choosing a contemporary context for the extrinsic pictorial background and the symbolism of his music, he removed it as far as possible from any suggestion of the present-day scene, making the setting, in the one case, the unreal world of a popular legend and in the other, the remote archaeological atmosphere of a prehistoric tale. But this is only a seeming paradox. The real, infinitely tragic paradox lay in the forecast of future events and the imminent fate of mankind : this Stravinsky unconsciously foresaw and foretold in the work. A tragic paradox indeed, because the very 'progress' of science and technology helped to bring about the dramatic irruption of the pent-up forces of dark, primeval barbarity. In the same way, positivist humanism engendered the drama of the triumph of the masses over man's individuality – the very faculty which both classical antiquity and Christianity had, each in its own way, made the focus and target of all moral value and every civilizing principle. This age-old civilization was suddenly placed in jeopardy by the encroaching hordes of latter-day barbarism, which is in no way different from the barbarism of antiquity, as was illustrated precisely by the symbolism of this great archaeological ballet of Roerich and Stravinsky. There are those who interpret Stravinsky's entire work in the light (or perhaps we should say, the shadow) of a negative philosophy which goes beyond the values of revelation and embraces also the whole field of human-istic illuminism. The reference here is to the extremist interpretation of Adorno, several of whose questionable theses and unacceptable conclusions I have already discussed in other writings. One of his contentions is that the adherents of the Viennese school of Schoen-berg, and they alone, took up the cudgels against the negative philosophy of the modern world, whereas Stravinsky is 'identified' with all that is destructive and regressive. I reject this argument absolutely, even though I have no wish to challenge Adorno's philosophical interpretation of the precise part played by Schoenberg and his two disciples in contemporary culture. All I take exception to is the antithesis which the author in his *Philosophie der neuen Musik* tries to establish between Schoenberg's rôle and that played by Stravinsky. I maintain that no case can be made out for the thesis put forward by Adorno that Stravinsky's art is reactionary, that it 'embraces' the negative forces and tries to 'exorcize' them by identifying itself with them. If at one particular time Stravinsky allowed his art to become identified with a tragically negative situation, he did so in order to give expression to this situation and thus to restore the balance on the basis of pure aesthetic reality. Be that as it may, whatever interpretation we give *The Rite of Spring*, its implications embrace so vast a field that any visual representation must inevitably restrict and cramp its significance. This statement is borne out by the fact that not more than a year after the disastrous 'first night' in the theatre, *The Rite of Spring* was given in concert form with tremendous success. In April 1914 *The Rite of Spring* and *Petrushka* were conducted for the first time in concert form by Pierre Monteux in Paris. From that date on *The Rite of Spring* has been recognized as a masterpiece. Tansman among many others regards it as 'the most significant work of our time', and Casella goes so far as to rank it in importance with Beethoven's Ninth Symphony.

The work has since been performed again in theatrical form, one of the best choreographic productions being that by Aurel Millos at the Teatro dell'Opera in Rome. Another was Massine's – produced first of all in Paris in 1920 by Diaghilev; there was a second production in New York in 1930 for the League of Composers. Stravinsky was not entirely satisfied with either, though he speaks highly of them in the *Chronicle of My Life*. But the true place of *The Rite of Spring* is the concert hall, as a work of pure music which requires no distraction for the eye. It is the kind of music that Alain calls 'music of such power that it suppresses every other object'. What Stravinsky himself wrote about another of his works (*The Fairy's Kiss*) would apply equally to *The Rite of Spring*:

This music has a much more difficult rôle. The music proper has to define what neither gesture nor words can express. Thus it is self-contained, and it sings, replacing the invisible with its own sounds.[7]

[7] A programme note quoted by De'Paoli, op. cit., p. 51, note 1.

V The Vocal Works of the Russian Period

In the earlier chapters we have followed Stravinsky's gradual development as an artist and his spectacular rise to fame with works of the stature of *Petrushka* and *The Rite of Spring*. The historical significance of *The Rite of Spring* with regard both to form and to its absolute value as music has already been pointed out. It is in every sense an 'extreme' work, in which expressiveness is raised to a white-hot incandescence, the emancipation of dissonances is complete, and the dynamic violence of the music is without precedent. But the most extremist feature of all is the thickness of the orchestral texture. It is interesting to note that the orchestra used by Schoenberg in the *Gurre-Lieder*, which was finished in 1911, surpasses in mere size the gigantic instrumental ensemble used in *The Rite of Spring*; but even before the orchestration of the *Gurre-Lieder* was completed, Schoenberg had already begun in the Chamber Symphony to react against the vogue for mammoth orchestras started by Wagner and continued by Strauss and Mahler. We find the same reaction in Stravinsky. Even before the orchestration of *The Rite of Spring* was finished he began writing the *Three Japanese Lyrics* for voice and small chamber ensemble – two flutes, two clarinets, piano, and string quartet, and it was not until many years later that he again used a symphony orchestra of normal size. As someone has said, it was as though the Wagnerian orchestra had exploded like a bomb in Stravinsky's hands when he composed *The Rite of Spring*. Before re-fashioning it, Stravinsky seems to have felt the need to take it completely to pieces and fit it together again bit by bit.

In the ten years following the composition of *The Rite of Spring* he wrote a whole series of works for small instrumental ensembles made up in each particular instance to suit the peculiar requirements of the work in hand. But however different the choice of instruments, the ensembles have one thing in common, namely the principle fundamental to all chamber music – the substitution of pure timbres used singly for the blending of timbres and massed instrumental writing peculiar to orchestral composition. Stravinsky used these particular instrumental combinations either on their own or in conjunction with solo voices or choral ensembles. Thus between 1912 and 1919 he produced a whole series of vocal works. Let us take first of all the *Three Japanese Lyrics* already mentioned. The lyrics on which these songs are based are three very short Japanese 'hai-kai' entitled 'Akahito', 'Mazatsumi' and 'Tsaraiuki'. Here once more the theme is the approach of spring, but a spring utterly unlike that depicted in *The Rite of Spring*, where the atmosphere is one of primitive, barbaric cruelty, as though the musical landscape were bespotted with scarlet patches from the blood of human sacrifice.

Spring in the *Japanese Lyrics* is carpeted with flowers, their milky whiteness merging with the melting snow. The fierce heat of *The Rite of Spring* has cooled down; the dense mass of sound becomes transparent as crystal; instead of the heavy compact timbres we get a glass fragility, a spidery line-drawing, like a Japanese print. As Stravinsky himself puts it: 'The graphic solution of problems of perspective and space shown by [the art of the Japanese] incited me to find something analogous in music.'[1] The dynamic multiformity of rhythm becomes a static uniformity of metre. In their aphorism-like conciseness, in quality of timbre, and in expressiveness, these pieces are distinctly reminiscent of Schoenberg's *Six Little Pieces*, op. 19, and even more of *Pierrot Lunaire*. In point of fact, a few months before he started the *Three Japanese Lyrics* Stravinsky was in Berlin and heard a performance of *Pierrot Lunaire*. He was profoundly moved by it, as he told Ravel, with whom he was collaborating at the time on a commission for Diaghilev to orchestrate and complete Mussorgsky's *Khovanshchina*. With Ravel, too, this first contact with Schoenberg's art bore fruit immediately in his *Poèmes de Mallarmé*. Indeed, in the case of both Ravel and Stravinsky, there is no doubt that the features reminiscent of *Pierrot Lunaire* should not be under-estimated (any more than they should be exaggerated) – first and foremost certain features of the musical configuration which do not alter the intrinsic tonal structure. The musical detail of the *Japanese Lyrics* also reflects that of *The Rite of Spring*. Compared with the latter, they are like the fragments of an immense meteor which has disintegrated, though its basic structure has remained unchanged. But the contrapuntal texture and the superstructure of timbre show an evident acquaintance with Schoenberg's brilliant piece.[2]

What has been said about the formal side of the *Japanese Lyrics*

[1] *Chronicle of My Life*, p. 78.
[2] For the influence of *Pierrot Lunaire* on Stravinsky, see pages 277–9.

applies to all the other vocal works of the period, with this difference, that in the other works the melodic line is not abstract as in
the *Japanese Lyrics* but is either taken direct from Russian folk-lore
or is based on the rhythmic and modal patterns used in ancient
Slavonic popular music. The first of the series, *Recollections of
Childhood*, consists of three short songs for voice and piano composed in 1913, about the same time as *The Rite of Spring* and the
Japanese Lyrics. Each of the three songs is dedicated to one of
Stravinsky's children. The first song, 'The Magpie', is dedicated to
Sviatoslav Soulima, the second, 'The Rook,' to his daughter Milena,
and the third, 'The Jackdaw,' to Theodore. According to Stravinsky
(*Chronicle of My Life*) the tunes are his own, the words being taken
from Russian nursery rhymes he had heard as a child, while the
piano accompaniment is vaguely reminiscent of the spontaneously
dissonant style of *The Rite of Spring*. One of the leading authorities
on Stravinsky, Boris de Schloezer,[3] calls these short songs one of the
most intimate expressions of Stravinsky's lyricism – a strange kind
of lyricism whose main characteristic is that the artist never expresses his own personality but sings the song of mankind, or more
precisely of 'a gregarious humanity, a collective being, "the people",
in whom all individual traits of personality are absorbed'. What de
Schloezer implies, in other words, is that in these pieces we again
have the same relationship between man and society that we found
in *Petrushka* and *The Rite of Spring*. There is this difference, however, that in these songs the relationship has lost all suggestion of
tragedy; it has become light-hearted as a child's game. De Schloezer,
and other critics like him, regard the impassive quality of Stravinsky's music as one of its most valuable attributes. On the other
hand, according to Adorno[4] 'objectivity' is the negative factor in
Stravinsky's art, an indication of the process by which the individual
loses sight of what is the real mainspring of his inner spiritual life.
There is no doubt some truth in both these views; but neither
should be taken too literally. The term 'objectivity', too, is open to
discussion. Surely the very title *Recollections of Childhood* is an
indication of the subjective feeling which Stravinsky has put into
the composition of the songs. Another prejudice which dies hard
among critics is the relationship between the music and the words
of the text. The great majority of writers on Stravinsky speak of the
three songs as the first of a series of vocal works in which the

[3] *La Revue Musicale*, December 1923.
[4] ibid.

poetic text is treated as a purely phonetic device. They allege that the composer makes use of the syllabic structure of the words only and completely disregards their meaning, and that to begin with he chose texts almost devoid of meaning. De' Paoli, for example, writes: 'They consist of three little tunes, neat and square, the words hardly making sense (in these songs we can already discern Stravinsky's tendency to regard the text from the point of view not of interpretation but purely of rhythm and sound).' (*Igor Stravinsky*, op. cit., p. 54.) This argument does not seem to me to hold water. The texts of the three songs, like those of *Pribaoutki*, the *Cat's Cradle Songs*, *Four Russian Peasant Songs*, *Recollections of Childhood*, and *Four Russian Songs* have as much sense, or shall we say nonsense, as ballads and popular songs, dirges or lullabies ever have. Nor is it true that Stravinsky has no interest in the texts. Notice the magpie tune in the first song; the way in which in the second song his accompaniment suggests onomatopoeically the hoarse cawing of the rook, and how in the third the joyful scampering of the chords in fourths suggests the pranks of the impudent jackdaw of Russian fairy stories. This, incidentally, is brought out even more vividly in the versions for small instrumental ensemble which Stravinsky made in 1933 and 1947, expanding the songs in places to suit the orchestral requirements.

After finishing the pieces mentioned above, and the stormy first night of *The Rite of Spring*, Stravinsky fell ill with typhoid fever, hovering for several weeks between life and death. As soon as he had recovered he took a short holiday at his house at Oustiloug in Russia, and then settled down in Switzerland, where he lived during the turbulent years of the First World War. But shortly before the war broke out he again returned to Russia. During this journey, the last he ever made to his native country, one of the regions he visited was Kiev, where he managed to get hold of some collections of Russian popular poetry, including the well-known collection of Kirievsky and Afanaziev. He also had a number of volumes of folk-lore sent to him from his father's library. The rest of the vocal pieces discussed in this chapter were obviously the fruits of this direct folk-lore inspiration. First of all *Pribaoutki*, written in 1914. The sub-title calls them *Chansons plaisantes*. They consist of four short pieces for voice and eight instruments: flute, oboe, clarinet, bassoon, and string quartet. They have an exhilarating if somewhat tart and piquant rustic humour; they are full of childish fun reminiscent of the *Recollections of Childhood*.

The *Cat's Cradle Songs*, written in 1915-16,[5] have the conciseness
of a set of aphorisms. They are scored for voice and three clarinets,
small E flat clarinet, clarinet in A, and bass clarinet. Noteworthy
here is the manner in which Stravinsky makes use of this unusual
trio of clarinets to produce an impression in sound of the physical
characteristics of the cat: lithe and sinuous, serene and stealthy.
The *Cat's Cradle Songs* may be reckoned as one of the most personal
and characteristic expressions of Stravinsky's lyrical style.

The *Four Russian Peasant Songs*, with the sub-title *Soucoupes*
(Saucers) were begun the year before the *Cat's Cradle Songs* but not
completed until the year after. They are four very short choral
works for equal voices ('On Saints' Day in Chigisakh', 'Ovsen', 'The
Pike', and 'Master Portly'). They are settings of tiny rhymes and
sayings like those which are, or used to be, sung in Russia about
Christmas time while the peasants told fortunes in tea-leaves poured
into a saucer. The original version of 1914-17 was for female chorus
a cappella. In 1954 Stravinsky produced another version for chorus
and four horns.

Stravinsky's half-amusing, half-nostalgic reminiscences of his salad
days, begun in *Recollections of Childhood*, recur in a new and most
successful form in the *Trois Histoires pour enfants*, written between
1915 and 1917. In these three delightful pieces the intimate bond
between music and text once again belies Stravinsky's alleged indifference to the poetic value of words. Notice how in the first little
story the piano accompaniment cleverly suggests the insistent, frantic
ringing of a little bell to warn the farmyard animals of a fire. See
the utterly charming way in which, in the second piece, the shower
of ninths and sevenths recalls the fluttering of ducks, swans, and
geese, and how very effectively in the third piece the alternation of
two notes in the bass suggests the heavy, clumsy walk of the bear.

One of the last works of Stravinsky's so-called 'Russian period' is
the set of *Four Russian Songs*, composed in 1918-19. Here again we
find features similar to those we have met with in the children's
pieces already discussed. Even in some of his later works, where
the theme is not in any way childish, we shall find similar
features typical of the children's pieces – tiny melodic phrases of

[5] This is the date given in *Igor Stravinsky. A Complete Catalogue of his
Published Works*, Boosey and Hawkes, London, 1957, p. 17. But as indicated
in Chapter III, footnote 3, the sketches for *The Rite of Spring* include several
(Nos. 110 to 113) for the *Cat's Cradle Songs* also. Hence Stravinsky must have
made a start on them not later than 1913, unless we prefer to think that he
later used up some odd pages that were left blank (there are others still in
the notebook) to jot down the sketches.

the utmost simplicity, stereotyped repetitions of rhythmical figures, and harmonic combinations with a deliberately naïve flavour and a sophisticated crudeness. The fact that such passages occur occasionally in works which are otherwise extremely complex has led one critic to make the charge that Stravinsky's works reveal positive symptoms of hebephrenia.[6] While such assertions should be taken with a grain of salt, it is undeniably true that certain of Stravinsky's works reflect neurotic phenomena typical of life today, traumatic experiences, nervous tensions, symptoms of schizophrenia, and again frenzied repetitions and positive musical obsessions. Something of all this is found even in works as apparently innocent as 'Canard', 'Chanson pour compter' and 'Le Moineau est assis', the first three of the *Four Russian Songs*. The same characteristics are even more accentuated in the heartfelt 'Chant dissident', the fourth in the group.[7] It is hardly surprising that sixty years ago the symptoms mentioned above should have produced the most violent reactions. But over the years the listener has gradually come to recognize in such works his own inner world, and has found more and more opportunities to obtain release by catharsis from the fetters of his own tormented sensibility.

[6] Weisengrund-Adorno, op. cit., pp. 115 et seq.
[7] In 1954 Stravinsky transcribed the first and fourth of these songs, along with two of the *Trois Histoires pour enfants* ('Berceuse' and 'Tilim-bom') for voice, flute, harp, and guitar.

VI The Nightingale

In the second chapter we saw how Stravinsky came to compose *The Nightingale*, and how he interrupted the work on it in the summer of 1909 when Diaghilev commissioned him to write *The Firebird*. The libretto for *The Nightingale*, written by the composer himself and his friend Mitusov, is based on the well-known story by Hans Andersen. The opera was to be in three acts, of which only the first had been completed when the work was interrupted. In 1913 the Moscow Free Theatre invited him to finish it. At first Stravinsky hesitated. He had hardly yet recovered from the emotion and nervous tension caused by the riotous first performance of *The Rite of Spring* and was still suffering from the after-effects of the serious bout of typhoid fever that had followed in its train. But it was not for reasons of health alone that he hesitated. He was greatly perplexed about the question of style. Four years had elapsed between the interruption of the work and the invitation to take it up again. Four years may not seem very much; but between 1909 and 1913 Stravinsky had covered an immense amount of ground in his stylistic development, and had covered it at a dizzy speed. The landmarks on the way are *The Firebird, Petrushka*, and *The Rite of Spring*. There is no question that the experience of composing these three masterpieces gave a new turn to Stravinsky's technique and language and profoundly affected it. There was no going back over the road he had taken between 1909 and 1913; he did not feel he could continue the work in the same vein in which he had begun it. On the other hand he had no desire to change the first act completely and begin the work afresh. If he had decided to complete it he would have had to leave the first act as he had drafted it in 1909 and write the second and third acts in the style he had evolved by 1913. This would have meant producing a work which was not uniform in style. Stravinsky obviously realized the difficulty, and explained it to the directors of the Free Theatre; but he was talked out of it and finally persuaded to settle down to the task. Stravinsky explains how he tackled the problem :[1]

[1] *Chronicle of My Life*, pp. 87-88.

As there is no action until the second act, I told myself that it would not be unreasonable if the music of the Prologue bore a somewhat different character from that of the rest. And, indeed, the forest, with its nightingale, the pure soul of the child who falls in love with its song . . . all this gentle poetry of Hans Andersen's could not be expressed in the same way as the baroque luxury of the Chinese Court, with its bizarre etiquette, its palace fêtes, its thousands of little bells and lanterns, and the grotesque humming of the mechanical Japanese nightingale . . . in short, all this exotic fantasy obviously demanded a different musical idiom.

The Nightingale was completed in the winter of 1913-14. In the meantime Stravinsky learned that the Free Theatre had gone bankrupt; but this did not hold up the first performance. Diaghilev had planned to produce Rimsky-Korsakov's *Golden Cockerel* during the season, so that the singers needed were available for the production of *The Nightingale*. Stravinsky's 'lyrical tale' was therefore included in the season of the Ballet Russe and was staged at the Paris Opera on 26 May 1914. The set was designed by Alexandre Benois, and the opera was conducted by Pierre Monteux.

The Nightingale is without doubt one of the most fascinating of Stravinsky's works, even though its unity of form is impaired by the difference in style between the act written in 1909 and those written in 1913-14. The composer himself tacitly admitted as much later, in 1917, when he arranged it as a symphonic poem entitled *Le Chant du rossignol*, making use almost exclusively of material from the second and third acts, and taking only 'The Fisherman's Song' from the first act. In 1920 Diaghilev used this orchestral version for a ballet which was performed at the Paris Opera with choreography by Massine and a set by Matisse. In comparison with the opera in its original form, the symphonic poem is without a doubt stylistically more homogeneous. But its conception as a vocal work is evident even in the purely instrumental arrangement. This is one of the reasons why I prefer the work in its original and complete form to the subsequent adaptation. The opera begins with an Introduction, its characteristic feature being the alternation of fifths and thirds in a gentle, regular pattern:

Larghetto (♩= 92)

The passage has a distinct affinity with Debussy's first nocturne 'Nuages' :

Incidentally this passage from Debussy is itself very similar to certain passages in the piano part of the third song from Mussorgsky's 'Sunless' cycle.

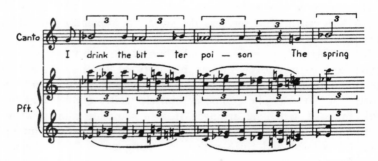

Hence it is quite possible that the link with Mussorgsky may be direct and not via Debussy.

A short transition brings us to the 'Fisherman's Song', heard as the fisherman sits in his boat waiting to hear the magical notes of the nightingale that sings every night with the approach of dawn. The nocturnal scene by the sea and at the edge of the forest is evoked in the music by means of chords of ninths and elevenths which betray the direct influence of Debussy's *Pelléas*, a work whose 'admirable music, so fresh in its modesty' aroused Stravinsky's whole-hearted enthusiasm.[2] The 'Fisherman's Song', with its clear diatonic modes and its harmonies in fifths, is related to Stravinsky's *Pastorale* discussed in the first chapter. A silvery cascade of trills, runs, and arabesques from the orchestra heralds the song of the nightingale – a sustained melodic phrase, full yet delicate and iridescent, sung by a lyric soprano, not on the stage but in the orchestra. A grotesque burbling from the orchestra and an ironically

[2] *Poetics of Music*, p. 58.

solemn motive from the bassoon give the signal for the entrance of a number of comic characters: the Chamberlain, the Bonze, the Courtiers, and the Cook, who have come to listen to the nightingale with the idea of inviting it to the Court to sing for the Emperor. The Courtiers mistake the lowing of a heifer and the croaking of the frogs for the song of the nightingale. The Cook shows them their mistake, and the wretched Courtiers despair of ever hearing the nightingale. The whole of this scene is depicted by Stravinsky with original and beautifully apt instrumental touches, even though not yet displaying all the raciness of which his grotesque vein was capable later. At last the nightingale appears. Now the trilling and burbling burst forth again from the orchestra and the coloratura soprano once more pours out her silvery arabesques. The Chamberlain sings a flamboyant song inviting the nightingale to follow him to Court. The nightingale agrees and perches on his hand; and they all make their way towards the Imperial Palace. The fisherman repeats his lay, and the curtain falls. A phantasmagoria of sounds irrupts like a torrent in the intermezzo between the first and second acts. Harp and horn glissandos, scintillating trills and tremolos from the whole orchestra explain why the subtitle of the intermezzo is 'courants d'air'. The stage directions read: 'The porcelain palace of the Emperor of China. Fantastic architecture. Decorations for a feast; lights everywhere.' During the preparations for the sumptuous tableau which follows, the chorus sings 'Bring light, bring light, oh quickly bring us light', and a thousand lights illumine the scene. Here the polyharmonic and polytonal fragmentation serves admirably to create a dazzling profusion of tonal planes which are brought to life in the rich, kaleidoscopic glitter of instrumental timbres. It can be argued that the music does not describe what is going on, does not create the atmosphere, indeed avoids any significant connection with it. This is no doubt true in an exterior and superficial sense. It would never have occurred to Stravinsky to use a recording of a real nightingale in his music or to resort to crude realistic imitation; but that does not mean that he has no interest in what is going on on the stage. On the contrary, as in *Petrushka* the music is fitted to the theme intimately and structurally. In this respect it is interesting to see how Stravinsky succeeds in rendering Chinese local colour. He does not follow mechanically the pattern of the pentatonic scale characteristic of Chinese music, but appropriates its structural principle, namely the absence of any semitone interval; and the different effects – the Oriental splendour, the ceremonious

austerity of the March, to the strains of which the Emperor enters
with his Court, and its elephantine grandeur – are created by the
use of this formal device. Once the nightingale begins to sing,
everything changes. The music again reverts to the use of semitones.
The melismata fall into a chromatic pattern, and the contrast with
the previous way of writing creates a wonderfully poetic atmosphere.
The full-throated song of a creature palpitating with life sends a
thrill through the stuffy, pompous courtiers:

The artless lyric tenderness of the scene dies away, and is followed
by a comic scene when the ladies of the Court produce hilarious
gargling sounds in an attempt to imitate the nightingale. The
grotesque element is equally predominant in the succeeding scene,
in which three Japanese emissaries arrive. The Emperor of Japan
has sent his brother the Chinese Emperor a mechanical nightingale.
This one does not sing, it plays like a musical-box:

Here Stravinsky does use the Chinese pentatonic scale in its strictly regular form, precisely in order to bring out the difference between the artificiality of the mechanical nightingale and the live, spontaneous singing of the real bird. Meanwhile, the latter has flown away leaving his musical-box rival in sole possession. The Emperor in a fit of rage banishes him from his kingdom. The orchestra again takes up the solemn march. The curtain falls slowly. Once again the fisherman sings his doleful ditty.

The third act follows without a break. When the curtain rises, the Emperor is discovered lying on his bed seriously ill. A chorus of ghosts appear on the stage, and at the bedside sits Death wearing the Emperor's crown and carrying his sceptre and sabre. The dying Emperor entreats the nightingale to return; it reappears and repeats its song from the second act, but in tones more melting and tender. Even Death is moved and after hearing the song gives the Emperor back his possessions one by one and disappears. The gentle 'Berceuse' of the nightingale brings peace to the ghosts of the dead and they betake themselves to their graves, while the Emperor is lulled into a soothing sleep. When the Courtiers arrive, to the strains of a funeral march, the Emperor rises and greets them all with 'Be welcome here'. As the curtain falls the nightingale flies off to the woods, where the fisherman sings his lay for the last time, in the simple key of C major. Here, as at the end of the other acts, this folk-tune contrasts with the unreal, fairy-tale atmosphere, like a return to the world of reality, as if to mark the end of a dream.

This music, as I have already said, is far removed from abstract formalism, and equally far removed from vulgar realism. I would place *The Nightingale* in the category of works of art which are properly described by the term 'magic realism'.

VII Return to the Spirit of Chamber Music

As has already been pointed out, after finishing *The Rite of Spring* Stravinsky did not compose for an orchestra of conventional size for nearly ten years. In the meantime he wrote a whole series of works for small chamber ensembles, the composition of the ensemble in each individual case being chosen according to the demands of the particular work. The instrumental combination in all instances has one feature in common, and it is a feature basic to the concept of chamber music in general, namely, the desire to exploit the individual quality of unmixed tone colours. Stravinsky used instrumental ensembles or isolated instruments alike, either in combination with solo voices or choral ensembles, or on their own. The vocal music of the period was discussed in Chapter V. Here we shall discuss the purely instrumental works, beginning with the *Three Pieces* for string quartet written in 1914.

Although very little known, these pieces are extremely significant as far as Stravinsky's stylistic development and inner artistic motivation are concerned. The first point of interest is the actual title of the work. Notice that Stravinsky does not call it a String Quartet, but Three Pieces for string quartet. The distinction is more than mere linguistic hair-splitting; there is a very real reason for it, one which throws light on an essential aspect of European musical history in the first decades of the twentieth century. From the eighteenth-century classical composers onwards the term 'quartet', like the term 'symphony', had become identified with 'sonata form'. This was based on the dialectical opposition of two distinct musical themes, with a parallel opposition between the tonal planes of tonic and dominant. As time went on, the working out or 'development' of the themes was carried to the point where sonata form dissolved into variation form. In addition, the dynamic tonal impulse due to the switching of the musical discourse from tonic to dominant and vice versa had lost its point, either because of a trend towards atonality or because of the polytonal and polyharmonic devices such as we find in Stravinsky from *Petrushka* onwards. As we have seen, by polytonal and polyharmonic superimposition Stravinsky brought together simultaneously elements which in the past could only be heard in succession. The classical sonata was based precisely on this succession or alteration of tonal planes. The moment succession became simultaneity, the sonata as such lost its *raison d'être* and its historical topicality. But as the terms 'quartet' and 'sonata' had become linked in common usage, composers like Webern and Stravinsky preferred to call their compositions 'Pieces for string quartet' when they were not written in sonata form. The word 'quartet' thus no longer refers to the form but merely to the nature of the instrumental ensemble.

The way in which Stravinsky handles this ensemble is also significant. The spirit of chamber music demands that the timbre of each separate part should be allowed its individuality. In the *Three Pieces* Stravinsky carries this principle to its logical conclusion. By making use of the different ways of attacking the strings, he achieves the utmost differentiation even in the homogeneous sonority of the stringed instruments. Thus in the first piece, the first violin is directed to rub the strings continuously with the whole length of the bow. The second violin is instructed to make 'extremely dry' sounds above the bridge, rather like a trumpet. Throughout the whole piece the viola holds a D, played either with the bow, *sul ponticello*, or pizzicato. The cello is treated as a percussion instrument. The structure of the themes assigned to the various instruments is also noteworthy. Throughout the entire piece, the first violin plays a figure based exclusively on these four notes:

which are arranged as follows:

The second violin at the beginning and at the end helps the viola to play its ostinato note. For the rest of the piece, it simply plays the following four notes, always in the same order:

The viola, as we have said, plays only a D; and the cello plays nothing but:

There is no development of the themes, no modulation. At no time do they constitute discursive elements between the various instruments. Each theme is rigorously confined to a strict area of the tonal compass of the piece, and is not allowed to go beyond a certain limit of tone colour. Stravinsky thus defies one of the fundamental principles of traditional chamber music and indeed of all music written for several voices or in several parts, namely the principle of dialogue between the parts. One of the chief means of establishing this was by the free interchange of themes and motives between one part and another and between one register and another continuously, each running through a series of harmonic planes and tonal sequences. The compass of the music and the instrumental structure were thus given maximum flexibility. Stravinsky makes them rigid. Once the thematic principle is removed, the tonal compass ceases to bind together the tonal groups contained in it, but as in a Byzantine mosaic or painting, it constitutes the aggregate of a whole series of geometrical segments or of solid pieces. This rigidity in the harmonic and melodic elements and the timbre is offset by the extreme plasticity of the rhythmic structure. The metric accents are constantly shifting, and as in the 'Danse des augures printaniers' the rhythm becomes an essential driving force in the musical context. The rhythmical current running through the music is what binds together these curious mosaic-like pieces. The compass within which the piece is written does not comprise the twelve notes: in fact the figuration of the four instrumental parts added together gives nine individual notes, always the same.

In this piece Stravinsky would appear to have moved very far away from the Schoenberg school. What he is really doing is anticipating one of the devices which Webern and those who came after him applied in some of their works, e.g. Pierre Boulez and, more systematically, Olivier Messiaen in his *Mode de valeurs et d'intensités* (1949) in which he extends the principle of structural rigidity to all the dimensions of the sound images. These devices consist of assigning every note to a given register, a strictly defined part of the compass, excluding all the octaves of those notes. Stravinsky is incidentally anticipating also some of the features of the last movement of his own Septet of forty years later, in which various series of notes, described as 'rows', have the specific function of delimiting, as each occurs, the sector of the compass over which the individual instrumental parts are to range. The comparison with Webern is particularly striking in the second of the *Three Pieces*, a composition in recitative form, with parts which could be described as 'expressionistic'. Of course, the parallelism is entirely fortuitous, since it is hardly likely that at that time either Stravinsky or Webern could have been acquainted with the other's music. It is nevertheless a significant indication of a natural bent in Stravinsky which makes the affinities with Webern we find in Stravinsky's latest works less surprising; it may also explain the tribute which Stravinsky paid to Webern on 15 September 1954, on the occasion of the tenth anniversary of his death: 'We must hail', he wrote, 'not only this great composer, but also a real hero. Doomed to total failure in a deaf world of ignorance and indifference, he inexorably kept on cutting out his diamonds, his dazzling diamonds, [of] the mines of which he had such a perfect knowledge'.[1]

The third of the *Three Pieces* for string quartet is very different from the other two. Here Stravinsky makes use of the homogeneous timbre of the strings to create a compact mass of sound. This resolves itself into a chorale which begins with the same notes as the Gregorian *Dies irae*:

[1] *Die Reihe* (Universal Edition: Vienna), No. 2, 1955.

Then come responses, like an antiphon to a psalm. The whole
piece has the hieratic austerity of a Byzantine icon. This is another
piece in which we find one of the essential facets of Stravinsky's
personality : the religious side. The *Three Pieces* for string quartet
never became very popular, although this does not detract from
their value.

Lindlar[2] finds pre-echoes of the Symphonies of Wind Instruments
in the *Three Pieces* for string quartet, and regards them as preparatory material for the *Symphony of Psalms* ('Wir stehn im Vorhof
der Psalmensinfonie'). This is why he stresses the importance of the
Three Pieces in Stravinsky's creative activity. Stravinsky himself was
always greatly attached to them, so much so that in 1917 he transcribed them for orchestra under the titles of 'Danse'; 'Excentrique';
'Cantique', adding in 1928 or 1929 a fourth piece, 'Madrid', which
turns out to be a transcription of a Study for pianola written in 1917.
We shall have something to say about this work later.

To proceed in chronological order, we come first to two sets of
piano duets (four hands). The first set, written in 1915, is called
Three Easy Pieces; the second, dating from 1917, consists of *Five
Easy Pieces*. The *Three Easy Pieces* are a March, a Waltz, and a
Polka. Stravinsky singles out one or two of the more hackneyed and
banal clichés of European music. Seen through the distorting mirror
of his acid humour, these musical commonplaces have a tragi-comic
drollery. The stiff, mechanical character of the works discussed above
is even more marked here. The bass part in these three pieces is
actually marked by the composer as 'easy', and in fact the player's
task could hardly be easier : through each of the pieces, all he has
to do is repeat one stereotyped little phrase from beginning to end.
Thus in the March the bass saws away at :

In the Waltz the old 'vamping' figure :

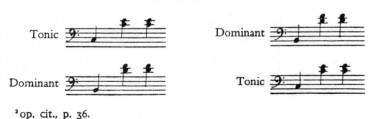

[2] op. cit., p. 36.

reappears with compulsive regularity, like a nervous tic. In the Polka the accompaniment is hypnotized by this little 'vamp':

surely the last word in banality. Even the rhythmic beat has ceased to show any sign of variation, and is petrified in a stereotyped, automatic squareness. The melodic line is as hackneyed and ordinary as anything in the musical stock-in-trade. The biting irony of these pieces is expressed mainly by means of a series of modal and tonal shifts; roguish off-key effects, twisting and slipping pitch. In the Waltz the 'colla parte' rubatos caricature the bad taste of the sentimental interpreter and accentuate outrageously the satirical character of the pieces. But Stravinsky's satire is not without a certain poetry of its own : it has the wistful, infinitely sad poetry of the barrel organ and the pianola. In the second set, *Five Easy Pieces*, these poetic aspects are more in evidence than any attempt at grotesque caricature. The Andante with which the second set opens is one of the most touching pieces Stravinsky ever wrote. The right hand, as in the other four pieces, plays a delightful tune, Russian in flavour. The Andante is the nearest thing to Ravel in all of Stravinsky's music. The second piece, too, 'Española', is not in any way a skit on Spanish music, but rather pays homage to it. The third piece makes a genuinely affectionate and poetic allusion to the sound of the ancient popular instrument of the Slavs, the balalaika, the Russian equivalent of the guitar or the mandoline. The fourth piece is a brilliant, spirited tarantella called 'Napolitana', an amusing tribute to Naples and Neapolitan music, for which Stravinsky always had a weakness.[3] It is only in the last piece that he pours out the venom of his satirical wit in Galop, a dance very much in vogue in nineteenth-century Paris. Stravinsky describes it as a caricature of the St. Petersburg version of the Folies Bergère, which he had watched in a demi-respectable night club in the Astrava. (*Dialogues and a Diary*, p. 41).

There is much more to every one of the pieces in both Suites than is suggested by the childishly didactic manner in which one part is written so that it can be played by the merest novice; as a matter of fact Stravinsky later turned them into two Suites for small

[3] In the *Chronicle of My Life* (p. 114) Stravinsky gives his impressions of Naples, where he spent a fortnight in 1917 with Diaghilev.

orchestra, rearranging the pieces in a different order, but without altering the fundamental harmonic and melodic shape. The description 'childishly didactic' is entirely appropriate in the case of the second series of *Easy Pieces*. On page 41 of *Dialogues and a Diary* Stravinsky says that he composed the five pieces as 'music lessons' for his children, Theodore and Mika, who were obviously given the easy parts to play while the more difficult parts were played by the teacher, in this case Stravinsky himself. However, he explains that 'the simplicities of one of the parts (of the three sections of the first series) were designed so as not to embarrass the small range of Diaghilev's technique', the pieces having been written for him. The pieces also had Diaghilev in mind as the object of a double caricature. The very notion of 'four-hand piano playing' was an ironical reference to the passion with which Diaghilev played piano duets with his lifelong friend Walter Nouvel. The *Polka* was intended specifically as a comic musical portrait of Diaghilev, whom he saw as 'a circus animal-trainer cracking a long whip'. In the 'ice-cream Valse', as Stravinsky calls it today, he 'tried to portray something of the spirit of Satie', to whom the piece is dedicated. Similarly, recalling the enthusiasm shown by Casella, as well as Diaghilev, for the *Polka* when he played it to them in 1915 in a hotel room in Milan, Stravinsky not only notes that Casella's genuine enthusiasm had led him to promise to write a similar piece for him (in fact it was the witty *March* which comes at the end of the *Three Pieces*), but he allows himself the rather malicious insinuation that this 'piece of popcorn' indicated a new path soon to be followed by Casella and that that same moment had witnessed the birth of 'so-called neo-classicism of a sort'. This insinuation may perhaps be seen as a last vestige of the dispute as to whether Italian neo-classicism was an offshoot of that of Paris, a controversy which had prompted Casella to write the famous article *Il Neoclassicismo mio e altrui* which appeared in issue No. 5, Year I, May 1929, of the magazine *Pegaso*.

With regard to the instrumental versions 'of the *Easy Pieces*, Stravinsky orchestrated the *Valse* for seven solo instruments immediately after composing the piano version. About the same time he arranged the *Polka* for cymbalom (the instrument he used later in *Ragtime for eleven instruments*) and small ensemble, and the *March* for eight soloists. These arrangements of the *Polka* and the *March* remained unpublished. The final chamber orchestra version (2 flutes, oboe, 2 clarinets, 2 bassoons, horn, trumpet, trombone, tuba, tympani and strings) of Suite No. 1 : *Andante, Napolitano, Española,* and *Balalaika*, is dated 1925. Suite No. 2 : *March*, *Valse*, *Polka* and *Galop*, for the same ensemble as Suite No. 1 plus a piano, was written in 1921 at the request of a Parisian music-hall director, who wanted it as an accompaniment for a short sketch.

The pieces written in the manner of a pianola were followed up in 1917 by a piece actually written for a pianola, the *Study for pianola* already mentioned. This, renamed 'Madrid', made up the *Four Studies* for orchestra, and like the second of the *Five Easy Pieces* it too is a tribute to Spain – hence the title 'Madrid'. Stravinsky went to Spain in 1916 to meet Diaghilev, who was on his way back from his first American tour with his company. Of this journey to Spain Stravinsky writes : [4]

Many of the musicians who had preceded me in visiting Spain had, on their return, put their impressions on record in works devoted to the music which they had heard there, Glinka having far outshone the rest with his incomparable *La Jota Arragonaise* [*sic*] and *Une Nuit à Madrid*. It was probably in order to conform to this custom that I, too, paid tribute to it. The whimsicalities of the unexpected melodies of the mechanical pianos and the rattletrap orchestrinas of the Madrid streets and the little night taverns served as a theme for this piece, which I wrote expressly for the pianola, and which was published as a roll by the London Aeolian Company.

Apparently the makers of cylinders for the pianola found it extremely difficult to make a roll that would reproduce this complicated score, so that it is almost impossible to hear it in its exact original form. In view of this difficulty, Stravinsky not only transcribed it for orchestra, but had his son Soulima make a version for two pianos.

The entire set of *Four Studies* had its first performance in Berlin in 1930. Stravinsky had given the first three separate titles. Study No. 1 (for woodwind) was called *Danse*. The second was called *Excentrique*, the reason for the title being that the piece had been inspired by the eccentric movements and postures of the great clown Little Tich. The third had the title of *Cantique* or *Canticle*, in keeping with its choral religious character. In *Themes and Episodes* (p. 33) Stravinsky says that *Hymne* would have been as good a title.

In the *Easy Pieces* Stravinsky took as his starting point a number of nineteenth-century dance forms. But *Ragtime for eleven instruments* and *Piano-Rag Music*, written in 1918 and 1919 respectively, are based on jazz. Stravinsky writes apropos of *Ragtime* : [5]

Its dimensions are modest, but it is indicative of the passion I felt at that time for jazz which burst into life so suddenly, when the war ended. At my

[4] *Chronicle of My Life*, pp. 116-17.
[5] ibid., p. 130.

request, a whole pile of their music was sent to me, enchanting me by its truly popular appeal, its freshness, and the novel rhythm which so distinctly revealed its negro origin. These impressions suggested the idea of creating a composite portrait of this new dance music, giving the creation the importance of a concert piece as in the past composers of their periods had done in the minuet, the waltz, the mazurka, etc.

More specifically, Stravinsky says in one of the *Program Notes*[6] that it was Ernest Ansermet who in 1918 brought him 'a bundle of ragtime music'. Incidentally, at the outset Stravinsky used both the spelling 'rag time' and the form with the two halves of the word joined, namely 'ragtime'; he later uses only the latter form.

Stravinsky says (ibid.) that he no longer regards *Ragtime for eleven instruments*, but *Histoire du Soldat* (which I shall discuss in the next chapter), as a 'portrait or snapshot of the genre'. He adds however that 'the portrait has faded, I fear, and it must always have seemed to Americans like very alien corn'. He feels that he had greater success with his 'essays in jazz portraiture' when in 1919 he had occasion not only to read through some jazz pieces but to hear live jazz bands, which made him realize that the main interest of jazz music lay not in composition but in performance, which implies an essential element of improvisation. In this sense he felt that he came closer to the spirit of jazz in his 'non-metrical pieces for piano solo and clarinet solo, which are not real improvisations, of course, but written-out portraits of improvisation'. The pieces in question are the *Piano-Rag Music* (written partly without barring) and the *Three Pieces for Clarinet* (the second of which is not divided into bars). It may seem odd that Stravinsky's leaning towards Bach coincided with his interest in jazz. But it need not surprise us; he admits in the passage referred to that 'jazz – blanket term – has exerted a time-to-time influence on my music since 1918, and traces of blues and boogie-woogie can be found even in my most "serious" pieces as, for example, in the *Bransle de Poitou* and the *Bransle simple* from *Agon*, the *pas d' action* (middle section) and *pas de deux* from Orpheus'. Details in these pieces do in fact suggest the blues and boogie-woogie (but elsewhere, as we shall see when we come to speak of *Persephone*, Stravinsky says that he was actually ten years ahead of boogie-woogie). On the other hand, he confesses that the pieces composed in the forties (at the beginning of his American period), namely *Circus Polka, Scherzo à la russe*, and *Ebony Concerto* were merely 'journey-man jobs I was forced to accept because the war in Europe had so drastically reduced the income from my compositions'. This was of

---

[6] 'Jazz Commercials' (*Dialogues and a Diary*, p. 87).

course not the first attempt to stylize the new American dances and incorporate the style into 'high-brow' music – the *Cake-Walk* from Debussy's *Children's Corner* was an earlier example. But Stravinsky's approach to jazz is altogether different. The aspects of jazz that interest him are its rhythmic principles and the instrumental technique of the jazz band, which is based on the idea of each instrument being a solo instrument in its own right, and hence has much in common with Stravinsky's own ideas on the use of instruments. In *Ragtime* particularly, Stravinsky concentrates on the peculiar jazz use of instruments like the flute, clarinet, horn, cornet, trombone, violin, viola, double bass, and percussion, adding to them the 'cymbalom' used ordinarily by gipsy orchestras. In *Ragtime* syncopated rhythm is used with the utmost freedom and fantasy; yet it remains characteristically a dance rhythm. In the *Piano-Rag Music* on the other hand, the function of the rhythm is more than purely dynamic; it assumes something of an expressive function. The jazz elements are broken down and crushed to a pulp, then reassembled as if processed by some diabolical machine. In the turbulent sea of clashing rhythms, a nervous, syncopated little theme appears from time to time, like a shoal emerging and quickly disappearing in the centre of a boiling whirlpool. More than in any other piece, the rhythmic violence in the *Piano-Rag Music* helps to raise the emotional temperature to a white heat.

The work was written in 1919 and dedicated to Artur Rubinstein, though he did not put it in his repertoire. Immediately following the composition of the *Piano-Rag Music*, Stravinsky wrote *Three Pieces for clarinet solo* for Werner Reinhart, a Wintertur industrialist and patron of the arts. Reinhart was a talented amateur and played the clarinet in the Wintertur orchestra. Whereas in *Piano-Rag Music* the main interest of the piece lay in the rhythm, here it lies in the melodic line. These pieces are in fact three pure melodies, each developing in a different way. The melodic curve recalls the sinuous chromaticism of the *Three Japanese Lyrics*, without lingering over recitative effects. The idea of writing a pure unaccompanied monody goes back to Bach's sonatas for unaccompanied violin. Thus in these *Three Pieces* for clarinet solo we see the first signs of a trend that was to assume great importance in the later phases of Stravinsky's work – his leaning towards Bach.

During the period covered by the present chapter Stravinsky also wrote several minor or occasional pieces. In 1917 when Diaghilev's company arranged a gala performance in Rome at the old Teatro

Constanzi (later the Teatro dell'Opera) for the Italian Red Cross, Stravinsky orchestrated the famous 'Song of the Volga Boatmen' for wind instruments. This took the place of the Russian national anthem, 'God protect the Tzar', which could not be played, as the Russian Revolution had taken place the February before, and the Tsar had just been forced to abdicate. Other works written for special occasions were the 'Souvenir d'une marche boche'. written in 1915 for the Belgian war orphans, and in 1918 the transcription of the 'Marseillaise' for violin solo. There are also several canons for horn, prompted by a different reason : his daughter Ludmilla was dangerously ill with appendicitis; and the Swiss doctor who saved her life, Dr. Roux, instead of sending in a bill asked to be paid in 'kind', i.e. music. As Dr. Roux was an amateur horn-player, Stravinsky wrote (1917) a series of duet canons for horn. The manuscript, as Robert Craft says,[7] 'one may hope still exists with the family of Dr. Roux, somewhere in the neighbourhood of Geneva'. In the same year he sketched out the only work he never finished, drafts for a series of songs, settings of Renaissance texts, entitled *Dialogue between Reason and Joy*. Sixteen years later Stravinsky made use of some of the ideas for these songs, and they became the central themes of *Persephone*.

[7] 'A Personal Preface', *The Score*, June 1957.

VIII Chamber Works for the Theatre

In two of the preceding chapters we have discussed the return to the chamber music outlook which is evident in Stravinsky's creative work in the period following the composition of *The Rite of Spring*. Let us now see what were the repercussions of this new outlook on the music he wrote for the stage. While he was living in Switzerland during the First World War, Stravinsky wrote two of his most original works – *Renard* and *The Soldier's Tale* – both of them stage works. Neither work fits into any of the regular categories of music for the theatre; they constitute an entirely new genre. *Renard* was begun in 1916. Stravinsky interrupted the work on it a number of times, completing it when Princesse Edmond de Polignac asked him to write a theatrical chamber work for a series of performances she was proposing to put on in Paris. The plot of *Renard* was adapted from an episode in the *Roman de Renard*. The Russian words are taken from the tales which Stravinsky had brought back with him from his recent visit to Russia, and the French version was a combined effort by the composer himself and the poet Ramuz, with whom he had become friendly. Incidentally it was Ramuz who translated *Pribaoutki* and the *Cat's Cradle Songs*, and wrote the words of *The Soldier's Tale*. Stravinsky calls *Renard* 'A Burlesque in Song and Dance', and the score contains the following directions:

The play is acted by clowns, dancers or acrobats, preferably on a trestle stage placed in front of the orchestra. If performed in a theatre, it should be played in front of the curtain. The actors remain on the stage all the time. They come on in view of the audience to the strains of the little March, which serves as an introduction, and make their exit the same way. The actors do not speak. The singers (two Tenors and two Basses) are placed in the orchestra.

Thus for the first time in the history of theatre music the singers are treated as mere instruments of the orchestra. Not only that, but the voice parts are not directly linked with any of the rôles being acted out on the stage; they are identified with one or other of the characters in the story – the Cock, the Fox, the Cat, or the Goat – as the occasion arises. At other times the voices comment on the action, or

are simply treated as instruments of the orchestra. The instrumental
ensemble consists of flute, cor anglais, clarinet in E flat, bassoon, two
horns, trumpet, and string quartet, drums, and the Hungarian, or
rather gipsy, cymbalom mentioned in the previous chapter. The
novelty of the cymbalom is explained by the fact that Stravinsky
heard Aladar Racz, a virtuoso on the cymbalom, play in a café in
Geneva. He became very enthusiastic about the instrument, and with
Racz's help he managed to obtain one and learned to play it.[1] In this
work the cymbalom plays quite a varied and important rôle. It
accompanies the Cock; it plays sustained reverberating pedal notes;
it marks the rhythmic accent, and in general it helps to create a
harmonic texture which binds the parts together. In between the
introductory March and its repeat, the Fox makes his appearance and
goes through two parallel scenes in which the same episode is repeated
twice : the Fox manages to fool the Cock, but the Cock is rescued by
the Cat and the Goat, who then celebrate their triumph in a dance.
At the end the Fox is killed.

The music is irresistibly comic and full of verve. The treatment of
the voices is especially amusing : in places suggesting 'four animals
let loose in the orchestra, like a hencoop in an uproar', to quote
André Schaeffner's description. From the point of view of linguistic
structure, the music in *Renard* is in the same category as *Pribaoutki*.
Taken as a whole, the work represents a conception of the theatre
which is the very antithesis of the Wagnerian ideal. Not only does
Stravinsky show no inclination to fuse the various musical, poetic,
and theatrical elements into one; he seems in fact to be trying to keep
them apart, or rather, he does not aim at an *a priori* synthesis of
these elements, but co-ordinates them into a series of complementary
relationships, so that each can fulfil its purpose quite independently
and hence with the maximum effectiveness.

During the First World War, Stravinsky was cut off from his native
country and went on living in Switzerland. The course of the Russian
Revolution made his exile permanent, and within a short time he was
penniless. His friends Ramuz and Ansermet were also in financial
straits. At this point Ramuz and Stravinsky hit upon the idea of trying
to make enough money to live on by starting up a sort of mobile
miniature theatre which could be easily moved from one place to
another and taken round even to outlying villages. Stravinsky tells the
story himself.[2] They found a backer to finance the scheme in Werner

---

[1] *Chronicle of My Life*, pp. 103-4.
[2] ibid., p. 130.

Reinhart, the amateur clarinettist mentioned in the last chapter. With his natural predilection for small instrumental ensembles – and having in any case no alternative – Stravinsky organized a group consisting of the instruments, high and low, most representative of the various families. From the strings he chose violin and double bass; from the woodwind, clarinet and bassoon; from the brass, cornet and trombone; and for good measure he added a large group of percussion instruments all operated by a single player – making up an 'orchestra in miniature' of seven players. It was for this 'orchestra' that he wrote *The Soldier's Tale*. The idea was that the players should be placed at the side of the stage in full view of the public, with a small rostrum for the narrator on the other side, and in the middle a space for the action, spoken or danced, to take place.

The plot of *The Soldier's Tale* was taken from the collection of Afanazyev's tales which Stravinsky had brought back from Russia. It is the story of a soldier who sells his violin to the Devil in exchange for a book which gives the answer to every question. The soldier spends three days with the Devil; in actual fact they turn out to be three years. When he returns to his native village, no one recognizes him, not even his mother and his fiancée, and he seeks consolation in the worldly wealth that the magic book helps him to acquire. But money does not bring him happiness. He throws the book away and goes back to his life of adventure. One day he hears that the King's daughter is ill, and that the man who can cure her is to have her hand in marriage. He makes his way to the capital to try his luck. In the city he meets the Devil who is on his way to the Court to try his luck too. He is carrying the soldier's violin with him. The soldier and the Devil have a game of cards and the soldier loses all his worldly wealth, but recovers his violin. The playing of the violin cures the princess and he marries her. The Devil swears vengeance if the soldier ever sets foot on his domain. After a time the soldier grows homesick and sets out for his native land, but the Devil captures him and carries him off before the very eyes of his grief-stricken wife.

The story is not specifically Russian. Similar fables are found in Grimm's fairy tales, and the libretto of the old operetta *Rip* is written on the same theme. The plot being international, Ramuz adapted it so that it could be located in any country. Thus in French the action can take place 'entre Denge et Denezy', in German 'zwischen Chur und Wallenstadt', in English 'twixt Rockhill and Lode' and in Italian 'fra Belsit' e Pieve al Mar'. On the musical side

Stravinsky tried to give the work a similarly universal character.
Instead of taking a purely Russian background as his starting point,
he draws his material from a variety of sources; from American ragtime to Argentine tango; from Swiss brass band to Spanish pasodoble;
from Bach's chorales and preludes to the Viennese waltz. Only the
violin theme, symbolizing the soul of the soldier, has a definitely
Russian flavour. All these heterogeneous elements are thrown into
the melting-pot, and the result is one of Stravinsky's most homogeneous and original works. All the incongruous elements are
assimilated, fused and reduced to the common denominator of the
composer's very personal manner. The music is conceived as a
series of separate numbers, as incidental music, as a suite played
simultaneously with the action or interwoven with the action as
read by the narrator or spoken by the actors. Stravinsky had asked
Ramuz to write the text in such a way as to make its narrative, epic
qualities stand out clearly. Only the main episodes, the highlights
of the action, are acted out on the stage. Whenever action is implied
in the narrative, the narrator is silent, except in the card-game scene,
where the soldier turns to the narrator and addresses him. The
orchestra, placed on the stage where the audience can see it, also
forms part of the visual action.

The whole work is divided into two parts. The first begins with
the Soldier's March as he returns home. An ostinato on the double bass
marks the rhythm of the rather ordinary march tunes played by the
cornet. The violin saws away irritably at the same old figure on the
open strings: the soldier feels he will never get home. He is footsore
and weary from his long trek. The second musical episode introduces
the stage action. The soldier tunes his fiddle and starts to play. The
Devil then appears to the strains of an Oriental melody played on the
clarinet:

The trombone and the cornet then begin to sneak in on the violin's
poetic melody, just as the Devil is trying to sneak in on the soldier's
soul. Next comes the narration of the various adventures, after

which a short Lento passage expresses the soldier's woeful state. In the third scene he throws his fiddle into the wings and takes out the magic book; meanwhile the fiddle tune is heard again briefly. The second part begins like the first with the Soldier's March. The soldier enters the King's palace to the sound of a pompous Royal March. There he meets the Devil, disguised as a successful violinist. The match between the Devil and the soldier is accompanied by a Little Concerto.

One of the motifs in this piece was inspired by a dream-sequence. Here is Stravinsky's own account of the episode:

Music has sometimes appeared to me in dreams, but only on one occasion have I been able to write it down. This was during the composition of *L'Histoire du Soldat*, and I was surprised and happy with the result. Not only did the music appear to me but the person performing it was present in the dream as well. A young gipsy was sitting by the edge of the road. She had a child on her lap for whose entertainment she was playing a violin. The motif she kept repeating used the whole bow, or, as we say in French, '*avec toute la longueur de l'archet*'. The child was very enthusiastic about the music and applauded with its little hands. I, too, was very pleased with it, was especially pleased to be able to remember it, and I joyfully included this motif in the music of the *Petit Concert*.[3]

At the end of the Little Concerto, the soldier recovers his fiddle from the Devil and plays the princess three dances in the modern style. In the first dance, a Tango, the violin is accompanied solely by percussion. With the entry of the clarinet, the princess rises up from her couch and begins to dance. The second dance is a sprightly Waltz; and the third a jolly Ragtime. Then follows the Devil's Dance. The devilish rhythm of the violin is too much for the Devil, and he falls to the ground exhausted. The princess and the soldier make fun of him and drag him off stage by one leg. With the Little Chorale the soldier and the princess fall into each other's arms. The Devil swears vengeance in a metronomically rhythmical couplet accompanied by the violin and double bass. Between the repeats of the Great Chorale, the narrator drops a few pearls of wisdom on the subject of happiness, and warns people not to want more than they already have lest they lose everything. This is of course exactly what happens to the poor soldier. Not content with winning the princess and a kingdom, he would now like to see his old home again. But

---

[3] *Conversations with Igor Stravinsky*, p. 17.

there is no going back – the past is taboo. Once he has stepped over the dread threshold, the Devil has him in his grip and carries him off, while the orchestra plays the Triumphal March of the Devil. The triumph in this piece is a triumph for the percussion. Little by little it silences all the other instruments. The violin holds out longer than the others and wrestles with it in a sort of doleful duet. Finally, even the violin succumbs and the percussion goes on alone to the bitter end. It is as though Stravinsky had gradually stripped every ounce of flesh from his music, reducing it to the bare bones, leaving only rhythm. In *Petrushka*, and particularly in the Finale of *The Rite of Spring*, rhythm was already on the way to becoming the symbol of the power of evil. In the Triumphal March of the Devil this is fully realized. Admittedly it is in terms of the grotesque; yet in spite of himself, the listener cannot help making the transition from the ridiculous to the sublime. Here we have yet another example of the eternal Faust theme – man sells his soul to gain wealth or esoteric knowledge. In this instance the theme is resolved in an utterly pessimistic way: man falls with no hope of reprieve; he is trapped and torn to pieces by the evil forces which gather about him.

IX The End of the Russian Period

The works discussed in the early chapters belong to what is commonly known as Stravinsky's 'Russian period', the majority of these works being based on popular themes taken from the wealth of Russian musical folk-lore. At times he uses popular melodies; but more often than not he makes up his own themes quite freely, modelling them on the modal and rhythmic patterns of Russian folk music. In either instance the material is used as the basis for an entirely novel stylistic approach. Its original scope is enlarged, and it virtually acquires a new meaning; in other words, the composer takes it over and assimilates it completely. This might suggest that the borrowed themes were used merely as raw material, and are not strictly essential features of the finished compositions based on them; the really essential feature is the metamorphosis which the material undergoes, the stylistic devices used and the way in which each work is conceived. This applies equally to the works of Stravinsky's Russian period and to those written later during his so-called 'neo-classical' period, when the 'raw material' was obtained not from his own native folk-lore, but from western folk music generally.

Of course, as has already been pointed out, even in the music of his Russian period Stravinsky did not confine himself entirely to Russian or Slav themes. In *The Firebird*, the *Three Japanese Lyrics*, and *The Nightingale* we find themes oriental in flavour, of the type favoured even by the nineteenth-century composers in Russia. In works like the *Easy Pieces for piano duet*, *The Soldier's Tale*, *Ragtime for eleven instruments* and *Piano-Rag Music*, Russian motifs are few and far between if they are found at all; instead, we get elements from a variety of sources. On the strength of this, some critics have questioned the validity of the epithet 'Russian' as applied to this particular period of Stravinsky's creative work. To my mind this is mere sophistry. It is true that the Russian influence is not the only influence, and in many cases it is not the dominant one. But taken as a whole these works do give evidence of both intrinsic and extrinsic features which justify the general label 'Russian' usually

given to them. This is only true, of course, so long as the term
'Russian' is restricted to the above definition and it is clearly understood that the individual periods of Stravinsky's creative activity
cannot be circumscribed or put into watertight compartments, but
overlap and are interwoven on a fairly general scale. This certainly
applies to the so-called Russian and neo-classical periods.

The latter period began in 1919 with *Pulcinella*, but came to
fruition only four or five years later. In the meantime Stravinsky
published two works which belong to the Russian period and mark
the end of his compositions in this manner – the comic opera *Mavra*,
written in 1921, and the choreographic scenes entitled *The Wedding*
(*Les Noces*), completed in 1923. 'Completed' is perhaps hardly the
word: it would be more accurate to say 'completed in their orchestral form', since a preliminary sketch was finished as early as 1917.
For this reason we can discuss *The Wedding* before the opera *Mavra*.
Stravinsky first conceived the idea in 1912, when he was working on
The Rite of Spring. Indeed, if we consider the two works together,
The Wedding may be regarded as the second panel of a diptych
taking its inspiration from the pagan rites practised in ancient Russia.
The Rite of Spring celebrated the propitiatory rite of the rebirth of
nature. The music seemed to express the release of sinister earth
forces, reducing mere man to a state of panic-stricken terror. *The
Wedding* describes the matrimonial rites of the peasants. Here mere
man will not be silenced; he sings and sings, hardly giving the
instruments a single phrase of their own, except for the pealing of
bells in the last twenty-one bars of the work.

Stravinsky describes *The Wedding* as 'Russian dance scenes with
song and music'. Here is what he has to say of the underlying conception of the work:[1]

According to my idea, the spectacle should have been a *divertissement*, and
that is what I wanted to call it. It was not my intention to reproduce the
ritual of peasant weddings, and I paid little heed to ethnographical considerations. My idea was to compose a sort of scenic ceremony, using as I liked
those ritualistic elements so abundantly provided by village customs which
had been established for centuries in the celebration of Russian marriages. I
took my inspirations from those customs, but reserved to myself the right to
use them with absolute freedom.

There are four scenes following each other without a break. In
the first scene, the action takes place in the house of the betrothed;
her companions are helping her to dress for the wedding and plaiting
her hair. The second scene is laid in the bridegroom's house, where

[1] *Chronicle of My Life*, pp. 174-5.

the bridegroom is seeking the family blessing. The third scene describes the departure of the bride and the distress of her parents. In the fourth scene we have the wedding feasts followed by the vigil of the parents outside the nuptial chamber. The words of the songs sung in this series of choreographic scenes, or 'stage cantata' as it might more appropriately be called, are taken from the folk-tales brought back by Stravinsky from his travels in Russia a short time earlier. In preparing the libretto for *The Wedding* Stravinsky made use chiefly of material from the book by Kirievsky (or Kireievsky). It is interesting to note what Stravinsky has to say about it.[2] 'Incidentally, Kireievsky had asked Pushkin to send him his collection of folk verse and Pushkin sent him some verses with a note reading: "Some of these are my own verses; can you tell the difference?" Kireievsky could not, and took them all for his book, so perhaps a line of Pushkin is in *Les Noces*.' The melodic themes, on the other hand, are all Stravinsky's own, with one single exception, namely the setting of the words 'jusqu'à la ceinture j'ai de l'or qui pend',

which is a popular melody commonly heard in the factories in Russia.

This is confirmed in *Memories and Commentaries* (p. 97) where Stravinsky points out that the theme of the proletarian song in question had been given him by his friend Stepan Mitusov 'at least ten years before he made use of it in the final tableau of *Les Noces*.' He also quotes the original model:

which he took over, slightly changing the melodic line:

[2] *Conversations with Igor Stravinsky*, p. 47.

Thus the workers' song theme not only fits perfectly into the
whole context of the music of *The Wedding*, but considering that
Stravinsky had known it for a long time before he composed the
work, it does not seem rash to assume that consciously or unconsciously he had derived from it the original cell from which the
entire composition was to grow. All the essential melodic structures
of *The Wedding* can be referred to this cell (a), its retrograde,
inverse, and retrograde-inverse forms (b) and to various other permutations of these forms – the groups of notes (c) and (d) – furnish
two examples of these permutations and combinations. The cell
structure of the melodic texture was analysed for the first time,
unless I am mistaken, by Victor Belaieff in his essay *Igor Stravinsky's
'Les Noces'* (Oxford University Press, London 1928). White (*Stravinsky*,
op. cit., p. 217) says that the original cell is the group I have indicated as (b), transposed down a major second. But he too fails to
analyse the relationship between the melodic structures and the
harmonic structures, which Stravinsky has linked together exceed-
ingly closely, even though not always obviously. Unlike what
occurred with *The Nightingale*, the very long period of gestation did
not mar in the slightest the compactness and complete coherence
of the work. As already said, the music of *The Wedding* was composed between 1912 and 1917, but another six years were to elapse
before Stravinsky finally orchestrated it. I have already explained
why for several years after composing *The Rite of Spring* he shied
away from the conventional orchestra. His original idea in *The
Wedding* had been to bracket together with the solo voices and the
chorus two diametrically opposed bodies of instruments, one consisting of winds and the other of strings, some playing pizzicato only.
He abandoned the device after writing a few pages of the score and
started off on a draft for a chamber ensemble similar to that used
in *Renard*. In a later version the wind was replaced by a harmonium
and the strings by a pianola and two gipsy cymbaloms as used in
Renard and *Ragtime*. Both the pianola and the harmonium were to
be electrically operated. This plan turned out to be impracticable

owing to the difficulty of synchronizing the mechanical instruments and those of the orchestra.

Work on *The Wedding* was constantly interrupted, but Stravinsky settled down to it again in 1921, having been urged by Diaghilev to finish it. Two more years passed, however, before the score was ready in its final form. The orchestration of the final version was four pianos and a large group of percussion instruments: four timpani, xylophone, bells, two tenor drums, two side drums, tambourine, bass drum, cymbals, triangle, and two castanets (*crotales*). For practical purposes the instrumental ensemble consists of percussion – even the pianos are used throughout with a hammering action. The sound effects produced by this unusual group of instruments are of incomparable splendour and brilliance.

There is some justification in Tansman's[3] comparison of the sonority of the instrumental ensemble of *The Wedding* with Javanese and Balinese music, which is also based on the percussive and resonant qualities of melodic instruments (xylophones) and others which produce 'pedal' effects (bells, gongs, anvils, etc.).

No less incomparable is the vitality of this music. But the irresistible, scintillating, and at times orgiastic exuberance, far from hiding the underlying tragic note, throws it into relief. It is as though the participants in these rites were singing, in fact shouting, so loudly in order to cover up the sense of misery and anguish they feel. All the characters involved play out their own drama: in the first scene the betrothed, weeping at having to leave her home and her companions; in the second scene the parents, with nothing further to live for, grieving over the loss of their daughter; then the bridegroom, seeking his father's blessing in a musical figure which is very reminscent of the Byzantine liturgy.

In the essay quoted above and in an expanded version in E. W. White's *Stravinsky, A Critical Survey* (1947), Victor Belaieff maintains that this theme is based on liturgical motives taken from a collection of Russian Christmas chants. This would mean that Stravinsky 'borrowed' two themes for *The Wedding* and not one, as he himself claims.[4] On the other hand, in the case of the liturgical motif Stravinsky probably transformed it to such an extent that he felt justified in claiming it as his own.[5]

---

[3] op. cit., p. 188. [4] *Chronicle of My Life*, p. 174.
[5] Casella (*Stravinsky*, op. cit., p. 87) speaks of a 'constant use of a Gregorian liturgical tune, easily confused with popular elements which quite commonly in Russian folklore adopt ecclesiastical scales'. He also says that this theme strongly confirms the religious aspect of *The Wedding*.

In the third scene, after the bride and bridegroom have left, the two mothers sing a lament imploring their children to return home; and in the last scene, after the Saturnalian music of the banquet, the bride and bridegroom express, along with the joy and emotion of a newly-wedded couple, their profound awe and trepidation at the thought that life must be renewed through them. This disquiet in the face of the twofold mystery of life ending and life beginning is the most significant feature of *The Wedding*.[6] In this respect it resembles *The Rite of Spring*, a significant component of that work also being the expression of the pain which overtakes mankind at the contemplation of the dread forces by which it is surrounded.

Stravinsky's Russian period virtually comes to an end with the composition of the comic opera *Mavra* in 1921, even though the orchestration of *The Wedding* was not actually completed until a year later. Apart from its intrinsic significance, it has a specific interest in that it represents Stravinsky's attitude vis-à-vis the Russian tradition from which he came and the western tradition into which he was being integrated. He took the plot from Pushkin's *The Little House at Kolomna*, dedicating the work to the memory of Pushkin, Glinka, and Tchaikovsky. In his own words:[7]

The genius . . . of our great poet Poushkin . . . in all its versatility and universality was not only particularly dear and precious to us, but represented a whole school of thought. By his nature, his mentality, and his ideology Poushkin was the most perfect representative of that wonderful line which began with Peter the Great and which, by a fortunate alloy, has united the most characteristically Russian elements with the spiritual riches of the West.

Diaghileff unquestionably belonged to this line, and all his activities have only confirmed the authenticity of that origin. As for myself, I had always been aware that I had in me the germs of this same mentality only needing development, and I subsequently deliberately cultivated them.

Was not the difference between this mentality and the mentality of the 'Five', which has so rapidly become academic and concentrated in the Beliaeff [*sic*] circle under the domination of Rimsky-Korsakov and Glazunov, that the former was, as it were, cosmopolitan, whereas the latter was purely nationalist? The national element occupies a prominent place with Poushkin as well as with Glinka and Tchaikovsky. But with them it flows spontaneously from their very nature, whereas with the others the nationalistic tendency was a doctrinaire catechism which they wished to impose. This nationalistic, ethnographical aesthetic which they persisted in cultivating was not in reality far removed from the spirit which inspired those films one sees of the old Russia of the Tsars and Boyars. What is so obvious in them, as

---

[6] Lindlar (op. cit., pp. 20-21) maintains that the ritual in the Russian peasant *Wedding* links together the magical in *The Rite of Spring* and the mystical in *The King of the Stars*. Fleischer (Stravinsky: Berlin–Moscow 1931) perspicaciously asserts that 'the more markedly ritualistic passages in the work give the impression of a funeral rite, of a Mass'.

[7] *Chronicle of My Life*, pp. 159-61.,

indeed in the modern Spanish 'folklorists', whether painters or musicians, is that naïve but dangerous tendency which prompts them to remake an art that has already been created instinctively by the genius of the people. It is a sterile tendency, and an evil from which many talented artists suffer.

This statement explains Stravinsky's purpose exactly and gives a hint as to the course which his creative art was to take from now on. Thus in conception *Mavra* belongs to the Russian-Italian tradition initiated by Glinka and continued by Tchaikovsky. The work is in one act and is divided into short scenes consisting on the musical side of arias, duets, and quartets in the manner of the old Italian opera buffa. Into this mould Stravinsky pours ingredients of Russian, gipsy, western, and jazz origin, though the over-all effect is unmistakably Russian. There is a strong suggestion of *bel canto* in the vocal line, and this contrasts violently with the harsh sonorities produced by the weird collection of instruments. The orchestra of thirty-four players is made up of four clarinets, four trumpets, three trombones, tuba, a small percussian section and only two violins, viola, three cellos, and three double basses.

Stravinsky wrote the music for *Mavra* without having a specific orchestration in mind. He only decided on the make-up of the ensemble in the light of the structure and character of the piece, after he had finished the first part. The orchestra used in *Mavra* reflects Stravinsky's especially keen interest at the time in ensembles of wind instruments, as also do the Symphonies of Wind Instruments, the Octet, and the Concerto for piano and wind orchestra. The disparity between the limpid vocal lines and the harsh harmonies and instrumental timbres paves the way for a series of hilarious effects arising from the repeated incongruities between the music and the action on stage. The farcical character of the action is admirably in keeping with the spirit of comic opera as Stravinsky understood it. The opera opens with Parasha singing an aria in which she reproaches her lover, a bold hussar, for being away so long. He answers in a gipsy love-song. In the next episode, Parasha's mother sends her to find a new servant to replace the old servant who has died. Parasha comes back, bringing with her a sturdy wench called Mavra who is none other than the hussar in disguise. Everybody is happy. The lovers sing a passionate duet, and then Parasha goes off with her mother. The bogus domestic takes advantage of their absence to shave. The women return suddenly and he is found out. There is a terrible scene with faintings and screaming. The hussar leaps out of the window and the curtain falls. In spite of the buffoonery of the story, here again the music has an underlying suggestion of melancholy and bitterness. The fact is, as André Schaeffner rightly points out, that throughout the whole course of his peregrinations Stravinsky carried in his soul the 'mental image of the Russia of his forefathers'.

X Neo-Classicism

In the earlier chapters we have had various indications of a trend towards neo-classicism in Stravinsky's style. Let us now look at the compositions which marked the beginning of this new and controversial period. His first work in the neo-classical manner is *Pulcinella*, a 'Ballet in one act. Music based on themes, fragments and pieces by Pergolesi'. The idea was first suggested to Stravinsky in 1919 by Diaghilev, who was anxious to put on a work on the lines of the *Astuzie femminili*, Respighi's arrangement of a piece by Cimarosa, and the highly successful *Good-humoured Ladies* written by Vicenzo Tommasini on the basis of Scarlatti's music. Diaghilev chose Pergolesi, having found a number of unfinished or at any rate practically unknown works by Pergolesi in the Naples Conservatoire, as well as several other manuscripts in the British Museum, including two three-act operas: *Il Fratello Innamorato* (1732) and *Il Flaminio* (1735), and twelve trio sonatas for two violins and continuo.

Stravinsky was immediately taken with the idea. As already mentioned, he was very fond of Naples and Neapolitan music, and as he says himself, especially of Pergolesi's 'Neapolitan music, so entirely of the people and yet so exotic in its Spanish character'.[1] A further attraction was that Picasso had been asked to design the sets and costumes and Massine was to be in charge of the choreography. The plot was taken from a manuscript dating from 1700 found in Naples. It describes how a number of young men plot to kill Pulcinella out of jealousy. When they think he is dead, they take his clothes and decide that each in turn shall visit his *innamorata* disguised as Pulcinella. But the wily Pulcinella has arranged for a double to impersonate him and to pretend that he is mortally wounded by his attackers. Pulcinella dresses up as a wizard and pretends to resuscitate Furbo, his double. The young men go off to meet their ladies in the belief that they are rid of Pulcinella, but he suddenly appears on the scene and marries off all the couples. Then he himself marries Pimpinella, while Furbo takes over his disguise and gives the couple his blessing.

[1] *Chronicle of My Life*, p. 135.

The ballet consists of eight tableaux. It begins with an Overture or 'Symphony' in the Italian style for orchestra alone, the material being taken from Pergolesi's first trio sonata.

The first tableau opens with a lilting Serenade sung by the tenor, who like the other singers is placed in the orchestra pit. The melody is that of Polidoro's Aria in Act I of *Il Flaminio*. The Scherzino, Allegro, and Andantino which follow are based on various movements from the second and eighth trio sonatas. The second tableau is divided into three parts – an Allegretto for soprano, taken from the cantata *Adriano*, an Allegro from Vanella's Aria in Act I of *Il Fratello Innamorato*, and an 'allegro assai' from the third movement of the third trio sonata. The third tableau, 'allegro alla breve', is based on a bass aria from the first act of *Il Flaminio*. The fourth tableau comprises an Andante (trio), a second Andante for tenor, Allegro for tenor and soprano, Presto for tenor, and Larghetto, all taken from Act II of *Il Fratello Innamorato*. Next comes an 'allegro alla breve' from the twelfth suite for strings. The scene ends with a Tarantella from the aria 'Contento forse viver nel mio martir'. The fifth tableau opens with an Andantino based on the well-known concert aria 'Se tu m'ami', and ends with an Allegro taken from the seventh sonata for harpsichord. The sixth is a Gavotte with two variations which is based on a gavotte Pergolesi also wrote for the harpsichord. The seventh tableau is recast from the third movement of the Symphony for cello and double bass, and the eighth consists of a Tempo di minuetto for soprano, tenor, and bass, from Don Pietro's Aria in Act I of *Il Fratello Innamorato*, and a brilliant 'allegro assai finale' taken from the finale of the twelfth trio sonata.

Stravinsky keeps Pergolesi's melodic lines for the most part intact, and only occasionally strings them together with a connecting passage of his own. He also keeps the original Pergolesi bass parts, though he treats them quite freely. On the other hand, Stravinsky's creative personality entirely dominates the harmonic tissue which clothes the eighteenth-century frieze traced by the basses and the melodic lines. Stravinsky's characteristic device of polyharmonic fusing of heterogeneous harmonic elements here consists mainly of a strong tendency towards the amalgamation of the tonic and dominant chords which are the chief means of articulation in the music of Pergolesi.

Stravinsky's frequent use of extraneous notes (including ostinatos) and of unresolved harmonic appoggiaturas creates dissonances which help to stiffen the musical fabric, to give it more of a punch without actually betraying the spirit and atmosphere of the original. Stravinsky is completely free in his arrangement of key, formal structure, and chronological order of the various pieces. Occasionally a piece is taken over lock, stock, and barrel, without any change in form; others are filled out or completely recast. Stravinsky's rhythmic peculiarities too manage to make themselves felt – the squareness of the rhythm is broken up; the symmetry of the metre is upset; the accents are displaced; the syncopations are accentuated; and the tempi are changed abruptly. And, of course, the instrumentation is pure Stravinsky.

Pulcinella, which was later turned into a Suite in eight parts for orchestra alone, without voices, was the first of a series of works in which Stravinsky, by more or less explicit references to the works of the great composers of the past, reconstitutes in the mirror of his own personal idiom a picture of the last two hundred years of western musical culture.

The work proved to be one of the main landmarks of what is known as neo-classicism as well as being one of Stravinsky's most controversial works. This 'music to the second power' as Boris de Schloezer calls it, consisting of or making use of borrowed themes, has ample precedent. The old *Missae parodiae*, the many transcriptions of Vivaldi, Marcello, etc., by Bach, and in a different way Liszt's 'paraphrases' come into this category, not to mention the classical theme and variations form. The essential feature of this type of music is that it is based either partly or wholly on already existing musical patterns. This does not imply *a priori* that the works are necessarily pastiches or hybrid in style. It is perfectly feasible for musical forms invented by composers of the past to be so completely transformed by contact with the taste and sensibility of an artist of a later age as to acquire new meaning and result in genuinely original works.

In some cases, the validity of the epithet 'neo-classical' as applied to Stravinsky's works in this category is questionable. Thus Craft, referring to *Pulcinella*, *The Fairy's Kiss*, and the Canonic Variations on 'Von Himmel hoch' in the chapter 'Trois œuvres anciennes recomposées' of his book *Avec Stravinsky*, writes: [2]

[2] *Translator's note:* The quotations from Robert Craft's interviews with Stravinsky used in the Italian text are taken from the French edition of 1957. Wherever possible, the equivalent passages are reproduced from the English edition *Conversations with Igor Stravinsky* (1959). Where a quotation from the French edition does not appear in the English version it has been translated or paraphrased.

These works are not in any sense neo-classical, nor are they a modernized version of the classics. It would be equally wrong to regard them as parodies or pastiches in the manner, say, of Busoni's *Arlecchino*. Sometimes they are pastiches and more, sometimes, they are nothing of the kind; they are interpretations, and in this case they are so skilful and so penetrating that we take as Stravinsky's own invention what is in fact pure Pergolesi, Tchaikovsky or Bach. What is noteworthy in these works is not so much Stravinsky's skill in imitating other composers as the means he uses to make them sound like Stravinsky. The double bass syncopated solo towards the end of the duet for trombone and double bass in *Pulcinella* and the fourth variation of *Vom Himmel hoch* with Stravinsky's instrumentation, are discoveries made by Stravinsky in Pergolesi and Bach.

Stravinsky's so-called neo-classical works presented something of a problem for the critical perspicacity of his commentators. For a time Stravinsky seemed with every new work to be facing the listener with a new challenge, a new world of experience to explore and appropriate. He appeared to be constantly straying from the path of logical development and continually changing his style. It only gradually became evident that this changeability merely represented the different facets of his personality, and that while experience was undoubtedly enriching it, fundamentally it remained the same. For all the apparent dissimilarity between *The Rite of Spring* and *Pulcinella*, the intrinsic shape of both works is determined by the same stylistic principle. In either case what the composer does is to take existing diatonic elements and present them in a new and original manner. This does not mean, however, that the transition from the Russian period to European neo-classicism took place without a profound crisis in Stravinsky's life and creative activity. In the short chapter entitled 'Change of Life' in *Themes and Episodes* he confesses that he had to 'survive two crises as a composer . . . The first – the loss of Russia and its language of words as of music'. The second was the crisis that followed his changeover from neo-classicism to twelve-note serialism. He says that as he continued to move from work to work he was not aware of either crisis or of any momentous change. In retrospect, however, he realized that it was 'Only after a decade of samplings, experiments, amalgamations' that he had found 'the path to *Oedipus Rex* and the *Symphony of Psalms*', in other words to the major masterpieces of our time.

Students of Stravinsky's work have produced a variety of theories to explain the underlying reasons why he gave up composing in the Russian manner. These are summed up fairly accurately in what Massimo Mila[3] has to say on the subject:

[3] *Breve storia della musica* (Bianchi-Giovini: Milan, 1946), pp. 302-3.

Stravinsky is a case in point. At the very moment when he was writing *The Wedding* (1917), at the peak of his compositions in the Russian style [he was] bold enough to undertake a prodigious task: having first of all transmuted the barbaric Russian elements, completely alien to western civilization, into a legitimate expression of art, he seizes upon the age-old tradition which forms the unconscious background of the European artist, and moulds it in his own personal manner. He endeavoured to embrace all the great characteristic musical movements of the past and to annex them in a steady assimilation of western civilization.

Another critic, De' Paoli,[4] sees the following series of landmarks in Stravinsky's 'assimilation' of western musical culture: in the Octet Stravinsky takes his inspiration from the Venetian Renaissance School via the art of Bach; for the Concertino and the Concerto for piano and wind orchestra his model was Bach himself; for inspiration in composing *Oedipus Rex* he went to Handel's secular oratorios; C. P. E. Bach provided a model for the Sonata; the Serenade was based on the late eighteenth-century style, while the main characteristics of *Apollo Musagetes* are nineteenth-century; the Capriccio marked a return to the brilliant piano virtuosity of Weber and Mendelssohn; and finally, *The Fairy's Kiss* is a tribute to Tchaikovsky.

The apparent similarities on which these comparisons are based should not be over-estimated, however. In the majority of cases Stravinsky employs the 'pre-existing' material (chords, harmonic groups, and melodic phrases) in such an entirely novel and original manner that it is hardly fair to speak of his neo-classical compositions as so many 'throwbacks' to Bach, Mozart, and Weber. It is going a little too far to bracket each of the compositions mentioned above with a specific classical model. For instance, I personally can find no trace of the influence of Bach in the Concertino for string quartet, whereas in any number of places the style suggests ragtime. The Concertino was written in 1920 for the Flonzaley Quartet; it consists of one movement in which the abstract lines of a 'sonata movement' can be discerned. The title Concertino is justified by the fact that the first violin plays an essentially 'concertante' part in the work.

At the beginning, the rising scales of C (major) and C sharp (phrygian), running parallel, merge in a band of sound keen as a razor. From the formal angle, the characteristics which go to create the thorny emotional landscape of this short work are a mass of gnarled, matted dissonances, searing contrapuntal effects, thin, disembodied melodic motifs; or at times, whole passages punctuated by two adjacent notes beating out an insistent, excited rhythm.

[4] op. cit., pp. 128-9, note I.

Nevertheless, the work by no means lacks the calm and gravity which is the key to the underlying meaning of so many of Stravinsky's works. The ultimate meaning of the Concertino is made clear by the marking 'sospirando', written no less than three times in the last bar of the score (see facing page).

Note in this last bar how enormously the emotional effect is enhanced by the absence of any preparatory crescendo of dynamics or expression. Markings like this would in themselves refute the alleged imperviousness of Stravinsky's 'objective' outlook to any subjective influence. Incidentally, Stravinsky himself recently pointed out the purely polemical nature of his earlier notorious and much-discussed dictum that music was 'powerless to express anything at all'. On page 101 of *Expositions and Developments* we read:

'That overpublicized bit about expression (or non-expression) was simply a way of saying that music is supra-personal and superreal and as such beyond verbal meanings and verbal descriptions. It was aimed against the notion that a piece of music is in reality a transcendental idea "expressed in terms of" music, with the *reductio ad absurdum* implication that exact sets of correlatives must exist between a composer's feelings and his notation. It was offhand and annoyingly incomplete, but even the stupider critics could have seen that it did not deny musical expressivity, but only the validity of a type of verbal statement about musical expressivity. A composer's work *is* the embodiment of his feelings and, of course, it may be considered as expressing or symbolizing them – though consciousness of this step does not concern the composer.'

In 1952, thirty-two years after the Concertino was composed, Stravinsky recast the work, orchestrating it for twelve instruments (flute, oboe, cor anglais, clarinet, two bassoons, two trumpets, tenor trombone, bass trombone, violin obbligato, and cello obbligato).

Stravinsky spent the summer of 1920 in Brittany, where he finished the Symphonies of Wind Instruments, dedicating the work to the memory of Debussy. It was written at the request of the *Revue Musicale*, then directed by Henri Prunières. The final movement, Chorale, was published in a piano version in the supplement to the *Revue Musicale* entitled *Le Tombeau de Debussy*; it was also later transcribed for an orchestra of wind instruments, excluding clarinets, for performance together with the *Symphony of Psalms*. The Symphonies of Wind Instruments is one of Stravinsky's most noble works, yet it is very seldom performed. No doubt the complete inwardness of the music largely explains why the work is so little known; it is absolutely devoid of any of the clever superficial tricks of dynamics and timbre which have contributed to the popularity of much of Stravinsky's music, even though they may not have been

essential features of the works. Stravinsky describes the disastrous
Queen's Hall performance of the Symphonies of Wind Instruments
conducted by Kussevitsky:[5]

> I did not, and indeed I could not, count on any immediate success for this
> work. It is devoid of all the elements which infallibly appeal to the ordinary
> listener and to which he is accustomed. It would be futile to look in it for
> any passionate impulse or dynamic brilliance. It is an austere ritual which is
> unfolded in terms of short litanies between different groups of homogeneous
> instruments. I fully anticipated that the *cantilene* of clarinets and flutes,
> frequently taking up again their liturgical dialogue and softly chanting it, did
> not offer [the public] sufficient attraction. . . .

It is a work of hieratic austerity; as André Schaeffner says, it is as
though Stravinsky, standing on the threshold of Italian art, were
taking a last long lingering look at the splendour of Byzantium. The
arrangement of the thematic material into blocks recalls *The Soldier's
Tale*. The piece is not a symphony in the classical sense, which
would imply the organization of its material in accordance with the
spirit of sonata form; hence the title – Symphonies of Wind Instruments, and not 'Symphonies for Wind Instruments'. Here Stravinsky
is using the term 'symphony' in its strictly etymological sense of
the 'symphonizing' or playing together of a group of instruments.
The work consists of three distinct movements played without a
break, like a series of short litanies, taken up in turn by each family
of wind instruments. Popular tunes and pastoral melodies alternate
with solemn passages; in particular, the Chorale which begins the
Symphonies and later constitutes the final fifty bars is of great
expressive intensity. It consists of a series of static vertical chords
recalling in structure the harmonies of *The Rite of Spring* and of
the finale of *The Nightingale*; in mood, it heralds certain passages in
Oedipus Rex and the *Symphony of Psalms*. The Symphonies of Wind
Instruments are yet another manifestation of Stravinsky's deeply
religious nature, and I happen to know that when Stravinsky was
making up a programme of his sacred music which was to open the
Nineteenth Venice Festival in St. Mark's Basilica, he thought of
including the final Chorale of the Symphonies of Wind Instruments,
as an introduction to the *Canticum Sacrum ad honorem Sancti Marci
nominis*. Stravinsky wrote a new version of the Symphonies of Wind
Instruments in 1947. Robert Craft[6] compares the two versions and
gives a detailed analysis of structure and form.

[5] *Chronicle of My Life*, pp. 156-7.
[6] *Avec Stravinsky*, pp. 108-116. (N.B. The English version does not include
this analysis.)

Stravinsky's predilection for wind instruments comes out in the Octet. In the first of the *Program Notes* included in *Dialogues and a Diary* (p. 39) Stravinsky states that the idea of writing this work came from a dream he had had, so that the *Octuor* as he calls it, offers a further example of how dreams inspired his work, in addition to those already mentioned in connection with *The Rite of Spring* and *The Soldier's Tale*. Following the composition of *The Soldier's Tale* Stravinsky wanted to write an ensemble piece which would not be incidental music like it but an instrumental sonata. But he had not even given a thought to an octet until one night he dreamed that he was in a small room surrounded by a group of instrumentalists who were playing some very attractive music. Stravinsky did not recognize the music and hence could not recall it next day, but he did remember very clearly that there were eight players and that they were playing bassoons, trombones, trumpets, a flute and a clarinet. He describes how he awoke in a state of great delight and anticipation, and he immediately set about composing the *Octet*, which was very rapidly completed during the year (1922).

The work consists of three parts. The first is entitled *Symphony*. The term is meant of course to be taken in the pre-classical sense, synonymous with overture. But the architecture of the calm, glowing *allegro moderato* which constitutes the bulk of it, following a short, slow introduction, gives evidence of a rediscovery of sonata form which Stravinsky used for the first time in the *Concertino*. The second movement takes the form of a theme and variations. The mood of the theme is elegiac and sombre, but gradually the light emerges through the most unimaginable series of ups-and-downs. It becomes first a march *à la* Rossini, then a graceful waltz played by the flute and accompanied by the brass, and finally it evokes the climate of tragic petrification of the prelude to the second tableau of *The Rite of Spring*. In the *Program Note* referred to above, Stravinsky says 'I derived the *tema* of the second movement from the waltz, which is to say that only after I had written the waltz did I discover it as a good subject for variations. Then I wrote the "ribbons of scales" variation as a prelude to each of the other variations.' The final variation is the climax to the entire work. It is conceived as a *fugato*, Stravinsky's plan being to present the theme in rotation by the instrumental pairs (flute-clarinet, bassoons, trumpets, trombones) 'which is the idea of instrumental combination at the root of the *Octuor* and of my dream'. The *Finale* emerges from the *fugato*, being 'intended as a contrast to that high point of harmonic tension'.

Stravinsky confesses that 'Bach's two-part Inventions were somewhere in the remote back of my mind while composing this movement, as they were during the composition of the last movement of
the Piano Sonata.' (I shall be dealing with this sonata in the next
chapter.) He goes on to say 'The terseness and lucidity of the
inventions were an ideal of mine at that time, in any case, and I
sought to keep those qualities uppermost in my own composition'.
Forty years later, Stravinsky (who is certainly not lacking in a sense
of self-criticism) felt that in the Octet he had realized his intentions
most accurately. Casella was right in regarding the Octet for Wind
Instruments as 'the most perfect specimen produced by Stravinsky
so far of the universal style which clothes in new terms and in new
forms the spirit of ancient classical art'.

XI The Piano Works of the Neo-Classical Period

Now that we have discussed the earlier works described as neo-classical and explained why they were so called and to what extent the definition is valid (incidentally, Stravinsky gave his opinion of this definition in an article published in *The Dominant* in 1927 and reproduced in nearly all the music periodicals), let us look at the piano compositions in which this new tendency gradually crystallized. We have already had occasion to note the important part played by the piano in Stravinsky's work from the very beginning of his career, not only as a solo instrument, but as an orchestral instrument used in a completely original way. Stravinsky himself speaks of a 'sort of refined Pavlovian reaction in which the piano acts as a catalyst on the raw material in the creative process'. As we have seen, the basic structural concept of *Petrushka* was inspired by the potentialities of the piano, which seeks in that work to impose its peculiar tone-colour on the whole orchestra. What is meant here is of course not the romantic sounds culled from the piano by nineteenth-century composers, nor the half-tint effects drawn from it by the French Impressionists. The cantabile quality of the melodies and the impressionist colour values tended rather to obscure the fact that the piano works on a hammer action, and that it is therefore by nature a percussion instrument. Instead of disregarding this quality, Stravinsky stresses and exploits it for his own purposes. His piano music is not worked out in an abstract manner and then adapted to the capabilities of the instrument; rather it is conceived with those capabilities in mind. It is as if he had penetrated to the very heart of his favourite instrument, the piano, and discovered its most intimate secrets. Considered in this light, *The Wedding* can be regarded as the apotheosis of the piano treated as a percussion instrument. In the first piano work of his neo-classical period, Stravinsky's use of the percussive quality of the piano is to a certain extent tempered by the use of legato and cantabile, the point being that while he preferred to exploit the potentialities of the piano, he nevertheless took advantage of the whole range of its resources. This is evident even in the apparently simple pieces *The Five Fingers*, eight very easy melodies on five notes, written in 1921. As the sub-title implies, the melodic line in each case remains within the compass of a series of five notes.

I have already pointed to Stravinsky's use of a somewhat similar technique in the first of the *Three Pieces* for string quartet. There, the peculiar method of subdivision of the tonal compass, by which the individual parts were confined in watertight compartments, seemed to be determined by an abstract arbitrary rule, whereas in *The Five Fingers* the adherence to the narrow compass has a practical purpose, namely, to spare the young pianist the necessity of shifting his hand on the keyboard. At the beginning of each piece and each section Stravinsky indicates what five (or in some cases four) notes will be used in the particular tune, thus anticipating actually on paper the serial technique he uses thirty years later in the Septet. However, more important than these technical details is the fact that the didactic nature of the pieces and their formal limitations did not prevent Stravinsky from achieving genuine artistic effects. The eight melodies (a gentle Andantino; an Allegro of the military band type; an Allegretto with the rhythm of a Russian dance; a Larghetto with the lilt of a Sicilienne; a cantabile Moderato; a tender, reflective Lento; a bouncy Vivo; and a tango marked Pesante) are worthy of a place in the gallery of children's pieces, to which Stravinsky himself contributed not a few noteworthy examples.

In its issue of Sunday, 21 May 1922, the Paris newspaper *Le Figaro* published a piano piece of 56 bars entitled *Valse pour les enfants improvisée au Figaro par Igor Stravinsky*. Eric Walter White reproduces this waltz in his book *Stravinsky, the Composer and his Work*, and says that the existence of the manuscript of the work is mentioned in *A Catalogue of Manuscripts* (1904-1952) *in Stravinsky's Possession*, compiled in 1954 by Robert Craft. On the manuscript, which has on the back a sketch for *Renard*, there is a note by Stravinsky reading 'sketch of the *Figaro Valse*, composed at Morges, 1916 or 1917'. The note would appear to indicate that the *Valse* belongs to the same period as the *Easy Pieces* for piano duet, the waltz from which resembles the *Figaro Valse* insofar as both have a two-bar ostinato accompaniment; but in expression the atmosphere of the latter is different, being vaguely reminiscent of Ravel's *Ma Mère l'Oye*. A certain neo-classical angularity also puts it stylistically in the same bracket as *The Five Fingers*, particularly in that here again we get a foretaste of a leaning (conscious or unconscious) towards certain serial-like practices. Here it is to be seen in the retrograde use and permutations of short series of notes, intervals, cells and musical figures. An in-depth structural analysis of this tiny and seemingly unpretentious piece might repay the effort, especially as a tell-tale pointer to the fact that Stravinsky's subsequent adherence to dodecaphonic serial technique is not so surprising after all.

Not long after composing *The Five Fingers*, Stravinsky settled down on Kussevitsky's advice to a really serious study of the piano, having decided to be his own interpreter in more difficult piano works he was thinking of writing. He made his début as soloist and interpreter of his own work with the Concerto for piano and wind orchestra or 'Concert pour piano suivi d'orchestre d'harmonie', as he called it in French. He finished writing it in April 1924 in Biarritz and played it for the first time in May of the same year at the Paris Opera, in a concert conducted by Kussevitsky. In the opinion of many critics this is one of the most baffling of all Stravinsky's works. Some criticize it as lacking homogeneity, and there is no doubt that Stravinsky has gathered together the most extraordinary ingredients. The introduction to the first movement has a monumental baroque grandeur suggestive of Handel; the Allegro which follows blends Bach and Scarlatti with jazz features. The second movement, a stately Larghissimo, recalls Vivaldi as well as Handel. In the middle of the movement the piano is suddenly hypnotized à la Erik Satie.[1] In places the figures are repeated with the automatic regularity of an incantation, creating a sense of suspension or blank amazement:

[1] Stravinsky was greatly impressed by the performance of Satie's *Parade* in Paris. He discusses the merits of Satie's work in his *Chronicle of My Life*, p. 154, where he says that Satie in turn wrote an article about him in *Vanity Fair* (February 1923) in which he says he greatly admires Stravinsky because he is a liberator who more than anyone else has set contemporary musical thinking free. He calls Stravinsky one of the greatest musicians of all time.

In the Finale also, characteristics of seventeenth- and eighteenth-century style are found side by side with modern syncopation. A variation of the stately introductory Largo recurs at the end of the piece as if to restate the basic emotional subject of the work. Unless I am mistaken, it was this Concerto that gave rise to the notion of Stravinsky's 'return to Bach'. I shall not repeat what I have already said on the validity of this remark, which Stravinsky's imitators very quickly adopted as their watchword. All I shall say is that in my opinion Stravinsky succeeds once again in this work in taking a vast variety of elements from outside and fusing them in the melting pot of his own personality. And, in the same way in which he can reconcile the most heterogeneous formal elements, in this Concerto he combines brilliant dynamics, achieved solely through movement and suggesting a lusty *joie de vivre*, with a sense of tragic grandeur.

In 1924, the year in which he completed the Concerto for piano and wind orchestra, Stravinsky wrote a piano sonata, which he performed himself in Venice in September 1925 at the Festival of the International Society for Contemporary Music. All the violence released in so many of the previous works, including parts of the Concerto, is here pent up, so that only the intensity of deep contained emotion remains. The Sonata is in three movements, the first and third having only metronome markings. In connection with this Sonata, Carl Philip Emmanuel and Johann Sebastian Bach, two of the models generally regarded as inspiring Stravinsky's neo-classical works (especially the forty-eight Preludes and Fugues and the Inventions) have often been quoted. De' Paoli claims that the Sonata is modelled on C. P. E. Bach's Sonata while agreeing with other critics that Stravinsky's admiration for J. S. Bach's Inventions has also directly influenced it. Stravinsky himself, apropos of the Adagietto, talks of a 'Beethoven frisé'. The dark tone of the phrase with which the two voices begin and end the first movement is suggestive of the passage consisting entirely of a single melodic line in unison in the finale of Chopin's Sonata in B flat minor. Casella[2] sees the arrangement in unison two octaves apart as a distant reminiscence of the beginning of Beethoven's *Appassionata*.

In fact, it would not be surprising if there were elements of Beethoven in Stravinsky's sonata in view of what he himself says:[3]

[2] op. cit., p. 128.
[3] *Chronicle of My Life*, p. 189. This statement is followed by a long digression on the art of Beethoven, championing its pure musical essence in the face of all the literary superfetations and ideological interpretations lavished on Beethoven's music and calculated to distort its fundamental character.

Though determined to retain full liberty in composing this work, I had, while engaged on it, a strong desire to examine more closely the sonatas of the classical masters in order to trace the direction and development of their thought in the solution of the problems presented by that form. I therefore replayed, amongst others, a great many of Beethoven's Sonatas.

But most comparisons of this kind are pointless, because as a rule the similarities and analogies are purely superficial. What is certain is that Stravinsky uses the term 'sonata' in its pre-classical, i.e. its etymological sense, to denote simply a piece to be played rather than sung. We can certainly not compare Stravinsky's sparse, threadbare fabric with C. P. E. Bach's almost romantic pre-Beethoven type of sonatas. The storm of rhythm which had raged in the earlier works has abated and the rhythm has sunk to an obsessive regularity. The web of sound in the first and last movements consists of two parts juxtaposed in a sort of argumentative relationship, as though they were criticizing each other.

The inexorable, regular, ostinato hammering in the one voice is offset by an expressive singing quality in the other. Thus, in the following passage, where the main theme of the first movement is introduced, the left hand plays staccato the whole time:

while the right hand plays 'legatissimo', a cantabile theme which recalls the 'Gloria' of a religious chant.

Harmonically, too, the voices are mostly separate, set off one against another: often, while one stays in the neighbourhood of the tonic the other is hovering round the dominant and vice versa.

The perpetual motion of the first and third movements of the Sonata does not slow down until the final cadences; the opaque, dissonant mass of sound resolves suddenly into a perfect concord, and the piece ends with an unexpected stillness and silence.

The Adagietto contains some of the most intense music in the whole of Stravinsky's work. There is a constant ebb and flow of expression. The player seems to launch into song only to be held up suddenly by the artificial device of a trill, as if giving way to an expressive impulse only to cool off its emotional heat in a little mechanical run, or in the gyrations of an arabesque. In the middle of this movement a quiet solemn motif stands out contrapuntally against a series of tight, nervous acciaccaturas:

This subtle chiaroscuro of emotion gives a curious fascination to a piece which at first sight might seem arid and sterile.

Some time after composing the Sonata, Stravinsky made his first tour in the United States; he had offers from a number of recording companies and signed a contract with one of them. This gave him the idea of writing a piano composition in four parts, each long enough to fill one side of a gramophone record. Apart from the practical consideration, he felt the urge to compose a work on the pattern of the eighteenth-century nocturne. This twofold stimulus produced the Serenade in A, in four movements, written in 1925. First we have a solemn introductory movement, Hymne; then a rhapsodic Romanza, which Stravinsky[4] describes as 'a ceremonial homage paid by the artist to the guests'. Casella[5] finds the opening bars of the Hymne extraordinarily like those of Chopin's second Ballade. The third movement, Rondoletto, is linked with the Finale and, as Casella says, 'it has a rhythmic sostenuto tempo and takes the place of the various dance pieces traditionally included in the serenades and suites of the time'. The fourth movement is a Cadenza Finale, which also serves as a solemn Epilogue. Unlike the Sonata, in which there was no tonal unity, the Serenade is entirely constructed round the note A. This note acts as a tonal centre or magnetic pole to which all the sounds have reference, without the device of the usual major and minor modes; hence the title 'in A' without mention of major or minor. Here we have explicit corroboration of what Stravinsky calls 'polar tonality' and 'extended tonality'.

[4] *Chronicle of My Life*, p. 203.
[5] op. cit., p. 133.

Many critics and musicians, including Alfredo Casella, consider the Serenade in A as Stravinsky's best composition for the piano.

In the four years following the composition of the piano works mentioned above, Stravinsky was invited more than forty times to perform his Concerto for piano and wind orchestra, and in 1928 he felt that the time had come to add another work in concerto form to his repertoire. Not wishing to compose a second concerto constructed on the same lines as the first, he decided to write a piece completely free in form. The result was the Capriccio for piano and orchestra (1929). The very title indicates the free, light-hearted nature of the work, for Stravinsky says of it:

I had in mind the definition of a *capriccio* given by Pretorius, the celebrated musical authority of the eighteenth century. He regarded it as a synonym of the *fantasia*, which was a free form made up of *fugato* instrumental passages.[6]

The freedom comes out in the essential relation of the parts as the musical discourse unfolds. The outward structure observes the classical division into three movements. The first is a Presto in G minor; the second 'Andante rapsodico' which harks back to the Adagietto of the Sonata; and the third is 'Allegro capriccioso ma in tempo giusto'. In the *Chronicle*, Stravinsky states that his model for this Capriccio is Carl Maria von Weber, in particular his well-known *Konzerstück* and his piano sonatas. The piano writing develops that of Stravinsky's earlier compositions to a point of virtuosity. Thematically, the Capriccio has something in common with the Tchaikovsky-like tunes in *The Fairy's Kiss*. In other respects, it looks forward to some of Stravinsky's later works like *A Card Game*, *Danses Concertantes*, *Scènes de Ballet*, and the Symphony in Three Movements.

[6] *Chronicle of My Life*, pp. 258-9.

XII The Neo-Classical Ballets

In the last two chapters we have described how Stravinsky's so-called neo-classical tendency came into being and finally established itself. This tendency reaches its climax in three ballets. The first, *Apollo Musagetes*, was commissioned by the Library of Congress in Washington in 1927. Stravinsky was asked to compose a ballet for a Contemporary Music Festival organized under the patronage of Elizabeth Sprague Coolidge. The duration of the work was to be under half an hour, and it was to be written for a small number of performers. Stravinsky took this opportunity to carry out a project which had intrigued him for some time, namely, to compose a so-called 'white ballet', i.e. a ballet based entirely on the abstract choreography of classical ballet without any psychological, narrative or expressive intent, and not using elaborate scenery or costumes, but danced only in monochrome ballet-skirts.

This uniformity of colour on the stage has its counterpart in the uniformity of tone colour in the music, which is played by an orchestra made up entirely of strings. Even its intimate structure is built up with this end in view. Polytonal superimposition is rare. We get any number of static perfect chords. Even the clash of dissonances does not produce violent dynamic effects; in fact they tend rather to give the harmonies a dry bloodless quality and to let down the tonal tension; and the melodic patterns, free from any traces of folklore but frequently borrowed from the composers of the past, from Lully to Delibes, Saint-Saëns and Tchaikovsky, seem to be sterilized and emptied of their original significance. The metrical structures are admitted to be based on the Alexandrine (Stravinsky once defined *Apollo Musagetes* as 'an exercise in iambics', or so Croft says – *Dialogues and a Diary*, p. 16). The hermetic quality of this music can easily induce indifference and boredom unless the listener senses the atmosphere of sublime tranquillity and liberation from all human passion. The static nature of the choreography is in keeping with that of the music; it is based exclusively on the plastic figures of classical ballet and is translated into the traditional forms of Pas d'action, Pas de deux, Variations and Coda.

The theme is purely allegorical: the Muses present their arts before Apollo for his approval. In the first tableau we have the Birth of Apollo, who is borne off to Olympus by two goddesses. The second tableau begins with the Variations of Apollo. Next comes the Pas d'action danced by Apollo and the three Muses most representative of the choric arts: Calliope, Polyhymnia, and Terpsichore. The three variations which follow describe the investiture of the Muses: Calliope is handed the 'stylus' and tablets symbolizing poetry and rhythm; Polyhymnia, a finger on her lips, personifies mime and rhetoric; and Terpsichore represents poetic rhythm and eloquence of gesture, and reveals the meaning of the dance. Following another Variation of Apollo and a Pas de deux danced by Apollo and Terpsichore, and a Coda in which Apollo joins the Muses, the ballet closes with an Apotheosis which discloses the two-fold origin of this and of all the other neo-classical pieces of Stravinsky, or rather it reveals an ambivalence characteristic also of the major works of Greek classical art, in which the sense of sublime serenity is often wedded to a sense of tragic fatality. In Stravinsky the tragic origin is all the more patent inasmuch as we realize intuitively that his serenity is not spontaneous but is willed, achieved at the expense of a violent effort to repress the strong forces of instinct which erupted with such overwhelming force in *The Rite of Spring*. *Apollo Musagetes* occupies a position diametrically opposite to that of *The Rite of Spring* in Stravinsky's work taken as a whole. In *The Rite of Spring* and *Apollo Musagetes* the two opposing dialectical forces of Stravinsky's personality are defined with absolute clarity – the first representing the instinctive nature of his genius, and the second, the rational will to control his musical material. Of all Stravinsky's works, *The Rite of Spring* is in every way the richest in contrasts of every kind – contrasting rhythms, symmetrical and asymmetrical, contrasts between heterogeneous harmonies, between melodies belonging to different tonal orbits, and between utterly dissimilar tone-colours. In *Apollo Musagetes* Stravinsky follows the very opposite course – he does his utmost to eliminate contrast completely, 'to proceed by similarity' and to reduce all the structural elements, timbre, rhythm, décor, and even choreography, based exclusively on the academic dance figures, to a common denominator. One of the passages in the *Poetics of Music* (pp. 80-81) is extremely significant in this respect:

Summing up: What is important for the lucid ordering of the work – for its crystallization – is that all the Dionysian elements which set the imagination of the artist in motion and make the life-sap rise must be properly subjugated before they intoxicate us, and must finally be made to submit to the law: Apollo demands it.

As already pointed out, Stravinsky has stated his preference for the principle of similarity (connected with 'ontological time') over contrast (connected with 'psychological time'); he prefers the classical approach, which according to him demands submission to the discipline of form, to the romantic approach which he sees as a rebellion against discipline; he favours Apollonian rather than Dionysian art. All this does not mean, however, that he categorically dismisses the other side. While he upholds his preference, he admits (ibid., p. 32):

Moreover, the coexistence of both is constantly necessary, and all the problems of art, like all possible problems for that matter, including the problem of knowledge and of Being, revolve ineluctably about this question, with Parmenides on one side denying the possibility of the Many, and Heraclitus on the other denying the existence of the One. Mere commonsense, as well as supreme wisdom, invite us to affirm both the one and the other.

And later (ibid., p. 79) he says:

We shall always find at the origin of invention an irrational element on which the spirit of submission has no hold and that escapes all constraint. That is what André Gide has so well expressed in saying that classical works are beautiful only by virtue of their subjugated romanticism.

Apropos of a statement by W. H. Auden describing Stravinsky as a complete Apollonian, Stravinsky himself asserted that there are both Apollonian and Dionysian elements in all his music.

Thus the choice of theme for *Apollo Musagetes* is by no means fortuitous, but has a symbolic meaning which Stravinsky explains when he points out the dualism implied in Nietzsche's antithesis of Apollo and Dionysus. If *The Rite of Spring* can be described as the most Dionysian of Stravinsky's works, *Apollo Musagetes* is surely his most Apollonian work.

I stated in Chapter IV that the avowedly tragic character of *The Rite of Spring* is bound up with the abasement and voluntary sacrifice of the individual to the community. As Adorno says,[1] in Stravinsky's neo-classical phase 'the individual is not merely bereft of the possibility of expression; he is even robbed of the dark secret of his own sacrifice'. But underneath the forbidding exterior of an impassive objectivity, we discern in Stravinsky's early neo-classical works a hint of repressed subjective expression. Hence the underlying sense of tragedy which continues to crop up sporadically until it finally takes shape in accordance with two spiritual principles successively: in the religious works the strivings of humanity abate

[1] op. cit., p. 135.

and are transmuted into the humble acceptance of the tenets of an unquestioning faith. In the music designed to entertain, all the tangles are unravelled in the abstraction of unalloyed diversion. Nothing remains to be despoiled or repressed since all vanishes into oblivion and utter escapism. These are the works which really mark Stravinsky's entry into the modern neo-classical Arcadia. A typical 'diversion' of this kind is a composition actually called Divertimento which is the symphonic suite from the ballet *The Fairy's Kiss*.

After he had finished *Apollo Musagetes* Stravinsky was commissioned by Ida Rubinstein to compose a ballet for her. The painter Alexandre Benois gave Stravinsky the idea of writing a work based on Tchaikovsky's music. Stravinsky liked the idea and wrote *The Fairy's Kiss* to mark the thirty-fifth anniversary of Tchaikovsky's death. The plot was devised by Stravinsky himself; once again he took his inspiration from a Hans Andersen fairy story, *The Ice Maiden*. The story tells how a fairy plants a magic kiss on a child and wrests him from his mother's arms. On his wedding day, the day of his greatest happiness on earth, the fairy snatches the youth away from this world and bears him off into eternity so as to preserve this happiness. Then the fairy gives him back his kiss. Stravinsky refers the allegorical meaning of this fable to Tchaikovsky whom he regarded as the darling of the Muses, more than any of the other Russian composers.

The choreography is similar to that of *Apollo Musagetes*, i.e. Stravinsky's purpose was to create a classical ballet in which the rôles of the Fairy and the other allegorical characters would be played by dancers in white ballet skirts dancing in and out among the tourists and country-folk against a Swiss village background. The melodic motifs, with one or two exceptions, are taken from Tchaikovsky's works, and Stravinsky uses them in the same way as he used Pergolesi's melodies in *Pulcinella*, except that here he refrains from distorting or parodying the themes.

His fondness for Tchaikovsky led him to compose one of his most tenderly lyrical works, in which nostalgia for bygone days is expressed quite openly. The Suite from this ballet, called Divertimento, as we have seen, comprises four parts corresponding to the four parts of the ballet. The first part is described as a Symphony; the second consists of a series of Swiss Dances; the third is a Scherzo; and the fourth a Pas de deux including an Adagio, Variations, and a Coda. As Alfredo Casella rightly points out,[2] *The Fairy's Kiss* antici-

²op. cit., p. 152.

pates various aspects of another ballet which Stravinsky wrote eight
years later, namely *A Card Game (Jeu de Cartes)*, a 'Ballet in three
deals', as the composer himself calls it. Unlike *Pulcinella* and *The
Fairy's Kiss*, *A Card Game* is not one of those works which can
really be defined as 'music to the second power', i.e. based entirely
on the re-moulding of musical figures taken from other people's
music – snippets from Viennese waltzes and band galops are found
side by side with phrases reminiscent of Haydn, Weber, Tchaikovsky,
Verdi, and Ravel, and indeed of the French operetta composer
Charles Lecocq. Stravinsky admits that he has borrowed motifs
from Rossini, Johann Strauss, Messager, as well as from his own
Symphony in E flat (see in this connection the 'Program Note' on
A Card Game in *Themes and Episodes*, pp. 34-39. He justifies these borrowings on the grounds that he wanted to suggest the atmosphere
of 'a concert by the Kursaal Band' like those that used to play in the
squares of spas and resorts in Germany where as a boy he first made
acquaintance with casinos. Stravinsky regarded *A Card Game* as in
many respects 'the most "German" of my works'. He even maintained
that the rhythm and instrumentation of the theme *alla breve* with
which each of the three 'Deals' of the ballet begins are an echo or
imitation of the tempo, timbre, and indeed the whole character of
the 'trombone' voice with which the master of ceremonies at one of
the German spas would announce a new game. Stravinsky's emphasis
on the German aspects of *A Card Game* must not make *us* lose sight
of its Italianate features. These are most evident in the third part,
where we get an almost literal quotation from the well-known motif
from Rossini's *The Barber of Seville*:

In Stravinsky this becomes:

The metrical structure of this theme is found also in passages like:

It would not be unfair to say that the metrical formula used in the
Rossini theme constitutes the nucleus of the whole of the final part
of *A Card Game*. The way in which Stravinsky uses Rossini here is
surely most important; for Rossini too was a composer more sensitive
to rhythm than to any other component of music. As he himself
said : 'Expression in music, all the power inherent in music, lies in
rhythm. Notes do not serve to give expression except in so far as
they constitute the components of rhythm.'[3] This might be said
equally of Stravinsky's music. But what is still more significant is the
timing of Stravinsky's citation of Rossini. In his hey-day, Rossini
expressed the pure joy of movement, diversion in music, in a completely direct dynamic manner. But in the music he wrote after he
had abandoned the theatre there was a sharp acid undercurrent.
With Stravinsky the very opposite took place. All the works of his
middle period have a dual fund of bitterness; they are amusing only
in appearance. In certain circumstances, Stravinsky's music throws
off this duality of meaning, as we have said. We then get works like
The Fairy's Kiss and *A Card Game*. The achievement of serenity and
of unalloyed joy could not be brought out more clearly than in the

[3] See Vlad, *Modernità e tradizione*, Chapter V.

quotation from Rossini's masterpiece. The disparity between *Apollo Musagetes* and *The Rite of Spring* is paralleled by that between *A Card Game* and *The Soldier's Tale*. The Devil appears in *A Card Game* too, in the guise of the Joker.

The subject of the ballet is a game of poker. In the first two hands the Joker butts in and stirs up all sorts of trouble. In the third hand the Joker is much put out because he is beaten by a royal flush of hearts. Here Stravinsky quotes a verse from La Fontaine :

> Il faut faire aux méchants guerre continuelle,
> (Ainsi que l'a dit le bon Lafontaine)
> La Paix est fort bonne de soi;
> J'en conviens; mais de quoi sert-elle
> Avec des ennemis sans foi?

In *The Soldier's Tale* it was the human element that suffered defeat. In *A Card Game* the losers are the forces of evil. Stravinsky's music is stripped of any vestige of philosophical meaning, direct or indirect. It is left free to throw itself wholeheartedly into amusement and undiluted *joie de vivre*. In *A Card Game* Stravinsky reaches the culmination of detachment from the responsibilities of life.

XIII The Dramatic Works on Classical Subjects

I have already spoken of Stravinsky's leaning towards the Mediterranean world and classical culture. His biographers and critics, Tansman[1] and Wörner[2] in particular, have not been slow to single out an element in his works which can definitely be identified as Greek. The earliest work which betrays a kinship with the landscape and spiritual climate of the Hellenic world is his opus 2, *Faun and Shepherdess*, dating from as far back as 1905-6 (see Chapter I). This same atmosphere also pervades the *Pastorale*, written in 1908. But it was only in the period between 1926 and 1934 that Stravinsky's penchant for the ancient world became explicit and recurrent enough to amount to a definitely 'Greek' phase in his work. The works included in this phase are the ballet *Apollo Musagetes*, the opera-oratorio *Oedipus Rex* and the melodrama *Persephone*, which will be discussed in this chapter, and the *Duo Concertant* which will be dealt with in the next chapter. There was a later extension of this Greek phase in the ballet *Orpheus* which will be discussed in connection with the music of Stravinsky's American period.

The best known of all these works is undoubtedly *Oedipus Rex*, an opera-oratorio in two acts on a libretto by Jean Cocteau, taken from the tragedy of Sophocles and translated into Latin by J. Daniélou. The idea of using a Latin text occurred to Stravinsky after reading Joergensen's book on St. Francis, where we are told that St. Francis used Provençal rather than his mother-tongue in moments of solemnity or when he was too overcome with emotion to express himself in ordinary everyday speech. Stravinsky felt that the corresponding language today would be Latin :[3]

A medium not dead, but turned to stone and so monumentalized as to have become immune from all risk of vulgarization . . . What a joy it is to compose music to a language of convention, almost of ritual, the very nature of which imposes a lofty dignity! One no longer feels dominated by the phrase, the literal meaning of the words. Cast in an immutable mould which adequately

---

[1] op. cit., pp. 218-20.
[2] K. H. Wörner: *Neue Musik in der Entscheidung* (Schott: Mainz, 1954).
[3] *Chronicle of My Life*, pp. 205, 210.

expresses their value, they do not require any further commentary. The text thus becomes purely phonetic material for the composer. He can dissect it at will and concentrate all his attention on its primary constituent element – that is to say, on the syllable.

In *Dialogues and a Diary* (p. 4) Stravinsky gives an even more significant explanation of this choice: 'I thought that an older, even an imperfectly remembered, language must contain an incantatory element that could be exploited in music'. (The entire first chapter of the *Dialogues* is particularly interesting because of the composer's repeated statements concerning his premises and concepts in the three works constituting the 'Greek trilogy'; *Oedipus Rex*, *Apollo* and *Persephone*.)

It was a similar desire for a static effect on the stage that led Stravinsky to choose a Greek tragedy. As we know, classical Greek tragedy prefers the extrinsic action not to take place on the stage; what is happening or is to happen should be narrated, while the stage action concentrates on the salient dramatic episodes. The specific choice of *Oedipus* is usually explained by the desire on Stravinsky's part to make use of a plot which everybody knows, so that the listener's undivided attention would be focused on grasping the musical values and nothing else. It is my belief, however, that the choice of *Oedipus* was determined largely by the affinity between the profound significance of the Sophocles tragedy and one of the essential mainsprings of action within Stravinsky himself. In the Prologue, whch is recited in French by the 'speaker', dispassionately, like a lecture, the spectators are given a running commentary on what is going on: 'Oedipus, unknown to himself, contends with supernatural powers: those sleepless deities who are always watching us from a realm beyond death. At the moment of his birth a snare was laid for him – and you will see the snare closing.' Here again, what Stravinsky is trying to express is the sense of tragic fate hovering over human destiny, the sense which pervades all the variety of poetic themes of his previous masterpieces from *Petrushka* to *The Rite of Spring*, *The Wedding*, and *The Soldier's Tale*. In *Oedipus Rex*, Stravinsky concentrates all his efforts on the inwardness of the drama. His aim is to get rid of all that is fortuitous, to purge it of all external spectacle. To this end all stage 'action' in the ordinary sense is eliminated. Apart from Tiresias the soothsayer, the shepherd, and the messenger, 'the characters remain in their built-up costumes and in their masks. Only their arms and their heads move. They should give the impression of living statues.' But even the three 'mobile' characters are not really creatures of flesh and blood, but walking travesties of human beings. The calf which the shepherd carries round his neck, his mask and his costume, are to form a one-piece 'shell' which hides everything but his arms and legs. The same applies to the messenger. The chorus is hidden behind a sort of bas-relief consisting of sculptured draperies, so that only the faces are visible. The protagonists in the drama stay absolutely still. They make entries and exits through trap-doors, or are veiled and unveiled alternately by special curtains. Here Stravinsky's tendency to make the tonal compass rigid, to petrify it and deprive it of its thematic perspective has a meaningful counterpart not only in the statuesque rigidity of the characters but also in the designing of the sets – one of the stage directions specifies that the stage should have 'no depth'. The whole action is to take place at the front of the stage.

This idea, which reduces the theatrical aspect substantially to a succession of frozen tableaux, would seem to be at variance with the very essence of operatic performance. In this respect it is significant that *Oedipus Rex* is described by the authors as 'an opera-oratorio'. The first performance was actually given in concert form, on 30 May 1927, at the Théâtre Sarah Bernhardt in Paris, under the auspices of the Russian Ballet, and it was not until 25 February 1928 that it was performed on the stage for the first time, with Klemperer conducting, at the Berlin Opera House. But even since then this work, which is undoubtedly one of Stravinsky's masterpieces, has found its way more readily into the concert repertoire than into the opera house. Nevertheless its performance on stage is not entirely without purpose, if only because of the very contrast between the way in which operatic characters normally act on the stage and the puppet-like immobility of the characters in *Oedipus Rex*, which makes them appear bereft of any semblance of 'real' existence, and as it were projects them on to the mythical plane. Their agogic passiveness is also symbolic of the hopelessness of resisting the fatal forces of destiny, which as we have seen overwhelms all the subjects either explicitly created by Stravinsky, as in his theatre music, or implied in so many of his concert works.

Tiresias, the messenger, and the shepherd are not exceptions to the symbolic intent already mentioned; in fact they tend to confirm it. They are the only ones who have any action to perform, and they themselves are not subject to Fate but are simply the instruments through which Destiny operates and is fulfilled. As far as the other characters are concerned, the musical characterization is so strong as to give the impression that their motivation, their dramatic impulses and their ineffectual gestures do nevertheless reflect real feelings of which the outward signs are repressed – the reality of these feelings is perceived as all the more intense below the surface because the conventional, outward manifestation is not seen. Thus in a sense Stravinsky overcomes the effect of abandoning the normal theatrical conventions in *Oedipus Rex* by resorting to what might be called 'secondary' conventions as compared with the usual ones. The attempt to project the drama on a static tragic plane has its effective counterpart in the diatonic structure of the music, which uses some of the most well-tried and even hackneyed tonal relationships. The work is orchestrated for a symphony orchestra; in fact this was the first time since 1914 that Stravinsky had used the conventional orchestra in composition. But in contrast to the works of the 1914 period, his new instrumental writing bears the mark of his experience with 'individualized' groups and with the analytical approach used in the chamber works written after *The Rite of Spring*. As Tansman says:[4] 'The combinations of timbres of *L'Histoire du Soldat* and of *Renard* appear in the symphonic structure in a significant and striking fashion, standing out from it like mobile bas-reliefs.' Outwardly the musical discourse is governed by the use of self-contained classical forms: aria, duet, and choruses. Within this formal framework the musical material is arranged in contiguous blocks with no thematic connection, to form a monumental edifice of sound. Frequently the rigidity of the rhythms is paralleled by the simplicity of the harmonies, except that in the dialogue between the messenger and the shepherd, Stravinsky abandons the continual shifting of the stress and the time-changes which are an outstanding feature of so many of his works. The rhythmic pattern results for the most part from the juxtaposition of long passages within which the rhythm does not change but proceeds with the inexorable regularity of a machine repeating the same metrical formula over and over again. Take, for example, the opening chorus in Act 1. The people of Thebes are imploring Oedipus, who has defeated the Sphinx, to save them from the plague. After the two exclamations ('Kaedit nos pestis' and 'Peste serva nos') at the beginning, the music settles down over a series of rhythmical ostinato bass figures. First of all the timpani, harp, and piano beat out a 6/8 rhythm, which remains throughout the whole piece the essential rhythm suggesting

[4] op. cit., p. 219.

Stravinsky

what Herbert Fleischer describes in the well-worn cliché of Beethoven criticism as 'Fate knocking at the door'. First we have a series of 6/8 quavers phrased in sixes; next come semiquaver figures, dotted quavers, etc. In the aria which follows, where Oedipus' nephew Creon announces the Oracle's reply, namely that 'the assassin is hiding in Thebes – at whatever cost he must be discovered', we get a more agitated rhythmic motif consisting of two semiquavers followed by a quaver (see p. 104).

Against this restless rhythmic iteration we have the solemn, peremptory declamation of the vocal line. Stravinsky does not hesitate to weave this round the simplest and most commonplace of chords, the tonal entity *par excellence* – the perfect triad of C major which is played on the trumpet arpeggiando as an accompaniment to Creon. Stravinsky uses the dominant on which the previous chorus ends to pave the way for it, without distorting it in the slightest or incorporating it in any polyharmonic complex, and manages in an almost magical way to give this most prosaic and hackneyed of all chords a dignity and a satisfying quality of which no one would have believed it capable any longer. I am not suggesting that this and other similar chords completely regain their pristine vitality; on the contrary – in order to rescue these worn-out harmonic devices from utter banality, Stravinsky is forced to deprive them of their organic tonal function and to sever them from their organic relationships in the musical context. The characteristic chords of the classical tonal system are not so much used in a new sense as 'fossilized', which gives them a dignity similar to that we seem to feel in the words of the dead language into which Cocteau and Stravinsky had their text translated. The vanity and weakness of character of King Oedipus, seen in the way in which he boasts that he can solve the riddle of the Oracle and promises to discover the murderer and drive him out forthwith, are rendered musically by an ornate melodic line full of flowery arabesques. The flexibility of this line contrasts with the stiffness of the following passage, in which the chorus resumes its regular quaver figure while waiting for the soothsayer Tiresias, 'the fount of truth', to answer Oedipus' questions. In an aria to be sung 'tranquillo ma ben articolato' against the constant grumbling of the bassoon till its part is taken over in turn by the cor anglais and the oboe, with the violins playing 'tranquillo' but with the same relentlessness, Tiresias refuses to answer :

As the 'speaker' has explained earlier, he already realizes that
Oedipus is the plaything of the heartless gods. Oedipus, infuriated
by Tiresias' silence, accuses him of plotting with Creon against the
throne. Then Tiresias speaks: 'The assassin of the King is a king.' The
function of the chord of C major in Creon's aria is now taken over
(see p. 107) by the chord of A minor, which is the starting point for
Tiresias' song of compassion with the victim of the impending tragedy.
As Tiresias proceeds to tell his story, particularly in the second part
of the aria 'Inter vos peremptor est', the harmonies become more
and more taut and acquire more complex and ambivalent tonal
functions. After a mournful reprise of Oedipus' aria, Queen Jocasta
appears, and the chorus bursts forth into a full-blooded 'Gloria' as
Act I comes to an end.

The second act begins with the previous chorus repeated, after
which the 'speaker' outlines the events of the next scene. The first
part of the scene is taken up by a long and elaborate aria by Jocasta;
its outward form is governed by its basic rhythmic structure – each individual part of the aria is based on a single, regular rhythmic formula.
After an introductory passage in which the vocal line is supported

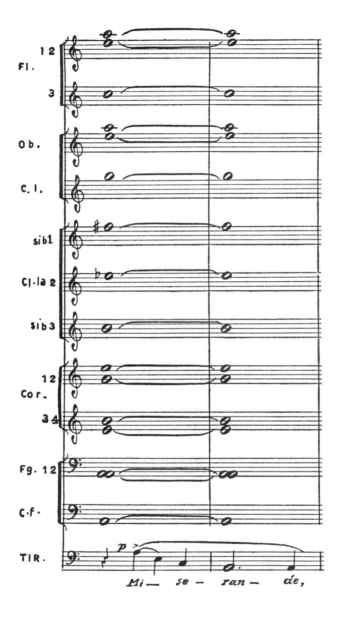

Mi— se — ran — de,

by sostenuto notes held by the flutes, and later by the strings, with harp and piano arpeggios, the first section of the aria is an unbroken succession of syncopated harp chords. The cold mechanical nature of this accompaniment brings out more effectively by contrast the persuasive warmth of Jocasta's melody as she reproaches the princes for raising their voices in a stricken city. A series of rapid triplets played by the clarinets gives a feeling of agitation to the passage in which she declares that she does not believe the Oracles, while a rhythmic figure like the 'Fate' motif in Beethoven's Fifth Symphony:

gives a dramatic quality to the middle section of the aria, in which Jocasta, in order to prove that the Oracles are false, asserts that the prophecy that Laius would be murdered by his own son was not fulfilled, but that Laius had been killed by thieves at the *trivium*, where the three roads to Delphi and Daulia meet. After a reprise of the first section, the chorus echoes the word 'trivium'. The insistent repetition of a chord of B flat cuts across the web of sound to signal the voice of Oedipus – the word 'trivium' has struck terror in him. He remembers how, on his way from Corinth before his encounter with the Sphinx, he killed an old man where three roads meet. If Laius of Thebes were that man, what then? Oedipus cannot return to Corinth, having been threatened by the Oracle with a double crime: killing his father and marrying his mother. He is afraid. The music expresses this fear wonderfully by the contrast between the inexorable hammering of rigid diatonic harmonies, and the chromatic and rhythmical vagaries of a melodic line which twists and turns this way and that, and is interrupted by fearful gasps and pauses.

At the height of his terror, Oedipus' voice is heard alone – only the menacing throb of the timpani intrudes upon the clipped phrases in which Oedipus tells Jocasta that he has killed an old man at the crossroads. At this point Jocasta's aria is taken up in 'tempo agitato'; the whirling triplets begin again more dizzily than ever. In contrast to Jocasta's admonishing and suppliant 'Cave oracula', Oedipus sings his 'Volo consulere' over an ostinato. The triplets finally disintegrate, and the shepherd and messenger arrive to announce the awful truth : Polibius is dead, but in fact he was only Oedipus's adoptive father; his real parents were Laius whom he assassinated, and Jocasta whom he has married, just as the Oracle had foretold. This highly dramatic scene between the shepherd and the messenger is, as we have said, the only one in the whole work in which the rhythm breaks through the rigid metrical formulas, and falls into the asymmetrical patterns Stravinsky had invented in the great works of his Russian period. This too is logically in keeping with the basic conception of the work, as we have described it. It is here in this scene that Fate is dramatically revealed and takes a hand. By virtue of that same equation which, as we have seen, establishes a symbolic relationship between the 'forces of destiny' and the rhythmical structure, the latter cannot remain *static* but must become *dynamic*; and this is in fact what happens. Once the messenger and the shepherd have gone, the music stops – only the timpani are left to break the silence periodically with two notes repeating like a nervous tic that most ordinary of all tonal relationships – tonic-dominant (exactly as in the *Easy pieces for piano duet*, though here there is no suggestion whatsoever of the grotesque or of irony to mar the sense of sublime tragedy which the scene creates); while the violins and the woodwinds play a series of short notes producing the musical equivalent of a shudder. In a triplet phrase, simple and infinitely expressive, Oedipus repeats to himself the awful truth : 'Natus sum quo nefastus est, concubui cui nefastum est – Kekidi quem nefastum est. Lux facta est.' The last three words are sung on the descending arc of a B minor chord, each separate note of the arpeggio gently passing through the domain of the perfect chords of a B minor, G major, then B minor again, and finally coming to rest on a chord of D major which is allowed to vibrate to the bitter end. In the whole history of music I know of few examples where such simple formal resources are made to express emotions so profound and intense. Formulas which have become completely ossified suddenly come to life again for an instant.

A simple minor triad recovers, perhaps for the last time, a power of expression it seemed to have lost decades if not centuries ago. Even the stone statue takes on a human quality at that moment – not for long, because it is galvanized into life only by a supernatural order of reality against which the human being struggles in vain. Oedipus' eyes see the light – but it is a light on which no human eyes can bear to gaze: Oedipus puts out his eyes with a golden pin; Jocasta hangs herself. The messenger has to tell of these happenings, almost too horrible for human nature to bear. 'He can scarcely open his mouth.' The chorus intervenes and shares in the commentary. Then Oedipus is 'driven gently, very gently away'. The man the people loved was not one who had sinned, but a victim of fate; Oedipus' exit is accompanied by the imperious affirmation of the 6/8 ostinato rhythm. The sheaf of instrumental sound narrows to the interval of a minor third, like a gramophone record running on and on in the same groove, until the sound dies away and the curtain falls.

In 1933, Ida Rubinstein, who had already commissioned Stravinsky to write *The Fairy's Kiss*, asked him to write the music for a play by André Gide, based on Homer's *Hymn to Demeter*. Stravinsky had never yet set a French text to music, except for the *Two Poems of*

Verlaine, and hence he hesitated to accept it. Finally he made up his mind to undertake the task, once he was convinced that he could base his music on the syllabic structure of Gide's text in the same way as he had treated the phonetics of the Latin text of Cocteau and Daniélou in *Oedipus Rex*. Stravinsky says as much in a statement concerning the way in which he had come to write *Persephone*, made on the occasion of the first performance in April 1934. In this statement he outlines his fundamental ideas on music generally and on theatrical music. Here is a passage from his statement:

I do not work outwards. My ideas about music are very different from what people think. Music is given to us to establish an order in things; to order the chaotic and the personal into something perfectly controlled, conscious and capable of lasting vitality. I cannot myself transform my conscious emotion into a rule. When we suddenly recognize our emotions, they are already cold, like lava. Any attempt to turn them outwards will be purely formal. I think I should tell the public that I hate any orchestral effects as a means of embellishment; they should not expect to be enthralled by seductive sonorities. I rejected the futility of mere brio years ago. And I hate pandering to the public. The masses demand that an artist should bring out and exhibit his inner self, and then they take it to be the noblest form of art and call it individuality and temperament. . . . I have used a normal orchestra, a mixed choir and a children's choir. The only solo voice is that of Eumolpus, the priest of Ceres at Eleusis. He unfolds the narration and controls the drama. Persephone's part is mimed, spoken and danced. It is worth noting just how this *parakataloge* fits in with my work as a whole. As the score stands, and as I hope it will remain in the musical archives, it forms a complete whole with the tendencies I had several times shown in my earlier works. *Persephone* logically follows *Oedipus Rex*, the *Symphony of Psalms* and my whole conception of a work in which the rejection of the spectacular in no way detracts from the individual value of the work. *Persephone* is my present form of this trend.

This statement requires some comment and explanation. In the first place, the definition of the work as a 'melodrama' is not to be understood in the ordinary sense of a 'play with music'. Stravinsky is using the term in the sense of a recitation with musical accompaniment. In point of fact *Persephone* is only partly melodrama in this sense and partly opera and ballet, inasmuch as it includes the parts of Eumolpus and the chorus, which are to be sung, as well as parts to be danced and mimed. (In *Dialogues and a Diary*, Stravinsky describes the work as 'a mask or dance-pantomime, co-ordinated with a sung and spoken text'.) The work is in a single act divided into three tableaux, the first called 'Perséphone ravie', the second 'Perséphone aux enfers' and the third 'Perséphone renaissante'. Except in one important point, the plot follows the Greek myth of Persephone, who is abducted by Pluto and becomes queen of the

Underworld. Her mother, Demeter or Ceres, goes to Eleusis where she is the guest of King Triptolemus. Ceres shows her gratitude by teaching the king how to till the earth, and gives him seed to sow. Then, through Jove's intercession, she persuades Pluto to allow Persephone to spend half the year in the Underworld with her husband, and half on earth with her mother. The symbolism of the myth is that of the seed which goes through its life cycle in the spring and summer and lies dormant in the autumn and winter. Gides's text emphasizes the symbol of the dependence of spring for its re-birth on the death of the seed. On this point the authors of *Persephone* have departed very considerably ·from the original myth. What they do is to alter the classical theme of Persephone's abduction by Pluto, making Persephone descend voluntarily into the Underworld. Persephone sees in the contemplation of a narcissus the tormented spirits of Hades, and is overcome by an irresistible impulse of charity. She sacrifices herself and goes down into the Underworld to console the shades and to brighten their eternal winter with her spring. The cruelty of human sacrifice, the blind self-immolation of the Chosen One in *The Rite of Spring*, is transfigured here by the enlightenment and gentleness of Christianity; for the impulse of charity which makes Persephone sacrifice herself is profoundly Christian.

The gap which separates the two concepts of self-sacrifice in *The Rite of Spring* and in *Persephone* shows what ground Stravinsky had covered along the road of his inner development in the thirty years between the composition of the two works. The fundamental consistency of this development, in spite of its ups and downs, transcends all the apparent external discrepancies between the works of each individual period. As we have seen, apart from his occasional recourse to religious themes, these periods were marked first by desperate, tragic pessimism, then by a vehement repression of the dramatic impulse, and finally by oblivion and escape into Arcadian bliss. In *Persephone* some of the most deeply hidden spiritual premises of Stravinsky's art have at last found full expression.

Although *Persephone* is a work about whose excellence in my opinion there can be no doubt, it would appear that Stravinsky regarded it as one of the least felicitous of his compositions. It appears also that he attributed the reasons which prevented it from being a resounding and continued success mainly to certain alleged or real shortcomings in Gide's text. In fact, in *Dialogues and a Diary* (p. 22) Stravinsky wrote 'My first recommendation for a *Persephone* revival would be to commission Auden to fit the music with new words, as Werfel did *La Forza del Destino*'; and he went on to single out some of Gide's verses which, taken out of their context, certainly do seem to breathe an old-fashioned spirit typical of what he disparagingly calls 'the Gide-Wilde age'. Personally I think that Stravinsky was rather unfair to Gide's text (just as he was unfair to the libretto written by Cocteau for *Oedipus Rex*). A particular type of imaginary and certain phraseology of Gide may seem outmoded and may have displeased Stravinsky, and may displease still more anyone who today takes an intellectual view; but there is no doubt whatever that it was precisely Gide's peculiar ethical and poetic approach to the myth of Persephone that caught Stravinsky's imagination and inspired him to write one of the tenderest and most meltingly human of all his works. And it is rather significant that he admits to a particular preference for the music to phrases which reveal the true moral basis of the episodes remoulded by Gide: 'the flutes in Persephone's final speech' and 'the final chorus (when it is played and sung in tempo, and quietly, without a general *crescendo*)' (ibid.).

The passages in question are in fact a musical setting of key statements in the text: 'I do not need an order and I willingly go where love leads me rather than faith. And I shall go step by step down the path which leads to the final human degradation.' However, it is also true that Stravinsky in the same paragraph expresses a fondness for a section like the lullaby *Sur ce lit elle repose* which precedes Persephone's awakening in hell in Part II. He wrote it originally for Vera de Bosset, his future wife, to Russian words of his own. I do not know what the words were so that I cannot compare them with Gide's text to which he finally fitted the music of this lullaby of love. At any rate the adaptation of language, the reclothing of the imagery, and the insertion of the passage into the context of the work seem to me to succeed perfectly and hence do not raise any particular critical problem. Such a problem might indeed have arisen in connection with the central G minor section of Eumolpus' second aria, likewise in Part II, where two flutes (*dolcemente cantabile*) and two harps (*sempre staccatissimo, presso la tavola*) accompany the phrase (similarly *dolce* and *cantabile*) with which Eumolpus narrates the episode where Mercury hands Persephone a ripe pomegranate to restore her desire for life and love. Stravinsky admits having taken it bodily from a 1917 sketch book, and observes slyly that no critic had 'cited [it] as stylistically discordant' (ibid). With all due respect to the composer, it must be said that no such discordance could be found for the very simple reason that there is none. The stitches in the garment seem perfect and hence practically invisible. Stravinsky also points out that nobody appears to have noticed that 'the two clarinets in the middle section of the Sarabande anticipate boogie-woogie by a decade' (ibid). In this case again, I do not think that failure to point out this detail implies a serious oversight; the similarity of the rhythmic module in the passage to that of boogie-woogie does not suggest an expressive mood that in any way resembles the commercial form of the dance of that name, except for the basic rhythmic beat.

This does not, however, by any means rule out the possibility that Stravinsky, who himself had been influenced by jazz, may in turn have sparked off some of the more recent developments in jazz music and may even have influenced some of the lightest of light entertainment music. Nor is there any reason to be surprised by the paradox that influences of the kind have been traced to a work in the 'sublime' manner such as *Persephone*. Like the tragic and the grotesque, the sublime and the ridiculous stand side by side more often than might be imagined in Stravinsky's works. And who is to say that it is not precisely because of a certain banality, transfigured or simply camouflaged, that his compositions of the Russian and neo-classical periods have been such a tremendous and lasting popular success? One of Stravinsky's peculiar virtues is his ability to give a certain aesthetic nobility to the commonplace.

XIV Works in Concerto Form

If this were to be a strictly chronological commentary on Stravinsky's work, now would be the time to discuss the *Symphony of Psalms*. But for the sake of convenience I have preferred to discuss this work in a later chapter devoted to the more important of the religious works, and to concentrate for the moment on the compositions in concerto form written between 1931 and 1938. The first of these is the Concerto in D for violin and orchestra.

While Stravinsky was in Wiesbaden, during a tour of Germany, he was asked by Samuel Dushkin and Dushkin's American patron, Blair Fairchild, through the director of Schott's, Willy Strecker, to write a violin concerto. Dushkin was to have the exclusive right to perform the work for a specified period, with Stravinsky conducting. After some hesitation Stravinsky agreed, and wrote the Concerto in collaboration with Dushkin, who advised him on the technicalities of the violin part. The Concerto for violin and orchestra is akin in conception to the Capriccio for piano and orchestra. The fact that the first and last movements are called Toccata and Capriccio indicates the free improvisatorial nature of the work; on the other hand, the very title of the two middle movements, Aria I and Aria II, indicates that the work is not one of mere withdrawal, since the word aria implies a certain expressive and cantabile quality. In both, Stravinsky's lyric vein is very much in evidence. In connection with these two Arias, Tansman and Ströbel have mentioned the name of Bach, Casella that of Weber, while others have even spoken of Tchaikovsky. Stravinsky himself agrees (*Dialogues and a Diary*, p. 47) that 'the subtitles of my Concerto – Toccata, Aria, Capriccio – may suggest Bach, and so, in a superficial way, might the musical substance'. He also says that he is very fond of Bach's Concerto for Two Violins, 'as the duet of the soloist with a violin from the orchestra in the last movement of my own Concerto may show'. Although there is no suggestion of actual borrowings, it would be fair to say that any thematic allusions there may be to works of the past are not used for grotesque parody effects. On the contrary, they seem to be rather a vehicle for the expression of wistful longing for the full expressiveness that music had once possessed. It can truly be said here that, in parts at any rate, Stravinsky drops his attitude of revolt against romanticism and abandons himself to the nostalgic 'recherche du temps perdu'. He also mentions that he regards the ballet *Balustrade* (1940) written by Balanchine and Pavel Tchelitchev to the music of the Concerto for violin as 'one of the most satisfying visualizations' of any of his works (ibid.).

Stravinsky's collaboration with Dushkin worked out so well that as soon as he had finished the Concerto he wrote the *Duo concertant*. Here again he consulted Dushkin on the technical aspect of writing for the violin. They gave the first performance together on 28 July 1932 for the Berlin Radio, and subsequently played it on a concert tour through Europe which had originally prompted its composition. Stravinsky explains the basic problems of the instrumental features of the work as follows:

After I had finished the *Concerto pour violon et orchestre*, which is as much an orchestral piece as a solo piece, I continued to explore the possibilities of the violin and especially its place in the chamber music ensemble. For years I had disliked the sounds produced in combination by the percussive strings of the piano and the strings vibrated by the bow. In order to be able to accept this combination of instruments, I felt I had to use the smallest possible grouping, i.e. as two solo instruments, so as to find a way of solving the instrumental and acoustical problems arising from the alliance of the two different types of strings. This is what suggested the *Duo Concertant* for violin and piano. The wedding of the two instruments seems to make for greater clarity than the combination of pianoforte with several stringed instruments, which tends to sound like an orchestral ensemble.

With regard to the spiritual background and the formal structure of the *Duo concertant*, he says that the work has a connection with Charles-Albert Cingria's tribute to the memory of Petrarch, one phrase of which struck him particularly:[1] 'Lyricism cannot exist without rules, and it is essential that they should be strict. Otherwise there is only a faculty for lyricism, and that exists everywhere. What does not exist everywhere is lyrical expression and composition.' As Oleggini says:

Stravinsky is referring to the lyricism of the bucolic poets of antiquity, and their conscious artistic technique which gave the *spirit* and the *form* to this *Duo concertant*. The theme he took runs through all five movements of the work, and these form a complete whole and produce what might be described as the musical parallel to the pastoral poetry of antiquity.[2]

[1] *Chronicle of My Life*, pp. 276-7.
[2] Léon Oleggini, *Connaissance de Stravinsky*, p. 201.

The Arcadian feeling for nature, even though displaced and suffused with other elements, is palpably evident in the two Eclogues which constitute the nucleus of the work. The initial Cantilena is imbued with a gentle melancholy; the writing, as De Paoli says, is 'strangely reminiscent of that of the early seventeenth-century composers for the violin'. The Jig is a brilliant virtuoso piece, and the Dithyrambe concludes the Duo on a note of transfiguration and ecstasy.

The Concerto for two solo pianofortes, like the Concerto for violin and orchestra and the *Duo concertant*, was the outcome of a practical necessity – Stravinsky wanted a concert piece which he could play with his son Sviatoslav Soulima. Father and son gave the first performance on 21 November 1935 in the Salle Gaveau in Paris for the Université des Annales. This is confirmed in *Dialogues and a Diary* (p. 74), and would appear to contradict his previous statement (p. 73) that the Concerto, like the later Sonata for Two Pianos, was written 'for the love of "pure art" '. He also says that 'The Concerto is symphonic both in volumes and proportions, and I think I could have composed it, especially the variation movement, as an orchestral work. But . . . I wished to incorporate the orchestra and do away with it. The Concerto was intended as a vehicle for concert tours in orchestra-less cities.'

The Concerto is one of Stravinsky's most impressive works, not only in its monumental architectural conception and the sumptuousness of the music but also in its intrinsic expressiveness, which reaches a solemn grandeur in the conclusion of the Fugue. In contrast, the Nocturne and the first and third Variations are little backwaters of serene, poetic delicacy which suggest that the assertions of not a few critics who find in Stravinsky a vein of pure and genuine lyricism are not so paradoxical after all, even though Stravinsky himself *(Dialogues and a Diary*, p. 75) says that 'the *Notturno* is not so much night music as after-dinner music, in fact, a digestive to the largest movements'. Obviously he has his tongue in his cheek, since the statement comes immediately after the revealing confession concerning the atmosphere he liked to steep himself in for stimulation and inspiration : 'I had steeped myself in the variations of Beethoven and Brahms while composing the Concerto, and in Beethoven's fugues. I am very fond of my fugue, and especially of the after-fugue or fugue consequent, but then, the Concerto is perhaps my "favourite" among my purely instrumental pieces.'

This is certainly one of Stravinsky's most 'straightforward' works;

it can be understood without any base of reference; it has no undercurrent of repressed emotion, nor is the music based on prefabricated thematic and stylistic elements. The listener feels that Stravinsky's fundamental state of mind in writing this music was a spontaneous, almost ingenuous enjoyment of 'playing', of 'music-making', which takes advantage of even the most subtle 'mechanical' resources of the instrument – hence the extreme dynamism and brilliance of the piece, which oddly enough enhances rather than obscures both the lyrical passages and those which express a genuine baroque 'pathos', in the finest sense of these words, with no pejorative implication.

The first movement in particular is fired by an impetuousness which in places gives the impression of a veritable contest between the two pianos. Casella describes the music as taut and close-knit; the two pianos do not 'converse' as they do in Mozart's famous Sonata; they are locked together the whole time like two wrestlers.

The interesting feature of the Variations which follow the Nocturne is also to some exent their peculiar construction; instead of developing from an explicit thematic statement, the theme is only allowed to emerge gradually, when it establishes itself as the theme of the Fugue. Like its model – Beethoven's Fugue in opus 110 – Stravinsky's too has a second part based on the inversion of the theme. Structurally the whole work is based on the principle of tonal unity around the polar note E, though it is achieved by means of an extremely varied modal scheme.

Stravinsky followed up the three compositions just discussed, and the ballet *A Card Game* (see Chapter XII), with another 'concertante' work, the Concerto in E Flat for chamber orchestra, associating the title with the estate of Dumbarton Oaks in the District of Columbia, U.S.A., whose owner Robert Woods Bliss had commissioned the work and had also borne the costs of the first performance given there on 8 May 1938. The Concerto in E Flat, as Stravinsky himself admits, is based on Bach's Brandenburg Concertos and the very first theme of the first movement is in a way an overt tribute to Bach :

Not that this theme is directly traceable to any of the themes of the
Brandenburg Concertos; but its general shape and the way it moves
is definitely reminiscent of the opening movements of the First,
Second, Third, and Fifth Brandenburg Concertos. But of course all
these similarities are reduced to a common denominator which is
unmistakably Stravinsky; in this instance it is recognizable in a
number of features going back as far as *The Rite of Spring* and *The
Wedding*. From the point of view of Stravinsky's later development
which ultimately led him to adopt serial writing, it is particularly
interesting to note that in the Concerto in E Flat the number of
extrinsic thematic references is 'offset by the intrinsic structural
motifs. As Ströbel rightly points out, each of the three movements
is developed from a single, minute interval, in a continuous and
consequential manner. The weird cadences of the Sonata also recur
here. Thus a shadow of disquiet is thrown across the peace and calm
which is still the dominant note of this first movement; the shadows
deepen in the middle section of the second movement, creating a
definite chiaroscuro effect in relation to the beginning and end

sections of the Allegretto. The first part and the figured repeat are among the wittiest and most amusing passages Stravinsky ever wrote. The motif used here reminds one of the phrase in the first act of Verdi's *Falstaff*, set to the words 'Se Falstaff s'assottiglia'. Stravinsky's comment comes in the form of deliciously lewd sounds from the bassoon, recalling the salacious sounds from the double-bassoon in the 'Tour de passe-passe' in *Petrushka*. In the final movement, 'Con moto', Stravinsky again succeeds in imbuing the musical discourse with that extraordinary polyvalence of meaning characteristic of so many of his more unusual works. This polyvalence makes the finale of the Concerto in E Flat seem at once serene and filled with a profound sense of anguish. The main theme of this movement sounds like a motif from one of Tchaikovsky's famous Symphonies recast by Stravinsky and given a dramatic panting breathlessness. 'L'ensemble souffle comme une machine' – as Oleggini says; this is Stravinsky's version of *Pacific 231*.

XV The Music of the American Period

As we have already seen, Stravinsky never returned to Russia after 1914. After the First World War, during which he lived mostly in Switzerland, he took up residence in France and became a French citizen. Between the two wars he made a number of tours in America, and in 1939 he was asked to give a series of lectures on the poetics of music at Harvard University; the lectures were later published in book form as *Poetics of Music*, already referred to. He was in the United States when the war broke out, and circumstances led him to take up permanent residence there; in 1945 he became an American citizen. From then on Stravinsky's entire creative activity was centred on America, even though in the 1950's and 1960's he paid frequent visits to Europe to conduct his own works.

It might be thought that the titles of this and the next chapter merely indicate the part of the world where the compositions to be discussed were written, and have nothing to do with the works as such. This is in fact largely true of the major works written by Stravinsky during the 'American' period. But he did write a whole series of works which directly and explicitly reflect his new environment. Stravinsky is decidedly not the type of composer whose music gives an exact picture of his private life. Thus, for example, in most of the works written around 1940 there is no trace whatsoever of the great sorrow he suffered in the loss of his mother, his wife, and his daughter, who all died within a short time of each other in 1939, while he himself contracted a serious form of tuberculosis. Nor is there any indication that the bloodshed and suffering of the war had any effect on the works of this period. It must not be concluded from this that Stravinsky's art lacks human quality. In the earlier chapters reference has already been made to the peculiar relationship which his music establishes between subjective human experience and objective musical reality. As we have seen, some of Stravinsky's works are designed as an opiate or a means of escape from reality, while others seemed to be coloured by the emotional residuum of tragic human experiences. But there is one thing which

Stravinsky's music never reflects – sentimentality. Outwardly Stravinsky's artistic approach has invariably been one of extraordinary sensibility towards the peculiar cultural background influencing it at any given moment. A great deal has been written about the close relationship between the individual phases of Stravinsky's musical development and the background of Russian culture; about the apparent or real parallel between his art and the manifold trends then taking shape in Paris, i.e. the Fauvisme of Matisse's circle, Cubism, Dadaism, the protean Picasso, and neo-classical objectivism as propounded by Cocteau. And there is no doubt that Stravinsky adapted himself admirably to the changing aspects of intellectual and artistic life in Paris, and came to be one of its decisive forces. The fact is that no other composer since Mozart has been gifted with such a prodigious power of assimilation as Stravinsky; no one since Mozart has been able as he has to use every experience that has come his way as grist to the mill in the development of his creative potentialities.

Culturally, America could not of course give him what Paris had given him. Moreover, Stravinsky's musical personality was by now substantially formed and was therefore less likely to be influenced by his new environment. But his natural adaptability, indeed his imperious 'urge' to adapt himself to his surroundings, had lost none of its force. America may not have had any profound influence on his style, but it certainly had a superficial influence, and gave a characteristically American slant to several of his works. This is evident in the very first work he wrote in the United States, a short Tango for piano. It was not the first tango he had written – there is one in *The Soldier's Tale* and another in *The Five Fingers*. There is in fact a distinct resemblance between the tango in this last-named work, composed in 1920 or 1921, and the one written in 1940 in America. But the distinguishing feature of the new work is an almost Gershwin-like light-heartedness, totally at variance with the inner meaning implicit in the earlier pieces, which makes the Tango perhaps the 'lightest' piece Stravinsky ever wrote. Apparently it was actually intended for a dance number or a popular song. But although it seems light in the context of Stravinsky's works, the Tango is not 'light music' in the commercial sense of the word. Hence it is hardly surprising that the composer's hopes of making a great deal of money out of it were not altogether fulfilled, in spite of a good send-off by Benny Goodman, who conducted a 'symphonic jazz' transcription (regular orchestra plus three saxaphones and guitar) made by Felix Guenther with Stravinsky's blessing, in July 1941 at Robin Hood Dell. In 1953 Stravinsky made his own orchestration of the piece for four clarinets, bass clarinet, four trumpets, three trombones, guitar, three violins, viola, cello and double bass.

The second work composed in the United States has a symbolical significance in regard to Stravinsky's attitude towards his adopted country, being a transcription for chorus of mixed voices and orchestra of the 'Star-Spangled Banner'. The arrangement created a furore. Its performance in Boston brought the police in, since under the Massachusetts State laws transcriptions of the national anthem are prohibited. Apart from this episode, this work is of no more than casual interest. During the same year, 1941, Stravinsky started work on a large-scale composition commissioned by the Werner Janssen Symphony Orchestra of Los Angeles – *Danses Concertantes*. As the title suggests, it is abstract ballet music, in the form of a series of dance-forms unrelated to any subject or any specific imagery, though two years later Balanchine wrote a choreography for it. It is the first work in which Stravinsky re-worked his own music rather than that of others. One writer on Stravinsky[1] describes the work as having 'the pleasing melodic quality of *Jeu de Cartes*, the harmonic and rhythmic concentration of *L'Histoire du Soldat*, the pulsating complexity of the *Dumbarton Oaks Concerto*, the wealth of modulation of the *Symphony in C*'. But as in all Stravinsky's 'syntheses', the components mentioned above are completely transformed.

In the *Program Notes*, included in the volume *Themes and Episodes* (p. 45) Stravinsky admits the influence of *A Card Game* as 'obvious', and adds: '. . . reactivated springs from my past work have continually nourished the present – which is one reason why I think my work deserves to be considered as a whole.'

The *Danses Concertantes* are in five parts. First comes an Introductory March; then a section entitled Pas d'action which in fact is a gay, humorous rondo. Next we have a Theme and four variations: Allegretto, Scherzando, Andantino and Tempo giusto, and a solo cadenza-like Pas de deux which leads into the finale section – a repeat of the initial March.

The *Danses Concertantes* were given their first performance in Los Angeles on 8 February 1942. Stravinsky's next composition was the merry *Circus Polka*, subtitled 'Composed for a young elephant'. The

[1] Tansman, op. cit., p. 242.

idea of this piece, already mentioned in Chapter VII, originated with Balanchine, who needed a short piece of music for an elephant ballet, in which one of the elephants which was to carry Vera Zorina, at the time Balanchine's wife, on its back. The music was first performed in a transcription by David Reksin for the Ringling Brothers' Circus Band of the famous Barnum and Bailey Circus. In the programme given by the Circus in the spring of 1942 at Madison Square Garden, New York, the work appeared as Display No. 18: 'The Ballet of the Elephants, Fifty Elephants and Fifty Beautiful Girls in an Original Choreographic Tour de Force.' It seems that at the outset the elephants were somewhat bewildered by Stravinsky's music, which was very different from the sugary waltzes and boisterous marches which constitute the musical stock-in-trade of circuses. However, they had plenty of time to get used to the Polka's dissonances, which disguise the conventional tonal relations, and its elisions and caesuras which break up the usual rhythmic squaring — the 'spectacular' ran for nearly 500 performances.

Stravinsky at once produced his version for conventional orchestra, and conducted it for the first time in 1944 in Boston. Shortly afterwards Paul Taylor used it for a choreographic work, with human dancers replacing the elephants. (Incidentally, this choreography was also seen in Italy on the occasion of the Two Worlds Festival in Spoleto in 1960.) However, even in its symphonic version, I find it hard to associate the piece with ordinary dance steps, where the essential, basic purpose is to create the illusion of overcoming gravity, whereas the *Circus Polka* evokes only too effectively the movements of the heavyweight among terrestrial fauna. This evocation is innocent of any intention to parody. The music is frankly witty and amusing, with none of the acid sarcasm of the 1915 Polka. There is nothing here to suggest a return to the 'aesthetics of the circus and the music-hall' which caused such a sensation and gave rise to so much controversy at the time of Satie's *Parade*, Milhaud's *Le bœuf sur le toit*, and Stravinsky's 1920 compositions. The Polka is innocent of any provocative intent, any hidden meaning or *double entendre*. Even in the quotation at the end from the famous Schubert *March militaire* there is every appearance of spontaneity without any hint of caricature or satire; Stravinsky's bitter irony has lost its sting.

In 1944 Stravinsky was invited by Billy Rose, one of the leading Broadway producers, to write the music for a show. The idea was to present the apotheosis of the 'Five Lively Arts', and Stravinsky's contribution was to represent 'serious' music; it was to be used for a classical ballet on the lines of *Giselle*, without any prearranged plot, but with an abstract dance action, prescribed by Stravinsky in accordance with a choreographic plan for which there is no precedent in any of his earlier scores of the kind. The result was the *Scènes de Ballet*, a suite of dance tunes. In conception the work is similar to the *Danses Concertantes*. It opens with a short Introduction followed by Dances for the *corps de ballet*, Variations for solo ballerina, First Pantomime, Pas de deux, Second Pantomime, Variation for Male Dancer, a Third Pantomime, another ensemble dance, and a triumphal Apotheosis. As Craft says in the 'Personal Preface', 'At the end of the manuscript score Stravinsky added the words "Paris n'est plus aux Allemands"; the whole jubilant apotheosis was written on the day of the Liberation'. On page 83 of *Dialogues and a Diary*, Stravinsky corroborates what Craft says, adding: 'I remember that I interrupted my work every few minutes to listen to the radio reports. I think my jubilation is in the music'. Thus we have here one of the few instances where Stravinsky admits that a particular emotional experience – in this case his feelings about war – is reflected in one of his works. The same cannot be said of the 'Souvenir d'une marche boche' or the 1918 transcription of the 'Marseillaise', in spite of the subject-matter.

Before it opened in New York, the entire show had its out-of-town opening – the customary practice in the United States – in Philadelphia. There was an amusing little incident in connection with this *avant-première*. After the preview in Philadelphia the organizers sent Stravinsky a telegram which read: YOUR MUSIC GREAT SUCCESS STOP COULD BE SENSATIONAL IF YOU WOULD AUTHORIZE ROBERT RUSSEL BENNETT RETOUCH INSTRUMENTATION STOP BENNETT ORCHESTRATES EVEN THE WORKS OF COLE PORTER STOP. Stravinsky wired back: SATISFIED WITH GREAT SUCCESS. The reactions of the producers are not recorded: but the *Scènes de Ballet* very soon abandoned the Broadway stage for the symphonic repertoire. They were given their first concert performance by the New York Philharmonic Orchestra in 1945.

In later life, Stravinsky took a somewhat critical view of this work, describing it as 'a portrait of Broadway in the last years of the war. It is featherweight and sugared – my sweet tooth was not yet carious then . . .' (*Dialogues and a Diary*, p. 82). In particular, the recapitulation of the *pas de deux* before the second Pantomime struck him as positively 'bad movie music' (ibid.). But he neither dismisses nor deprecates the work, even though only the exultant Apotheosis 'and, especially the voicing of the chords in the intro- duction to it, with the repetition of the upper line in canon and in different harmonic contexts' seems genuinely the outcome of a real and urgent inner need on his part.

What Stravinsky offered the Broadways producers was not a jazz work; but he did actually write for jazz band – the *Ebony Concerto* which Woody Herman and his orchestra performed for the first time in Carnegie Hall, New York, in March 1946. The work was written for a jazz orchestra of the Woody Herman or Duke Ellington type, i.e. it is scored for the whole saxophone family, clarinet, horn, five trumpets, three trombones, piano, harp, guitar, double bass, and percussion. There is a virtuoso solo clarinet part specially written for Woody Herman. There are three movements: Allegro Moderato, Andante, and Moderato. The work as a whole is in keeping with Stravinsky's plan (spelled out in the *Dialogues*, p. 86) to write 'a jazz *concerto grosso* with a blues slow movement'. Stravinsky's use of jazz technique in *Ragtime, Piano-Rag Music* and *The Soldier's Tale* and other compositions written about 1920 has already been mentioned. In those early works, what he borrowed from jazz was essentially its rhythmic principles, which he broke down, tore apart and fused together again, making them independent nuclei from which the musical discourse sprang into being. These nuclei being severed from the ordinary melodic and harmonic con- nective tissue of jazz, the pieces in question could not strictly be called jazz music. But the *Ebony Concerto* is a genuine jazz work, while at the same time it is authentic Stravinsky. He does not adapt himself to jazz; rather he takes it over and gives it his own cachet, inventing it afresh without straining its resources. The rhythm, for all its tremendous variety and plasticity, has ceased to be auton- omous. As Tansman rightly says: 'On the contrary, it is the melodic material here that defines the rhythmic movement.'[2] The taming of the rhythm robs it of its demoniacal character, so that it does not spoil the pleasing effect which is at once the virtue and the limita- tion of the *Ebony Concerto*.

[2] op. cit., p. 260.

XVI Other Works of the American Period

Let us now look at some of the other works which Stravinsky wrote in America between 1942 and 1947. The first of these bears the title *Norwegian Moods*, but in *Expositions and Developments* (p. 66, note 1) the composer says the work is 'misnamed because of my poor understanding of English'. He preferred to call it *Quatre pièces à la norvégienne*. The subtitle describes the pieces as *Four Episodes for Orchestra*. They are episodic in form because they were originally designed as incidental music for a film on the Nazi invasion of Norway. Stravinsky undertook to write the music for the film, but refused to make any concession whatever to American commercialism or its methods. In other words, he was not willing to agree to any tampering with his music by so-called 'arrangers'. In the similar situation mentioned in the last chapter, the Broadway producers finally gave in when Stravinsky refused to budge; but Hollywood held out, so that Stravinsky withdrew the music which was already on the stocks and turned it into a composition in its own right.

The four episodes of which the work consists are 'Intrada', 'Song', 'Wedding Dance', and 'Cortège'. To match the local colour of the film it was to accompany, Stravinsky used a number of Norwegian folk-tunes. It was in fact the first time for twenty years that he had resorted to the use of folk themes. This may well have been prompted by reasons bound up with the original purpose of the work; on the other hand, the allusion to folk motifs in the Sonata for two pianos, composed in 1943-4 (begun before the *Scènes de ballet* and completed immediately after) seems without any doubt to have been prompted by an inner need. In that connection, there is surely some significance in the fact that the Sonata was not commissioned or requested from any outside source, but was composed 'for the love of "pure art" ', as Stravinsky says in the *Dialogues* (p. 73). Several of the themes on which the Sonata is based are unmistakably Russian in character; but perhaps this statement needs qualification: the Russian flavour is not produced by picturesque splashes of local colour; on the contrary, the themes are completely devoid of local colour. The 'Russian' feeling comes solely from their

peculiar brand of expressiveness. To illustrate this we need only look
at one or two of the themes removed from their polyphonic context
so that we see only their melodic shape.

Incidentally, it was because he wanted to give the four lines of the
musical texture more clarity and a cantabile vocal character ('to
voice' them, as he says – ibid.) that Stravinsky decided to write the
Sonata for four hands rather than two as originally intended. Here
is the second theme of the first movement (*Moderato*):

and farther on:

The theme of the Four Variations which make up the second
movement is announced by this utterly simple diatonic period,
archaic in flavour:

The two themes of the final Allegretto have the same modal purity:

Obviously these themes sound somewhat different once they are embedded in a harsh contrapuntal texture. But dissonances like those resulting from the superimposition of the various polyphonic strands, with the theme quoted below balanced upon them:

do not distort its contours; in fact they endow it with a deeper significance. The astringency of the harmonic intervals mingles with the suavity of the melody to give the evocation of the Russian *melos* a sense of nostalgic yearning which, far from destroying its sweetness, heightens its effect. Thus in the Sonata we get a feeling of veiled longing for a native land lost forever, and for the far-off days of childhood; perhaps too for certain landmarks along Stravinsky's own artistic path. Like the *Danses Concertantes*, this little Sonata for two pianos is one of the works in which Stravinsky's 'recherche du temps perdu' embraces even aspects of his own art.

Shortly before writing the Sonata, Stravinsky wrote an *Elegiac Chant* in three parts – a funeral 'Ode' dedicated, as we saw earlier, to the memory of Natalia Kussevitsky, the wife of the famous conductor and the founder of the Edition Russe de Musique which published many of Stravinsky's early works. In subject and expressiveness, the Ode is reminiscent of the Symphonies of Wind Instruments composed twenty years earlier in memory of Debussy. In places the harmonies go back to *The Rite of Spring*. But they have lost their bitter sting and gaudy colour. Static harmonies and monochrome timbres are deliberately cultivated in the emotional landscape which Stravinsky conjures up in the Ode. The three movements are 'Eulogy', 'Eclogue', and 'Epitaph'. In the Eclogue the expression of grief is tempered by a lyrical feeling of nature. Originally the work was composed for one of the hunting scenes in the Orson Welles film of *Jane Eyre*; but it was not used in the film simply because once again Stravinsky could not see eye to eye with the producers. In the Eulogy and the Epitaph, the expression of grief is more intense, though it does not at any point go beyond the bounds of a disciplined dignity.

A year after he composed the Ode, Stravinsky wrote another *In Memoriam* – the *Elegy* for solo viola (there is also a version for solo violin). It is a short piece, dedicated, as already mentioned, to the memory of Alphonse Onnou, the founder and viola-player of the Brussels 'Pro Arte' Quartet which did so much to popularize modern works for quartet. The instrumental problem which Stravinsky tackles – and solves in a highly original manner – in this work is the problem inherent in all compositions for an unaccompanied stringed instrument, namely the achievement of a real polyphonic texture while using no other means than those of an essentially monodic instrument. Because of the elegiac character of the piece, Stravinsky wished to avoid any abruptness or violence of accent. Hence he eschewed the use of the device of plucked chords, restricting himself to double stopping to produce a two-part harmony. Thus in its inner musical structure the *Elegy* is a 'two-part invention'. In outward form it approximates to the *da capo* aria. There is a first section, a middle fugato episode, then the first section is repeated.

The underlying spirit of the Elegy and Ode, no less than the actual titles and subtitles of the pieces, heralds a new trend in Stravinsky towards subjects dear to classical antiquity. The most significant manifestation of this new tendency is the ballet *Orpheus* which he completed in 1947. As was said in an earlier chapter, it is in this ballet that the Greek ingredient in the art of Stravinsky comes most noticeably to the surface. In its formal structure, in the relationship between the music and the literary subject, *Orpheus* looks back to *Apollo Musagetes*, except that the musical material of *Orpheus* shows no trace of borrowings of the type discussed in relation to the earlier work. Its archaisms may suggest an occasional vague allusion to Monteverdi. We know that about the time when he was writing *Orpheus*, Stravinsky made a thorough study of the music of Monteverdi and his contemporaries. But in writing the ballet he avoided any direct borrowing and any thematic parallelism with Monteverdi.

The ballet is in three scenes. The first begins with a sustained Lento motif for the harp, placed above a chorale-like melody, austere yet full of feeling, played by the strings (see page 134). Stravinsky uses a modality oscillating between Dorian and Aeolian, and a stately, hieratic expression, to give tremendous dignity and a sense of remoteness in time. The sound of the harp, played 'près de la table', is the sound of Orpheus' lyre. On the stage, Orpheus laments for Eurydice in a motionless posture, his back turned to the audience. The woodwind entry marks the arrival of Orpheus' friends, who come to offer their condolence, and Orpheus begins his Air de danse. Then follows the brooding Dance of the Angel of Death, in which the Angel conducts Orpheus to the Infernal Regions. During the Interlude, the Angel and Orpheus reappear in the gloomy realm of Tartarus. In the second tableau we get the Pas des Furies, their 'agitation' and their 'threats', to quote the subtitles. The music contemplates them in figures which express disquiet without ever approaching a loud burst of sound. The tempo and expression marking of the Pas des Furies is 'Agitato ($\downarrow = 126$) in piano'. In Stravinsky's own words, 'the music for the Furies is soft and constantly remains on the soft level, like most of the rest of this ballet'.[1] The Pas des Furies is followed by another Air de danse, Recitative and Aria, the song with which Orpheus moves the Gods of the Lower World to pity. In the second Interlude the tormented souls of Tartarus stretch forth their fettered hands to Orpheus, pleading with him to go on singing his soothing song; and Orpheus resumes his Aria. The Underworld is moved to tears, and its wrath is placated. The Furies surround him, blindfold him and hand Eurydice over to him. This Pas d'action by the *corps de ballet* is followed by a Pas de deux

[1] Quoted by Ingolf Dahl in the article 'The New Orpheus', *Dance Index*.

danced by Orpheus and Eurydice in front of the curtain. When it is finished, Orpheus tears off the bandage from his eyes, and Eurydice falls down dead. In the third Interlude which follows, Orpheus returns from the underworld, and the Bacchantes seize him and tear him to pieces. It is only in this dramatic Pas d'action that the music becomes violent. The fits and starts in the rhythm, the sudden strident sounds emitted by the whole orchestra as if from the effects of a bout of Dionysian intoxication, suggest for a moment a somewhat debilitated and watered-down version of Stravinsky's manner in *The Rite of Spring*. But only for a moment: in the third tableau the music reverts to its detachment of expression and its Apollonian dignity. The harp takes up its initial theme, while the two horns intone in fugato style but always *mezza voce* a majestic chant offset by the thin tone of a solo violin played *sul ponticello*, and a muted trumpet. This is the Apotheosis of Apollo. 'Apollo appears. He wrests the lyre from Orpheus and raises his song heavenwards.' This is Stravinsky's own note on the final tableau of the ballet.

XVII Return to the Symphonic Form

The fundamental structure of most of the works we have discussed up to now has been based on principles different from and in some respects the very antithesis of those which during the classical period governed symphonic music, and, in a general way, the larger forms of European music.

From the time when the classical sonata form became the normal pattern of European music, musical composition was based on development from specific thematic figures. Taken as a whole, every work could be regarded as an organic entity resulting from the proliferation of individual musical 'cells'. Such classical pieces, especially classical symphonic works, possess a definite, intrinsic dynamism in every feature. The works of Stravinsky we have examined so far, with the exception of his very earliest juvenilia, have for the most part the very opposite characteristics; their internal structure is rigid and static. Stravinsky makes no use of the classical technique of thematic development; his music makes no attempt to lead on from one musical image to another, but juxtaposes or in many cases opposes them in stiff squared-off blocks. He even renounces the dialectical relationship between harmony and tonality, based on the distinction between dissonance and consonance. By massing together chords of various types, he deprives them of their specific tonal pull. The harmony too becomes static. In Stravinsky's music the tonal compass is the sum of a number of harmonic blocks, segments of melody belonging to different tonal orbits, and different 'magnetic fields' as it were. The multiplicity of focal points in Stravinsky's harmonic perspective, the juxtaposition of heterogeneous blocks, and the geometric rigidity of structure, all go to make up what I would call the cubist element in his art. To call this art static may seem strange to those who think of Stravinsky as the composer of some of the most frenziedly dynamic works in the entire history of music. The static quality is intrinsic; it is a question of melodic and harmonic structure. As I have already had occasion to point out, a practical illustration of the symbolic projection of this static quality is to be seen in the stage characters of *Oedipus Rex*, which are conceived as living statues. There is some truth in Tansman's description of *The Rite of Spring* as 'a universe of stone', or a 'gigantic stone bas-relief hurled madly through space', as others have called it. This metaphor hits off most aptly the way in which the intrinsically static structure of Stravinsky's music is given a bewildering dynamic animation from the outside by being associated with the autonomous forces of rhythm; and the reason why the release of the rhythmic forces turned on the music is so violent is precisely to counteract its essenial fixity and to make up for the lack of structural dynamism. Stravinsky's music gets its discursive eloquence from rhythmic accentuation. This is why it invariably suggests dance measures even when it attempts to free itself from all external phenomena. The fact that Stravinsky is the greatest ballet composer of all time is not due to his lucky meeting with Diaghilev; rather, this meeting helped to bring to fruition a feature inherent in Stravinsky's art. In the earlier phases of his career he might have been described as the ideal ballet composer and the anti-symphonist *par excellence*. Even at the height of his 'neo-classical period' he seemed a very long way from a 'return to the symphonic form'. As I have already said repeatedly in the preceding chapters, he uses the term 'symphony' in its strictly etymological sense simply to designate an 'ensemble'. Symphonies of Wind Instruments meant a composition for a 'collection' of wind instruments; Symphony of Psalms meant a 'collection' of pieces on texts taken from various Psalms. But suddenly in 1940 Stravinsky astonished the musical world by producing a Symphony which was a real symphony in the classical sense of the word. This was the Symphony in C, commissioned for the Chicago Symphony Orchestra by Robert Woods Bliss, who had previously commissioned the Dumbarton Oaks Concerto. The manuscript score has a dedication similar to that of the Symphony of Psalms: 'This Symphony, composed to the Glory of God, is dedicated to the Chicago Symphony Orchestra on the occasion of the Fiftieth Anniversary of its Existence.' Of all Stravinsky's 'turnabouts', whether they happened literally, virtually or only seemingly, his 'return to the symphonic form' in this new work is certainly the one which had the strongest impact on his musical language. Here he not only adopts the thematic exposition and the technique of development inherent in this form, but he adopts them in a most consequential and rigorous manner, i.e. he accepts the cyclic form based on a single motif or thematic idea which permeates the whole work – in this case

the basic motif is an extremely simple figure consisting of the three
notes B, C, G:

This is the germ cell of the entire Symphony. It is introduced in
its most elementary form by the strings:

But before this, the first note B is given a rhythmic scansion, which
as played by the timpani:

is seen to be an allusion to the rhythm of the main motif of Beethoven's Fifth Symphony:

Incidentally, there is an obvious reference to this famous motif in
A Card Game, written two years before he even began to write the
Symphony. It comes in the passage for two oboes:

But this quotation of Beethoven's best-known rhythmic motif is not the only legitimate grounds for arguing that the Symphony was influenced by Beethoven. His influence, as indeed that of Haydn as well, is evident from the very basic concept of the work. Stravinsky admits as much. In *Themes and Episodes* (p. 42) he writes 'those two celestial powers stand behind the first, and even the pastoral second, movement far more significantly than [Tchaikovsky].' However, a certain relationship between Stravinsky's Symphony in C and Tchaikovsky's Symphony No. 1 can be detected in a sort of parallel between the theme that grows out of the cell motif we are discussing and the opening theme of the Tchaikovsky work. It might perhaps also be argued that Beethoven's influence is to be found in Stravinsky in a form filtered through Tchaikovsky, as it were. But to revert to the way in which the main theme of the first movement of Stravinsky's Symphony is built up, after the initial statement by the strings, the basic motif is taken over by the wind instruments in a broader transposed form, then returns to its original form played by the whole orchestra. After being tossed backwards and forwards between the wind instruments and the strings, the motif is introduced in other metrical variants:

and :

and again :

until finally the oboe weaves around this nucleus of three notes the complete figure of the first theme of the first movement of the Symphony.

Thus the theme itself is already a sort of 'development' from a basic thematic cell. After a re-statement of the theme by the whole orchestra, there is a short transitional passage leading to the second thematic group which alternates between the sub-dominant key of F and the key of G major and minor. This second thematic group is based on a variety of figures, but in all instances they derive from the original motif. The figure in F :

is simply a permutation of the three original notes, so that instead of B, C, G :

we get G, B, C :

or in its transposed form :

By now it is clear that we have a cell similar to the germ cell of *The Wedding* – a perfect fourth divided into a major third and a minor second (in the *Wedding* cell, the same interval of a fourth consists of a minor third and a major second). Also, the manner in which the three notes constituting the cells in question are subjected to serial-type treatment and permutations is very similar. But the way in which they are used is different – in the Symphony they conform to the principles and the spirit of sonata form development. Thus the G minor motif :

is the original motif in a disguise which unmistakably recalls Beethoven. Another F major motif :

is derived from an inversion of the cyclic motif.

As all these are presented they are altered, developed and interwoven in a variety of ways, in accordance with the formal shape
of the classical sonata movement. Stravinsky follows up the exposition with a general development and concludes the movement
with a repetition of the themes in the fundamental key of C. In
view of what I said at the beginning of this chapter, it is highly
significant that this first movement of the Symphony in C is the
only composition on anything like a large scale in which Stravinsky
refrains from making even the slightest change of rhythm. The
entire movement is written in two halves. Since the piece is built up
on the intrinsically dynamic pattern of the sonata form, Stravinsky
does not need to resort to polymorphic changes of rhythm to make
it extrinsically dynamic. This first movement marked 'Moderato
alla breve' is followed by a 'Larghetto concertante' in F major. This
is in three parts: a rapid, agitated central section sandwiched
between two long sections with a melodic line entrusted for the most
part to the oboes, which are thus used as solo instruments. The third
movement, Allegretto, runs straight on from the second movement.
It is a kind of scherzo. Like the Minuetto this Scherzo also represents
within the framework of the Symphony a vestige of the spirit of
the dance characteristic of the old suite. Stravinsky gives free rein
to this spirit in the third movement and achieves a metrical variety
similar to that of the Finale of *The Rite of Spring*. The second part
of the Allegretto is in the form of a complex Fugue with inversion
and retrograde variants. The Finale, 'Tempo giusto alla breve', is
introduced and framed by a Largo in the form of a chorale for
bassoons, accompanied by the brass. Here, as in the other movements,
the musical figures are related to the original motif, the initial group
of three notes B, C, G. The kinship is sometimes obvious, at other
times it can be discovered only on close examination. The reason
why I have dwelt at some length on the structure of this Symphony
is that in it we find a hint of some of the formal trends later
crystallized in Stravinsky's more recent works and almost incredible
to anyone who has not followed the composer's development step
by step.

In the Symphony in C specifically, the structural links referred to
suffice to ensure the substantial unity of the work, clearing up from
within a seeming discrepancy between the first two movements,
composed while Stravinsky was still in Europe, and the last two,
written after he had moved to the United States. The composer
himself in *Themes and Episodes* (p. 43) recognizes that there is a

marked schism between the 'European' and the 'American' movements of the work, which he says are 'very different in spirit and design'; and he points out that some of the bars in the third movement 'would not have come to my ears in Europe' and that the passage beginning at No. [145] of the Finale 'would not have occurred to me before I had known the neon glitter of the Californian boulevards from a speeding automobile'. Perhaps facetiously, he adds that he regards this passage as 'perfect movie music for a Hollywood traffic scene'. Apart from the obvious confirmation of his realism, stressed already in connection with *Petrushka*, this statement further confirms Stravinsky's capacity for being influenced, as pointed out at the beginning of the chapter on his American compositions. Without any doubt, the last two movements of the Symphony in C are also genuinely 'American' in the sense in which I have used the adjective. The passage referred to by the composer is still more reminiscent of Gershwin, suggesting a counterpart to *An American in Paris*, since Stravinsky refers to himself as 'a Parisian in Hollywood'. But leaving aside the witticisms and the metaphors, we need only look a little more closely at the saucy 'street music' motif of the trumpet solo at No [145] to realize that it is nothing more than yet another variant on the Beethoven-like opening of the first movement. Here it is transformed so that while on one side bowing to Gershwin, on the other it not only continues to keep the rhythmic shape of the root motif of Beethoven's Fifth Symphony (merely doubling the long note), but it now adopts the same melodic intervals (descending thirds) as well. A similar unity in diversity can be discerned by an analysis of the entire finale, which illustrates how and why the coherence of the work is maintained in spite of the schism – the geographical gulf, almost – between the two series of movements in the work. On the other hand, if we recognize the new meaning given to the main motif throughout the Symphony we can challenge the viewpoint of people like Ansermet,[1] who contends that the Allegro from the Symphony in C is not really and truly a symphonic movement but merely 'a portrait of a symphonic allegro', his argument being that the motive does not 'germinate' and hence does not develop in the spirit of true symphonic form, but turns back incessantly upon itself, its novelties adding nothing to its inherent significance. Incidentally, the whole of the large section of this important if debatable book devoted to Stravinsky

[1] *Les Fondements de la musique dans la conscience humaine*, La Baconnière: Neuchâtel 1961, Notes, pp. 177-8.

would warrant more thorough discussion than is possible within the scope and limits of this book. Let me merely recall Ansermet's key thesis in regard to Stravinsky and his art. It hinges on his assertion that Stravinsky's urge to create music is purely aesthetic and that consequently there is a flaw, in human terms, in the relationship between the composer and his work. For that reason, he argues, Stravinsky's music does not have the same value as experience, as personal revelation and statement, as music originating in self-expression, and hence it is not comparable, let alone superior, to that of the great masters of the past from Bach to Debussy (ibid, pp. 285-6). Leaving aside the question of the validity or otherwise of value judgements of this kind, let us dwell for a moment on the problem of the human relationship between Stravinsky and his music. On this point the composer himself in *Themes and Episodes* (pp. 40-45) presents us with a series of confessions which are all the more impressive in that they come from a man who, in spite of his apparently extrovert social behaviour and great worldly charm, was always extremely reserved and unforthcoming in regard to his real inner life. Speaking of the Symphony in C Stravinsky first of all recalls that the work came about during the unhappiest period of his life when, as already described at the beginning of Chapter XV, he was stricken with tuberculosis and lost a mother, a wife and a daughter. He says 'I cured myself or at least forgot about myself by composing the *Dumbarton Oaks Concerto* and the *Symphony in C.*' After describing how he heard the news of Mika's death on the railway station at Turin towards the end of 1938, he says 'I think it is no exaggeration to say that in the following weeks I myself survived only through my work on the *Symphony in C* – though I hasten to add that I did not seek to overcome my personal grief by "expressing" or "portraying" it "in" my music'. And after telling how the death of his wife and his mother had happened within a short time, he further confesses that 'for the third time I was able to live only through my composition, though no more than before were the sections of the *Symphony* written in these dark days an attempt to free myself from my feelings'. Thus it is clear that the Symphony in C, as a whole, with its serenity and its optimism, is the complement at the ideal level of the real, human situation experienced by its composer as he composed it. The only direct reflections of this are the brief interjections of the sombre chorales played by the bassoons in the last movement.

The very opposite is true of the Symphony in Three Movements written only a few years later. Although it was composed at a time when Stravinsky had passed through a critical period from the point of view of his health, and had rebuilt his family life, and when the war was coming to a successful end, this Symphony turned out to be one of his most dramatic works, a direct reflection of the experience of grief by the individual and society. Thus in Stravinsky's creative work, moments of escape do not exclude but alternate with moments of catharsis, just as in Mozart the supreme catharsis of the *Requiem* is offset and counterbalanced by the escapist pages written in the last year of his life – from the 'canarie' waltzes and sleigh bells to the bells in *The Magic Flute*.

But before we discuss this new Symphony, let us turn to the *Scherzo à la russe* written in 1943-4. This composition too owes its origin and its *raison d'être* to work on a film begun by Stravinsky but not carried through. The musical material from which the *Scherzo à la russe* was to be moulded had been intended originally for a film on the war in Russia. When the film project was abandoned, Stravinsky reorchestrated the piece for Paul Whiteman's Band, one of the main promoters of the 'symphonic jazz' from which works like Gershwin's *Rhapsody in Blue* emerged. The jazz version of the *Scherzo à la russe* (performed for the first time in the context of the 'Blue Network Program') seems to have found little favour and was soon overshadowed by the version for regular symphony orchestra which Stravinsky himself conducted at San Francisco in March 1946. Changing the work's instrumental garb was indeed not sufficient to provide the *Scherzo* with intrinsic jazz qualities which it did not possess and could not be given, since it had been conceived as a symphonic piece. (This is in fact why it is discussed in the present chapter.) The formal structure of the composition is that of a classical scherzo, with two trios. While the theme of the scherzo suggests the Russian dance in *Petrushka*, the motifs of the trios are akin to the Russian-sounding motifs of the *Sonata for Two Pianos*. Stravinsky's nostalgic feeling for his native land fitted in admirably here with the need for background music in keeping with the subject-matter of the film. He was therefore perfectly willing to meet the requirements, but only within the limits of 'incidental music' or 'stage music' in a theatrical sense and not by writing specifically 'film music', in other words music taking account of the peculiar requirements of a movie film. In *Memories and Commentaries* (p. 108) Stravinsky says he is well aware that this conception is quite wrong from the film industry's point of view, but he adds quite firmly that it is as far as he will go. The reasons that prevented him from making a direct contribution to the literature of film music are to be sought only partly in the attitude and mentality of Hollywood producers; they are also attributable in part to the unswerving determination thus stated quite categorically. In the absolute this may be debatable; but in the specific case of Stravinsky it was no doubt based on a single-minded personal conviction.

In 1945, a year after the publication of the *Scherzo à la russe*, Stravinsky published the Symphony in Three Movements. Chronologically this was his third symphony, the first being opus 1, the very first work he produced, and the second being the Symphony in C just discussed. The Symphony in Three Movements was first performed in January 1946 by the New York Philharmonic Society, to which it is dedicated. It was begun in 1942, and was originally conceived as a symphonic work with the piano as solo instrument. Its structure as it was produced shows traces of this; in passage after passage of the first movement the piano part is all-important. In the second movement the *concertante* part is taken over by the harp, while in the final movement, 'Con moto', it is filled out for piano and harp. Thematic exposition and symphonic development technique as used in the Symphony in C are used here also to achieve a musical texture of great density. The Symphony in Three Movements also develops organically from an original germ which is explicitly formulated in the following passage for solo horns:

This germ is made up of three notes:

which represent a perfect diatonic chord minus the fifth, written out melodically. In the phrase which follows the opening flourish of the Symphony:

this cell is presented in the form of a harmonic figure in the chords played by the strings:

simultaneously the major:

and in the minor:

The notes F-A flat-F, and F-A natural-F which make up the chord are identical with the cyclic motif found at the beginning of Brahms's Third Symphony and forming the basis of the work:

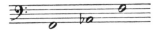

or in its harmonic garb:

This is an extremely significant borrowing, though Stravinsky uses it only for more or less structural purposes. It does not engender

any obvious melodic similarities to Brahms's Symphony. With regard
to the shape of the first movement of the Symphony in Three Movements, it should be pointed out that it follows quite strictly the
pattern of the classical sonata movement as found in the first Allegro
of Beethoven's Fifth Symphony. The second movement, Andante, is
in the form of a *da capo* aria which is linked to the Finale Con
Moto by a short Interlude. Some students of Stravinsky's music
maintain that this Symphony is one of his key works, one of the
highest peaks of his artistry. For example Tansman[2] finds in it

the eruptive explosiveness and the breathtaking pulsation of certain fragments
of *The Rite of Spring*, the active rhythmic movement of *Petrouchka* and *Les
Noces*, the constant charm of the melodic spontaneity of the *Jeux de Cartes*,
the lightness and animation of the *Octet* or the *Capriccio*, the astonishing
plasticity of the timbres for which the utilization in concertino of diverse
groups originates in *L'Histoire du Soldat*, the moving tension of the *Symphony
of Psalms*, the peaceful serenity of the *Apollon-Musagète*, . . . and finally the
discursive virulence of the *Concerto for Two Pianos*.

All these components are reduced to a structural common denominator based on the symphonic writing of Beethoven and Brahms.
Incidentally, when Robert Craft[3] asked Stravinsky 'What music de-
lights you most today?' Stravinsky replied that he liked to play
the English virginalists, Couperin in the Brahms-Chrysander edition,
Bach, the Italian madrigals, Schütz, Ockeghem, Obrecht, and Haydn,
and that when he was composing, 'to put myself in motion . . .
Beethoven quartets, sonatas, and especially symphonies like the
Second, Fourth and Eighth, are sometimes wholly fresh and delightful to me'.

Stravinsky's attitude towards Brahms and Beethoven, the two
great symphonic craftsmen of the nineteenth century, can be judged
in its proper perspective in the light of the expressive values embodied in his Symphony in Three Movements. He gives his own
explanation, somewhat cautiously perhaps, as to what these values
are in a programme note written for the first performance of the
Symphony. Although he stresses that it is absolute music which is
not to be regarded as the expression of any specific 'programme', he
says that it is certainly possible to find traces of impressions and
experiences coloured by 'this our arduous time of sharp and shifting
events, of despair and hope, of continual torments, of tension, and at
last cessation and relief'.

In later life Stravinsky grew less reluctant to admit the emotional

[2] op. cit., pp. 263-4.
[3] *Conversations with Igor Stravinsky*, p. 127.

and imaginative content of his music and its roots in his personal, human experience. Referring to this same Symphony in particular, he says in *Dialogues and a Diary* (pp. 83-5) – admittedly expressing his thoughts in somewhat sibylline language – 'It both does and does not "express my feelings" about [world events]', yet he allowed it to be called a 'war symphony'. 'It was written under the sign of them . . . with out participation of what I think of as my will, they excited my imagination.' Incidentally, this statement fits neatly into the theory of unconscious or involuntary expression of which Massimo Mila is an ardent champion. He goes on to say that 'the events that thus activated me were not general, or ideological, but specific: each episode in the Symphony is linked in my imagination with a concrete impression, very often cinematographic in origin, of the war'. Only after completing the composition of the third movement did he realize that it 'actually contains the genesis of a war plot . . . The beginning of that movement is partly, and in some – to me wholly inexplicable – way, a musical reaction to the newsreels and documentaries that I had seen of goose-stepping soldiers. The square march-beat, the brass-band instrumentation, the grotesque *crescendo* in the tuba – these are all related to those repellent pictures'. Again he goes on to recall an ugly scene of assault by a squad of Brown Shirts he had witnessed in Munich in 1932.

In the third movement, says the composer, 'In spite of contrasting episodes . . . the march music is predominant until the fugue, which is the stasis and the turning point. The immobility of the fugue is comic, I think – and so, to me, was the overturned arrogance of the Germans when their machine failed. The exposition of the fugue and the end of the Symphony are associated in my plot with the rise of the Allies, and perhaps the final, albeit rather too commercial, D-flat sixth chord – instead of the expected C – tokens my extra exuberance in the Allied triumph. The figure . . . developed from the rumba in the timpani part in the introduction to the first movement . . . was somehow associated in my imagination with the movements of war machines. The first movement was likewise inspired by a war film, this time a documentary of scorched-earth tactics in China. The middle part of the movement – the music for clarinet, piano and strings . . . – was conceived as a series of instrumental conversations to accompany a cinematographic scene showing the Chinese people scratching and digging in their fields.'

What Stravinsky does not indicate is the impression of war that inspired the middle movement. I would say that the sweet, serene *cantabile* mood of the *Andante* would at most suggest a contrast with the climate of war, a kind of oasis of peace and hope amid the flashes of guns and bombs.

As a matter of fact, Stravinsky had said earlier (*Expositions and Developments*, p. 77) that he had used for the *Andante* music composed for the 'Apparition of the Virgin' scene in the film *Song of Bernadette*, based on Franz Werfel's book on the life of Bernadette of Lourdes. Werfel had managed to persuade Stravinsky to embark for the nth time on the task of writing film music; but like the earlier attempts, this one too came to nothing because in the end Stravinsky was not prepared to accept the 'conditions, business and artistic' of the producer. There is no record to show how far the music intended for the apparition scene in the film was reshaped or modified before being incorporated into the Symphony. Stravinsky merely says that 'this music became the second movement of my *Symphony in Three Movements*'. In *Dialogues and a Diary* he makes two further remarks that are worth noting. With regard to the formal substance of the Symphony he says that 'perhaps Three Symphonic Movements would be a more exact title'. The other remark concerns the very essence of the music. As if he were afraid he had said too much and revealed more than he intended, he rounds off his comments as follows: 'In spite of what I have said, the Symphony is not programmatic. Composers combine notes. That is all. How and in what form the things of this world are impressed upon their music is not for them to say.'

A critical analysis and exegesis of the way in which this relationship of meaning between music and the hard facts of life would undoubtedly be of the utmost interest, but it would involve problems on which scholars never have been and never will be in agreement. What does seem to be an incontrovertible fact is that in the final analysis the greatness, the strength and the intrinsic importance of a piece of music are measured in terms of the existence, the quality and the intensity of the relationship it is intuitively felt to have with the world. And my intuition did not betray me when I contended that there is such a relationship in the major masterpieces of Stravinsky, even at a time when he persisted in minimizing and vehemently denying that there was any imaginative and expressive power in his music. Aesthetic reality is often at variance with his preconceived theoretical dicta, and at times with his *volte-face* performances. Hence basically it is not unduly surprising to find that so much of the music that Stravinsky claims is non-expressive actually has far more power of expression than the music of composers who were anxious to proclaim their programmatic expressive designs even before they took on a musical shape.

Here it may be well, however, to recall the dialectics of Stravinsky's creative rhythm – his habit of following up a work, or a series of works highly charged with tragedy and drama by composing works that imply non-involvement and escapism. Thus in contrast to the dramatic human involvement characteristic of the Symphony in Three Movements, the Concerto in D for string orchestra, written in 1946 for the Basle Chamber Orchestra, conducted by Paul Sacher, is a light, vivacious work, more in the nature of pure entertainment or even escapism. The musical discourse trips along with a gay, carefree lilt. The opening theme:

is strongly reminiscent of a theme from Emerich Kalman's *Gypsy Princess*. But after the first few bars, this theme is set against a modally equivocal harmonic background which changes its meaning:

The vague chord which supports the accompaniment:

consists of the inverted major :

and minor :

forms of the selfsame thematic nucleus from which Stravinsky built up his Symphony in Three Movements. The alternation of the F sharp and F natural within this harmonic motif is used by Stravinsky as the melodic nucleus on which to base not only the first movement, but the second, 'Arioso andantino', as well, and even part of the final Rondo. Thus the organization of the musical material in this Concerto is similar to that already discussed in connection with the two Symphonies. Hence it was not only for reasons of chronology that the Concerto in D was omitted from the discussion of works in concerto form in Chapter XIV, and kept for the present chapter for consideration along with the works which mark Stravinsky's return to the symphonic form.

XVIII Stravinsky's Religious Music

In Chapter XII I said that while the sense of tragedy which per-meates the works written about the time of the First World War continued to crop up sporadically in later works, it gradually merged with two distinct spiritual currents. In the pieces written purely as entertainment the tragic element gives way to an all-pervading spirit of gaiety. In the more serious works, the only course was to return to those values which, as we have said, the tidal wave of latter-day barbarism had momentarily swept away – the values of the Hellenic world and of Christian civilization. Thus under the cloak of the many avowed 'returns' to musical forms and styles of the past which had a superficial impact on Stravinsky's music, 'returns' of far deeper significance were penetrating to the very core of his art. The outward sign of the 'Greek' influence on Stravinsky is seen in his choice of subjects and episodes belonging to classical mythology and literature. The 'Christian' influence was late in making itself felt, and except in the *Symphony of Psalms* it was less obvious and less conspicuous, though to my mind it is more intimately bound up with Stravinsky's real spiritual character.

While his 'Greek' works seem to me an identification on a purely abstract, ideal plane with the spirit of Greek art, his religious works reflect experience of life at its most real and most palpable; the kernel of his personal *Erlebniss* as a human being, and the key to its ultimate meaning. Fundamentally Stravinsky was a profoundly religious man. Highly significant in view of this assertion is the revelation he makes in *Expositions and Developments* (pp. 72-7) that before leaving the Gymnasium he had abandoned the Russian Orthodox Church completely – a rupture he repaired in 1926 after several years of spiritual preparation and spurred on by an interior need rather than 'reasoned into my disposition'. And it was precisely in 1926 that he wrote his first sacred work – the *Pater Noster* which I shall have occasion to discuss below.

The religious side of Stravinsky, and particularly the way in which this comes out in his music, has not been properly appreciated by most of his commentators, or else it has been ill-judged and even misinterpreted. I myself have put forward views on this subject which in the light of a more thorough examination of Stravinsky's works now strike me as mistaken, though possibly the misconception is due in part to the seeming paradox inherent in some of Stravinsky's own theoretical writings. I am thinking in particular of what I wrote on the alleged 'anti-mystical' conception of music propounded by Stravinsky in the *Chronicle of My Life* and modified later in the *Poetics of Music* in favour of explicit adherence to the noumenal conception of music.[1]

In the same way, I accepted the opinion of Stravinsky's biographer and friend Alexander Tansman that

> Stravinsky's attitude toward the mystery of the Divinity remains hidden in the very depths of his soul; it would never occur to him to display it in his everyday living, and even less so in his art. Music stops where prayer begins . . . Stravinsky's religious music, then, should be considered as a sort of professional offering from a musician for the purpose of glorifying the Divinity, a sort of musical *ex voto*; yet it has no illustrative or literary relationship with the great order of things, it is not a transcendental and exalted transcription in sound by a mystic describing his vision.[2]

It should be made clear that in the passage from the *Chronicle of My Life* referred to above (p. 69), Stravinsky does not actually take a stand against the mystical conception of music as such. Taking as his starting point a performance of *Parsifal* which he attended with Diaghilev at Bayreuth in 1912, Stravinsky launches out vehemently against what he calls 'this unseemly and sacrilegious conception of art as religion and the theatre as a temple'. Far from making these criticisms from the aesthetic standpoint of secular illuminism, he attributes the confusion of the theatre with 'the sacred and symbolic ritual which constitutes a religious service' to a trend of the times 'when the openly irreligious masses in their degradation of spiritual values and debasement of human thought necessarily lead us to utter brutaliza-

---

[1] One clear if incidental reference to the basic importance of the religious factor in Stravinsky's work is to be found in De' Paoli's *Igor Stravinsky*, op. cit. pp. 131-2, note 1. I myself tried to pinpoint the significance of Stravinsky's sacred music in an article published in *La Rassegna Musicale*, year XII, no. 3, Rome, July 1952, and later included in my *Modernità e tradizione*, op. cit. I also took up the subject in *Le Musiche religiose di Igor Stravinsky* written in conjunction with Robert Craft and Alessando Piovesan (Lombroso, Venice 1956). The theory of 'radiation' (*kernstrahlige Perspektive*) as embracing the religious aspect (*das Kultische*) in Stravinsky's work as a whole constitutes the basis of Lindlar's book: *Igor Stravinskys Sakraler Gesang*, op. cit. Lindlar cites something I wrote, and also the book by Fleischer, but he completely ignores De' Paoli.
[2] op. cit., p. 129.

tion'. In this connection, he paid a tribute to the spirit of 'a society like that of the Middle Ages, which recognized and safeguarded the primacy of the spiritual realm and dignity of the human person . . .',[3] while elsewhere in the passage of *Chronicle of My Life* (p. 92) he sets forth his own conception of music as having 'the sole purpose of establishing an order in things, including, and particularly, the co-ordination between *man* and *time*'.

In the *Poetics of Music* Stravinsky not only maintains this conception, but distinguishes two categories of time, 'psychological' time and 'ontological' time, and explains that he prefers the latter since it allows music to partake of the nature of 'ontological reality'. Although he does not pretend to an 'illustrative or literary relationship with the great order of things', nor to the 'transcriptions' or 'descriptions of his conception of the mystery of the Divinity' referred to by Tansman, he ascribes a very much more responsible and arduous task to music, namely as 'a form of communion with our fellow man – and with the Supreme Being'.[4] If Stravinsky admits the possibility of music in general as being capable of fulfilling such a function, it would surely be absurd for him to deny such a possibility to religious music proper. Indeed, it is in his sacred music that his religious outlook is expressed in its purest and most explicit form with nothing of the mystic or the heterodox aesthete, but ready to see the characteristic traditions of the Easern and Western Christian Churches brought together under the banner of catholic universality.

The number of Stravinsky's works composed before 1950 which were inspired by sacred texts is not great. Apart from the *Symphony of Psalms* and the *Mass*, there is only a group of three short *a cappella* choruses and a very short cantata, *Babel* – a mere fifty minutes of music all told. But the intrinsic significance and the scope of these works within the framework of his music as a whole seem to justify the view that a study of these religious works is the key to Stravinsky's real self and to the logic of his entire development.

Stravinsky's religious works differ at once from the majority of modern or even romantic and classical works of a similar kind in that they are conceived with an eye to their particular purpose and the ideal place for their performance. The major composers of the last two hundred and fifty years have been wont to dramatize liturgical texts, interpreting them in music in psychologically very diverse ways, and the musical cathedrals they have erected in dimensions alone

---

[3] *Poetics of Music*, p. 75.
[4] ibid., pp. 18, 142.

are far too huge for even the most solemn divine service. Bach's B
Minor Mass lasts nearly three hours, and Beethoven's *Missa Solemnis*
hardly less. Such works – and this does not in any way detract from
their outstanding absolute value – cannot be described as ideally
suitable for inclusion in the actual celebration of the divine service.
Their proper place is in the concert hall and not the church. If a
musical composition is to meet the requirements of the liturgy, it
must of necessity be inspired by an absolute and dogmatic faith;
and in the light of this faith all the impulses of the spirit, all the
upheavals and torments of the emotions must be calmed down,
resolved and sublimated into the devout and serene contemplation
of the divine mystery. This is precisely what has been done in the
Stravinsky works intended expressly for the divine service – namely
the *Three Sacred Choruses* and the *Mass*. It is noteworthy, I think,
that in the interviews with Robert Craft, Stravinsky adopts as a
motto for the book Kassner's phrase: 'In the Kingdom of the Father,
there is no drama but only dialogue, which is disguised monologue.'

In *Themes and Episodes* (p. 31) Stravinsky speaks of the role of
religion in his life and in his music specifically with reference to
the *Three Sacred Choruses*. Here he gives the date of his conversion
as 1925 – earlier than in *Expositions and Developments* – and he says
that 'the bad music and worse singing in the Russian Church in
Nice . . . eventually provoked me into composing something of my
own. I knew nothing of the traditions of Russian Church music at
that time (or now), but instinctively I sought older roots than
Bortniansky, our classic composer in the genre, who, after his long
stay with Galuppi in Venice had been wholly converted to the
Italian style . . . My pieces probably fuse early memories of church
music in Kiev and Poltava with the conscious aim to adhere to a simple
and severe harmonic style, a "classical" style but with pre-classical
cadences. I should add that apparently all traditions of Russian
church singing are decrepit nowadays, for which reason I rewrote
the *Credo* in June 1964, spelling out the rhythm of the *faux bourdon*'.

The *Three Sacred Choruses* are explicitly designed for the Russian
liturgy. They were written at different times: the Pater Noster in
1926, the Credo in 1932 and the Ave Maria in 1934. They are three
very short pieces for choir *a capella* written in the spirit and style of
traditional Russian church music. From the point of view of Stravinsky's spiritual development it is interesting to note that the first
edition of the Pater Noster, Credo, and Ave Maria, published by the
Edition russe de musique S. et N. Koussevitsky, was printed in

Russian only, with the indication 'for the Divine Office', whereas in the Boosey and Hawkes catalogue only the Latin text is referred to. I think I am right in saying that this Roman Catholic version of the *Three Sacred Choruses* was written in 1949, shortly after Stravinsky finished the Catholic *Mass* in 1948. Lindlar claims that in addition to being influenced by the classical models of the Russian liturgy, the Credo is also linked with the early forms of *accentus* as defined by Vogelmaier in *Musicae activae micrologus* (1517).

From the time of writing the Credo in 1926, Stravinsky had had the idea of composing a Mass; but twenty years elapsed before he carried out the project. In the meantime he wrote two other works of a religious nature, though they were designed not for liturgical use but for concert performance. The first is one of Stravinsky's best-known works and a masterpiece – the *Symphony of Psalms*, written in 1930. The circumstance which occasioned it was a request by Serge Kussevitsky for a symphony to celebrate the fiftieth anniversary of the founding of the Boston Symphony Orchestra; but the deeper *raison d'être*, its inner spiritual meaning, is revealed in the words with which the dedication to the Boston Orchestra begins : 'Cette Symphonie composée à la gloire de Dieu . . .' Thus here again the mainspring of the work is faith and the desire to offer to God the fruits of his labours; but nevertheless it is essentially a highly dramatic work. The emotional background of the *Symphony of Psalms* is reflected in Stravinsky's choice of three of the Psalms of David (he began to work on the Slavonic version, but changed over to the Latin version of the Vulgate). He treats them in the true spirit of the Old Testament. Man's relation to God, as revealed in the sacred Mosaic texts, is not illumined by grace, which will only be won for the Christians by the advent of the Redeemer. But even to them, grace comes only at very special moments, and it is only on such occasions that faith has the power to solve all the problems of existence, to ease the dramatic tensions of human life, and to calm the turbulence of the spirit. Otherwise faith can only offer the consolation of hope in answer to prayer and invocation, thus bringing into focus on the emotional plane the dramatic atmosphere of alternate struggle and passivity of the Old Testament, where the pain and suffering of life are real and down-to-earth. This is what I mean by the 'spirit of the Old Testament' which pervades the *Symphony of Psalms*. Before the hymn-like grandeur of the finale we get dramatic invocation, fervent prayer, and anguished questioning, contrary to Tansman's assertion quoted earlier that with Stravinsky 'music ends where prayer begins'. What, after all, if not a prayer, is the passage in the first movement – which serves as a Prelude to the Double Fugue of the second movement – when the choir sings 'Exaudi orationem meam Domine' on two adjacent notes? Moreover, the composer says explicitly in *Dialogues and a Diary* (p. 78) that : 'The rest of the slow-tempo introduction, the *Laudate Dominum*, was originally composed to the words of the *Gospodi Pomiluy*. This section is a prayer to the Russian image of the infant Christ with orb and sceptre. I decided to end the work with this music, too, as an apotheosis of the sort that had become a pattern in my music since the epithalamium at the end of *Les Noces*.' This reference to the last movement is equally valid for the beginning.

The motif with which the woodwind accompanies the vocal line is the basis for the later movements; we find it in the first subject of the Fugue and in the thematic design of the last movement.

Note that the three movements which make up the *Symphony of Psalms* follow each other without a break, and that as in the case of the Symphonies of Wind Instruments the term 'symphony' is used here too merely to indicate an 'ensemble' of musical strands and does not imply any particular form in the classical sense of the word. As I said earlier, the basic structure of the music has no connection with 'sonata form'; the first movement is a Prelude, and the second a Double Fugue for voices and instruments. The theme of the instrumental Fugue is stated by the oboe and is then taken up by the flute. Oboes and flute then also play the first development of the Fugue, in a soft organ-like register which stays in the 'celestial' high registers. The vocal 'human fugue', as Stravinsky calls it, then descends gradually towards the lower register to make what he describes as 'the most overt use of musical symbolism in any of my music before *The Flood* (*Dialogues and a Diary*, p. 77). The subject of the vocal Fugue :

is stated by the sopranos, contraltos, tenors, and basses; then a *stretto* from the second Fugue leads into a passage for choir *a cappella*, which is followed by the *stretto* from the first Fugue. The 'act of hope' which makes up the second movement is followed by a final Alleluia, a sort of Hymn of Praise on the text of Psalm 150. The expressive meaning of this noble piece is rendered by the juxtaposition of contrasting musical motifs. The Alleluia does not burst forth with the sense of redemption, as in a nineteenth-century finale; after the initial organ-like chords played by the winds, the choir intones the Alleluia almost timidly, with an extremely simple musical motif, making a short crescendo and decrescendo like a sigh. Even the Laudate begins laboriously, with a thrice-repeated little thematic figure which rotates slowly over a bass punctuated with inexorable solemnity by the timpani, harp and two pianos substituted throughout the whole work for the complement of violins and violas. Gradually the voices, which began almost as if issuing from the depths of the human body bowed beneath an everlasting burden, seem to float aloft in ecstatic contemplation of the 'firmament'; the rotating movement spreads to the whole orchestra and comes to a halt on the straightforward major chord, while the choir sings, piano, with a kind of rapt reverence, the word 'Dominum'. A clamorous fanfare of horns and bassoons seems to summon to prayer, with imperious gestures, flashing rhythmic figures, tempestuous scales, and glissando effects, poor downtrodden humanity which 'out of the depths' has turned its eyes to heaven. Of this passage Stravinsky writes (*Dialogues and a Diary*, p. 78): 'The *Allegro* in Psalm 150 was inspired by a vision of Elijah's chariot climbing the heavens; never before had I written anything quite so literal as the triplets for horns and piano to suggest the horses and chariots.' The Laudate takes up again the initial motif on two adjacent notes as in the first movement. Very soon this narrows to a single note, repeated under the lash of the percussion with a martellato accompaniment played by an orchestra in which every instrument seems suddenly to have joined the percussion section. The forlorn Alleluia with which the work began is taken up again and leads into a reprise of the whole of this part, followed by a melting, tranquillo song with an undulating melodic line. This is picked up gradually by all the voices and all the instruments in a gradual crescendo. Suddenly, at the height of this crescendo the music becomes 'molto meno mosso' and 'piano subito' and enters a new realm: the 'Laudate Eum in cymbalis bene sonantibus, Laudate Eum in cymbalis jubilationibus', intoned on a motif of adjacent notes repeated like an incantation to the accompaniment of the trumpets and strings, rises with ineffable solemnity over a new, rotating ostinato bass of timpani, harp, and two pianos.

The music revolves for a considerable time in the circular orbit in a strictly regular movement, with a hieratic Byzantine grandeur, set free from all emotional upheaval and human frailty. The last echo of the opening Alleluia dies away on a perfect chord of C major whose perfection remains unmarred. Again in the *Program Note* from *Dialogues and a Diary* (p. 78) Stravinsky says that, although such statements embarrass him, 'the final hymn of praise must be thought of as issuing from the skies, and agitation is followed by "the calm of praise" . . .'

Stravinsky's other biblical work, the cantata *Babel*, is invested with the same dramatic quality of conception, if not of expression. While the *Symphony of Psalms* is universally known and is in the regular concert repertoire, *Babel* is still almost entirely unknown in Europe. It was designed as part of a collective work based on texts from Genesis, commissioned in 1944 from a number of well-known composers living in the United States by Nathaniel Shilkret, American composer and patron of the arts. The Prologue was written by Schoenberg, *The Creation* by Shilkret himself, *The Fall of Man* by Tansman, *Cain and Abel* by Milhaud, *The Deluge* by Castelnuovo-Tedesco, *The Message* by Ernest Bloch, and *The Tower of Babel* by Stravinsky. Other episodes were to have been written by Bartok, Hindemith and Prokofiev, but this part of the plan did not materialize. The entire cycle was performed for the first time at Los Angeles in October 1946.

This short cantata, whose general shape is described by Craft as 'that of a passacaglia in which a fugue serves as one of the variations'[5] consists of a brief solemn introduction, followed by a fugato fragment, and then by a choral part and an animated orchestral finale which as it were cancels out the polyphonic structure which has gone before. The way in which the polyphonic architecture of the fugato is built up contrapuntally is obviously symbolic of the building of the Tower, the finale representing its destruction. The words of God are entrusted to the choir, on the principle that the Divine Word should not be 'represented' by an individual human voice. By giving it to the entire choir to sing Stravinsky makes it a mere quotation. He also studiously avoids putting a musical halo, as it were, round passages which might suggest the supernatural or even create an atmosphere of mystery. Incidentally the choral technique just mentioned is used by Schoenberg in *Moses and Aaron*, by Dallapiccola in *Job*, Benjamin Britten in *Abraham and Isaac*, etc.

[5] 'Music and Words' in *Stravinsky in the Theatre* (New York, 1949).

Lindlar sees the choral representation of Jehovah-Elohim (plural) as corresponding to the primitive idea of the plurality of the Divinity in the Old Testament. In my opinion, certainly as far as Schoenberg, Stravinsky, and Dallapiccola are concerned, any such correspondence is purely fortuitous.

Four years after finishing *Babel* – in 1948 – Stravinsky finally published the *Mass* which had haunted him for so many years. It is highly significant that the *Mass* is one of the few works which Stravinsky composed without any external prompting, or without being commissioned to write it, but simply to satisfy an inner urge. It is also significant that a composer of the Orthodox faith, as Stravinsky is, should have written a Catholic Mass and one actually designed for liturgical use. There is no doubt that it is intended to be performed as part of the Roman service. This is clear not only from the fact that it is written in Latin, and from its character and length – it lasts seventeen minutes, which fits in perfectly with the time normally taken to celebrate the Catholic Mass – it is also proved conclusively by the fact that the intoning of the Credo is assigned to a priest, and reproduces exactly, without accompaniment of any sort, the traditional Gregorian melody which begins the first, second, and third Credos of the Ordinary of the Mass in the Catholic Church:

cre-do in u-num De-um

The fact that Stravinsky composed a Catholic Mass is not due to circumstances of the kind which, for example, led the Protestant Bach to compose a Latin Mass – Bach was after all in the service of a Catholic prince at the time. If we think back to some of Stravinsky's manifestoes of the past, one of his main preoccupations was a word which speaks volumes: the syllable. All he looked for in the text of *Persephone* was 'syllables, beautiful strong syllables'. It might be argued, therefore (and I myself have used the argument in the past), that it was merely the Latin text that attracted Stravinsky. He shows a special predilection for the Latin language from the time of *Oedipus Rex* and the *Symphony of Psalms* onwards; in fact in the score of the latter he specifies that the text is not to be translated, but must always be sung in Latin. In any case, Stravinsky's own explicit statement on the subject removes all possible doubt as to the real, profound, and intimate reasons why he wrote the *Mass*.

In an interview he gave on the occasion of the first performance of
The Rake's Progress in Venice, Stravinsky was asked whether his
conception of freedom was similar to the Catholic conception; his
unequivocal reply was yes. But there was nothing surprising about
it, he said, since he was brought up with a profound admiration for
Catholicism partly as a result of his spiritual education and partly
by inclination, being far more Western than Eastern. His Orthodox
religion, he said, was very close to Catholicism, and it would not
be surprising if he became a Catholic one day. What attracted
Stravinsky to the Catholic Church must have been that universality
which is one of its great claims and which is lacking in the somewhat
parochial nationalist outlook of the Orthodox cult. In *Expositions and
Developments* (p. 65) he cites other reasons that led him to compose
a Roman Catholic Mass. It 'was partly provoked by some Masses of
Mozart . . . rococo-operatic sweets of sin', he says. Whether this
description is justifiable, or whether it is to be ascribed to some
Cecilian musical bigotry, is immaterial. The significant point is that
his reaction to the Mass was to decide that he had to write a Mass
of his own, and, as we have seen, his inner self had been ready to do
so for some time. As far as I am concerned it is equally significant
that the Mass he wanted to write should be 'a real one' – a Mass for
liturgical use. This would not have been possible in the Russian
Church, since Orthodox tradition proscribes the use of musical instruments in its services; in any case Stravinsky says he can endure
unaccompanied singing in only the most harmonically primitive
music (which his *Three Sacred Choruses* in fact are). The *Mass* could
certainly not be classed as 'harmonically primitive', even though the
flavour was to be largely archaic. In its underlying ethos, this *Mass*,
like the *Three Choruses*, has a certain palaeo-Christian aspect. In the
Three Choruses it is the spirit of Byzantine music; in the *Mass* it is
the Gregorian modes; but it must be emphasized that while in ancient
ecclesiastical music the levelling-down of expressiveness is due in part
to the patina that comes with age, in Stravinsky's liturgical works the
quality is used consciously as a feature of the musical colouring. It is
achieved in the main through an almost complete diatonic stillness.
The musical fabric is woven with modal threads which hardly ever
combine in polytonal or polyphonic knots; sometimes they fall into patterns on the lines of the early polyphonic forms – descant and faburden
– and combine in free contrapuntal clusters innocent of any model. The
resulting clashes of dissonance, which at one time Stravinsky would
have used to produce explosive, violent sensations, no longer generate

dynamic effects; they are used to absorb the harmonies, whittling away their traditional function, performing a kind of blood-letting which relieves their tonal tension. It is this refining process, this clarifying of the classical harmonic entities that helps to create in the *Mass*, as in the Finale of *Apollo Musagetes* and in certain passages of *Persephone*, a sense of sublime calm, of freedom from the bonds of human passion.

It is noteworthy, however, that whereas in the Finale of *Apollo Musagetes* the static, petrified quality, and the awe-struck stupefaction are shot through with a sense of anguish, we feel in the *Mass* that tranquillity and detachment are not the result of a resigned and hopeless pessimism – but stem from Stravinsky's profound religious faith. This faith is not devoid of love, compassion or poetry; but its chief quality is a humility not to be found in any religious work of any of the great composers over the last two hundred years. The extraordinary humility with which Stravinsky approaches the liturgical text is seen not only in the architectonic conception and the expressiveness of his *Mass*; it is also apparent in the musical material he uses to build up the fabric. To the choir of male voices and children's voices Stravinsky adds a homogeneous body of only ten wind instruments – two oboes, cor anglais, two bassoons, two trumpets, and three trombones. No one who listens to this work can fail to agree that the instrumental combination is exactly right, the thin, sharp sonorities of the wind blending perfectly with the choral mass. The peculiar ensemble rules out from the outset any attempt to achieve colour. What it does is create an unusually contemplative, austere musical atmosphere which is at once felt to match the underlying theme of the work perfectly. In the same way, there are no 'virtuoso' soloists; the solo passages, *ad lib* in the Gloria and *obbligato* in the Sanctus, are entrusted to single voices which detach themselves for a brief moment from the anonymity of the choral mass. The way in which Stravinsky has managed to create such profoundly and intensely significant musical imagery with such economy of means, without stepping outside the bounds of absolute discretion of expressive utterance, is little short of miraculous. Notice the sense of joy and of restrained jubilation in the Gloria and the Sanctus, produced without any other means than the subtlest shift of the metric accents and a few unobtrusive inflexions in the curves of the melismata. In these passages the frenzied asymmetrical rhythms of the pagan *Rite of Spring* seem to have been toned down and transmuted, and the blind cataclysmic earth forces seem to have been tamed once and for all, and assimilated into the 'Higher Order' of dogma which Stravinsky mentions in his writings.

The *Mass* was written in 1948, and in its essentials it exactly fits Stravinsky's theory, discussed earlier, of what sacred music should be. Nor is there any doubt that it was composed, not for concert performance, but for the Church. As the composer himself says, it 'appeals directly to the spirit' and is liturgical and unadorned. He contends that liturgical music, other than the 'academic' type, has almost disappeared, and the tradition has been lost, citing the example of the crude Victorian harmonization of the beautiful Gregorian chant. In point of fact, his desire to see his *Mass* actually used for the celebration of Mass was fulfilled during the Donaueschingen Festival in 1958.

Let me recapitulate briefly what Stravinsky's conception of sacred music is: in the first chapter of the *Poetics of Music* and again at the end of the last chapter, he makes a statement which is the key to all his previous statements on the subject. He defines the deep meaning of music, and its essential aim, as being 'to reveal itself as a form of communion – with our fellow-man and with the Supreme Being'. He thus recognizes that the principal virtue of music is as a means of communication with God; and in so doing he at last aligns himself explicitly with the noumenal conception of music, which is observed, at times perhaps unconsciously, in all his greatest works. This is the conception which has at all times accounted for the mysterious prophetic quality, the underlying truth of all great intellectually constructed works, from early Flemish art through the *Art of Fugue* to twelve-note music. This is the mysterious quality referred to by Hanslick in the famous dictum quoted earlier: 'the spiritual content of music can only be preserved by denying its sentimental content'; and I repeat, it may well be that here we have the explanation of the many paradoxes in Stravinsky's music, and in modern music generally. Who knows but under cover of this same metaphysical principle, viewed in its proper chronological perspective, and stripped of the morphological distinctions which today loom so large, the European music of our time may one day be seen in its ideal spiritual unity.

XIX Culmination and End of Neo-Classicism: The Rake's Progress

In the music written during his first ten years in the United States, Stravinsky appeared to stress his archaic neo-classical trend very strongly. If we except works like the Symphony in Three Movements and the *Ebony Concerto*, it could fairly be said that over these ten years he was steadily simplifying his music, stripping away the trappings and ornaments, and giving up not only the frequent use of polytonality but in many instances even the polyharmonic devices he had begun to use in his early masterpieces. This particular phase of diatonic simplification – and indeed his neo-classicism generally – reaches its climax in the three-act opera *The Rake's Progress*.

Stravinsky began writing the opera in 1948, as soon as he had finished the *Mass*, and completed it in 1951. On 11 September 1951 it was given its first performance in the Fenice theatre in Venice, as part of the Fourteenth International Contemporary Music Festival. Prior to the performance in Venice, he made a statement concerning the way in which he conceived and composed *The Rake's Progress*. He said that for many years he had been toying with the idea of writing an opera on an English text, i.e. based on English prosody, just as he had made use of the peculiar prosody of Russian in *The Nightingale*, *Mavra*, and *The Wedding*, of French in *Persephone*, and of Latin in *Oedipus Rex*, the *Symphony of Psalms*, and the *Mass*. Five years earlier, at a painting exhibition, he had been struck by Hogarth's series of narrative pictures, which reminded him of a succession of scenes from opera. Some time later, in the course of conversation with Aldous Huxley, his friend and neighbour in Hollywood, the question of composing an opera in English had come up, and Huxley suggested W. H. Auden as librettist. In 1947, after completing *Orpheus*, he told his publisher, the late Ralph Hawkes, of his idea of writing a full-scale opera. Hawkes was enthusiastic, and in due course commissioned Auden to write the libretto. Auden joined Stravinsky in Hollywood in November of the same year. They agreed on the plot, a moral tale in three acts based on the series of Hogarth drawings known as *The Rake's Progress*; and they sketched out the plot, the action, the scenes, and the characters. Auden asked Chester Kallman to collaborate with him, and in March 1948 the two librettists handed Stravinsky what he regards as one of the finest librettos ever written.

Stravinsky worked on the opera for three years. When the news spread around, the press came out with various conjectures as to the kind of work it was likely to be, in the light of his earlier operatic ventures with *The Nightingale* and *Mavra*. His own view was that in its musical structure, in its approach to the use of aria, recitative, chorus, and ensemble, and in its tonal relationships, it followed the traditional classical lines.

Auden too has given his views on the underlying principles governing the libretto. He says in essence that the story of the young man who is lured to his destruction by the temptation of the fleshpots was a favourite theme in eighteenth-century England. In writing the libretto, the librettists kept the main episodes of Hogarth's drawings – the unexpected legacy and its dissipation, the marriage with an ugly old woman, the auctioning of the Rake's belongings, and his final confinement to bedlam. To these they added three well-known mythical episodes – the story of Mephistopheles; the card-game in which the Devil loses his supreme confidence in himself; and the story of the three wishes – in the opera Rakewell's desire for wealth, happiness, and virtue, with its counterpart in temptation : the desire for pleasure, the desire for untrammelled freedom of action, and the ambition to become the saviour of the world.

With such a wealth of mythical elements making up the plot, the *dramatis personae* are, inevitably, composite characters. Thus the hero Tom Rakewell embodies features of various classical operatic characters – Don Giovanni, Faust, and Herman in Tchaikovsky's *Queen of Spades*. The heroine recalls Gounod's Marguerite and several other heroines of romantic opera. Nick Shadow, Rakewell's servant and evil counsellor, is Mephistopheles and Leporello rolled into one, with something of Iago thrown in. Like the plot and the characters, the music itself can also be linked to various traditional trends which derive certain features from Mozart's *Don Giovanni* and *Così fan tutte* manner, others from Gluck's *Orpheus*, others again from Rossini, Donizetti, and Verdi. A noteworthy feature throughout is the singable quality of the voice parts and the transparency and sobriety of the instrumentation, which is conceived in many places on chamber music lines.

The opera is divided into three acts, each of three scenes. The first act is introduced by a short flourish of horns and trumpets. As the composer himself says: 'not an overture, or a prelude in a real sense, but simply the equivalent of "on va commencer".' The first scene of the first act takes place on a spring afternoon in the garden of the country house of Trulove, the father of Ann, Tom Rakewell's betrothed. Ann and Tom sing an idyllic duet – which turns into a trio with the entrance of Trulove – in praise of nature, spring, and love.

The voice part, based on a naïvely simple and expressive figure:

is interlarded with instrumental passages which have a delightfully Mozartian flavour. One motif in particular recurs:

a favourite motif of Mozart, who used it in almost the identical form in the Andantino of the well-known C minor Fantasy (K.475):

in the second movement of the G minor Symphony (K.550):

and elsewhere. Stravinsky's more or less textual quotation of this motif is in itself enough to establish the eighteenth-century atmosphere of the work.

In the 'recitative secco' which follows, Trulove offers Tom a position in a counting-house. Tom turns down this offer in a recitative followed by a vigorous aria in which he confesses that he cherishes more ambitious desires and plans: his goal is to achieve happiness as a gift from fortune, without effort on his part. An arabesque on the harpsichord:

signals the entry of Nick Shadow, the Devil himself. In a recitative, Shadow informs Tom that he has inherited a fortune from an unknown uncle. Then comes a quartet, following the pattern dear to the nineteenth-century opera composers. Tom in his elation begs Shadow to remain in his service; Ann rejoices in their good fortune; Trulove urges Tom to be prudent; and Nick tells him he must hasten to London to settle the formalities of the inheritance. Nick and Trulove go off to find a coachman. Ann and Tom converse in a touching duettino which has the simplicity of melody reminiscent of an old English folk-tune. In a new recitative, accompanied alternatively by solo harpsichord and orchestra, Tom asks Nick what recompense he expects for his services. Nick evades the issue: at the end of a year and a day Tom is to judge how much he has done for him, and pay what he feels to be just. Tom agrees; there is no special accentuation or inflexion in the music to suggest that by agreeing the hero of the opera is putting himself in the power of the forces of evil which will ultimately drag him to destruction and drive him out of his mind. The phrase with which Tom seals the pact is the very same hackneyed device used regularly in the music of the past at the end of a recitative:

The accompanying figure in the arioso which follows immediately afterwards has an equally old-fashioned and almost commonplace look about it:

Only the odd slight dissonance here and there gives the passage a feeling of sourness and disenchanted melancholy. In the Terzettino, again, the music is on an altogether conventional level which actually suits the conventionality of the stage situation depicting the general leave-taking. But an indication of the disruptive force set in motion is seen in the 'disassociation' of the voices – the characters sing together less in the Terzettino, and more one against the other, in 'asides', as the composer himself indicates expressly in the score. Finally, with a simple G major arpeggio sustained by a drum roll, Nick announces to the audience, like the' barker at a fair: 'The Progress of a Rake begins!'

The second scene takes place in London in Mother Goose's brothel. A chorus of harlots and young bloods drink to Venus and Mars. In this chorus, and particularly in its orchestral introduction, we recognize once again the inimitable Stravinsky in his brilliant *Card Game* vein. The bantering, free-and-easy, uninhibited gaiety of the brothel's habitués is both expressed and at the same time satirized by the music, with the same verve that marks so many of Stravinsky's most famous but not particularly profound passages. This is perhaps the last time that Stravinsky let himself go in this way.

In the Recitative and Scene, Nick explains for Mother Goose's benefit how he has led Tom into vice. Tom answers all their questions but refuses to answer when the question of true love comes up. The cuckoo-clock strikes one. Nick makes a sign and the clock goes back an hour. The riotous chorus of prostitutes and young men start up again. In a second recitative Nick introduces Tom to the ladies. Then comes a Cavatina in which Tom laments his betrayal of love and implores the God of Love to help him. His song has an elegiac, chopinesque quality, heightened by the crowding of dissonant intervals in the accompaniment. Then the chorus of harlots invite Tom to forget his worries in their embraces. Mother Goose asserts her claim on the grounds of seniority. As Tom and Mother Goose go off, the harlots and the young bloods form a double row for them to pass between. Nick drinks to Tom and wishes him happy dreams in a sleep . . . from which he will not awake. Here again the music studiously avoids stressing or underlining the episode.

The third scene, like the first, takes place at Trulove's country house. It is an autumn night, and there is a full moon. In a beautiful Recitative and a most expressive Aria, Ann pours out her woe at not hearing from Tom. Here the conventional melodic patterns, the hackneyed bag of tricks for accompaniment and the strait-laced rhythmic formulas are moulded to fit the direct expression of genuine emotion. Ann's character, dignified and profoundly human, is depicted and expressed by the music. Her father calls her – she answers in another simple, moving recitative. She cannot abandon Tom to his fate; he is weak and he needs her help. In the Cabaletta which concludes the act, Ann expresses her love for Tom and announces that she has made up her mind to go and find him. The Mozartian motif of three descending notes quoted earlier is taken up again with a change of rhythm, and gives vitality to a musical fabric which is a curious synthesis of eighteenth-century devices and typical Stravinsky.

The first scene of the second act is set in London. The music begins with an Aria, which has a short Recitative in the middle. Tom, seated at breakfast, tells how bored and sick he is of the idle life he is leading. In the Recitative, Aria, and Duetto Finale which follow, Nick, again heralded by the thematic arabesques on the harpsichord, persuades Tom to ask for the hand of Baba the Turk – a bearded wench, so repulsive to look at that even tough soldiers faint at the sight of her. This is the second temptation to which Tom yields – to assert his complete freedom by a meaningless, foolish act.

The second scene is laid in front of Tom's house. Musically it consists of Ann's Recitativo-Arioso, a duet by Ann and Tom, a Recitative by Baba the Turk, a Trio, and a Finale. When Ann reaches London she sees Tom and Baba arrive in a sedan chair. Tom informs her that Baba is his wife; Ann is heart-broken and runs away, while Baba shows off her flowing beard to a cheering crowd. The third scene is in Tom's living-room. Baba sings an Aria, with the mechanical iteration of a grotesque 'perpetuum mobile', followed by a coarse Canzoncina. Tom is irritated by her chatter. They have a fight, which is expressed musically by a series of frenzied musical figures. Tom quietens Baba by clapping his wig inside out over her head. After a short Recitative in which he gives vent to his despair, Tom falls asleep. Then follows a Pantomime in which the music seems to be going round and round aimlessly. Nick brings an extraordinary contraption into the room. Tom wakes up and tells how he has dreamed of a machine which will save the human race from want by changing shells and stones into bread. Nick convinces him that his dream has come true and that the machine can be made to work.

When the third act opens, again in Tom's room, a crowd has gathered for the sale by auction of all Tom's belongings. Baba is sitting where she was left at the end of the second act with the wig still on her head. Ann arrives to inquire after Tom. The auction begins, and proceeds with a dazzling whirl of sounds. The town crier takes the wig off Baba's head. At that moment the voices of Nick and Tom are heard outside. Tom shouts from the wings: 'Old wives for sale!' Baba and Ann recognize the voices. Baba implores Ann to find Tom and to bring him back to his senses. She herself will go back to the fairground.

The second scene is set in the graveyard. Nick's undertaking to serve Tom for a year and a day is fulfilled; the time is up, and Nick has come to claim his wages. What he wants is not money, but Tom's immortal soul. Tom is to kill himself with a weapon of his own choosing. But first he is given a last chance: he may stake his soul on a game of cards. The card game between Nick and Tom takes the form of a Duet accompanied at first only by the jangling sounds of the harpsichord. Once again the association of music with the forces of evil is expressed by means of rhythm. In this Duet it has the obsessive mechanical effect and the insistent iteration of an 'ostinato perpetuo'. To bring out the rhythmic elements alone, Stravinsky again neutralizes the harmonic effects by means of continual polytonal superimposition and criss-crossing.

Little by little, as Nick loses the game, the rhythm broadens, and the polytonal clashing and jolting subsides. In the end, the strength of Ann's love helps Tom to win and to save his own soul. But in expiation of his sins he loses his reason. The last scene, in London, finds Tom in Bedlam. He thinks he is Adonis. Ann comes to visit him and he takes her for Venus. Ann sings him to sleep with an utterly sweet, tender, simple lullaby, and goes off swearing to be true to their love for ever. Tom wakes up, and with the names of Venus and Orpheus on his lips he dies.

Since, like *Don Giovanni, The Rake's Progress* is a 'comic opera', Tom's death in the mad-house is followed by an epilogue, in which the main characters come out in front of the curtain, remove their wigs and sing the moral of the tale. As in *Persephone*, so in *The Rake's Progress* Stravinsky deals with a fundamentally Christian theme – the same theme that dictates the destiny of the Da Ponte-Mozart libertine. Man is the victim of dark, cruel forces which rule, tempt, and crush him. But he can be saved by a miraculous act of love, a manifestation of Christian 'caritas'. But salvation means redemption of the soul only. To satisfy the implacable law of justice, the libertine has to pay the penalty and lose his life and reason.

XX Towards Twelve-Note Music

The Rake's Progress appeared to put the final seal on Stravinsky's leaning towards neo-classicism. His return to the forms and philosophies of the past is more clearly in evidence in this work than in any of his earlier works, in respect both of its intrinsic form and of the detail of the musical texture. It might confidently have been expected that from now on the trend of Stravinsky's composition would be towards a more and more marked simplification of expression and a more and more archaic, plain and unadorned diatonic musical language. It hardly seemed likely that at the age of seventy he would produce out of the hat yet another of those surprises with which time and time again throughout his career he has shocked the musical world. In fact, apropos of *The Rake's Progress* Stravinsky is claimed to have said: 'This is the end of a trend.' Such a statement would seem to be at variance with the whole tenor of the interview given by Stravinsky in Venice, in which he said he thought a great deal of *The Rake's Progress* as being sound and 'authentic', justifying further work along the same lines. Possibly in the former case what he had in mind was the end of a stylistic period and in the latter simply the possibility of further development in the direction of opera as a sequel to *The Rake's Progress*. It is significant that Nicolas Nabokoff speaks of the work as the forerunner of a new era in the evolution of the opera form. Today, twenty years after the first performance of *The Rake's Progress*, this view has not really been corroborated. On the other hand, the thesis I myself propounded in an essay on Stravinsky as an opera composer entitled 'Stravinsky's *The Rake's Progress*, the Last Classical Opera' (*Rassegna Musicale*, year XXXII, No. 2-4, Turin 1962) has not been refuted. Be that as it may, Stravinsky must soon have realized that *The Rake's Progress* actually did indicate that he had reached a dead end and that there must be a change of direction. Realization of this caused the second crisis in his life as a composer. In the section of *Themes and Episodes* entitled 'Change of Life' already quoted in connection with the two crises which he said he 'had to survive . . . as a composer' when he changed over from his Russian phase to his neo-classical phase, he makes an extremely important and significant confession on this point. While he was working on his final major work (*Requiem Canticles* – or the Princeton Requiem, as he called it at the time), he dictated the following: 'Crisis number two was brought on by the natural outgrowing of the special incubator in which I wrote *The Rake's Progress* (which is why I did not use Auden's beautiful *Delia* libretto; I could not continue in the same strain, could not compose a sequel to *The Rake*, as I would have had to do). The period of adjustment was only half as long this time, but as I look back on it I am surprised at how long I continued to straddle my "styles". Was it because one has to unlearn as well as to learn, and at seventy the unlearning is more difficult? However that may be, the slow climb through in the 1950's eventually brought me to *Movements*, which I now see as the cornerstone of my later work.'

The present chapter is concerned with the adjustment Stravinsky speaks of here. This new phase begins with the first work composed after *The Rake's Progress* – the Cantata for soprano, tenor, female chorus, and a small instrumental ensemble. It also includes the Septet, the *Three Songs from William Shakespeare, In Memoriam Dylan Thomas*, the *Canticum Sacrum ad honorem Sancti Marci Nominis*, the ballet *Agon* and other recent compositions; and it opens up new possibilities of future developments which may well have a decisive influence on the art of music today. Let us repeat once again: the main problem, on the solution of which the very survival of music as a coherent form of aesthetic expression would seem to depend, is to restore to music the unity of language it had lost as a result of the post-Romantic dilemma. At that point a parting of the ways seemed inevitable, with no possibility of compromise between out-and-out chromaticism as advocated by the Viennese school and the polydiatonic trend of which Igor Stravinsky is certainly the most brilliant and most authoritative exponent. In the face of twelve-note music, the polydiatonic school had begun to take on the appearance and fulfil the function of an 'alternative choice' in modern music, to establish itself as one of the main musical currents, even though today we may question its capacity for further development. At all events, with the passage of time, partly because of an inherent narrowing tendency but mainly owing to the fact that it became identified with neo-classicism, the art of the principal representatives of the polydiatonic school has tended to shrink into a more and more restricted mould, whereas the tendency of twelve-note music in Webern, and still more in his followers, has been to expand. The manner of its expression foreshadowed not only development beyond dodecaphonic music proper, in the sense of an articulation of the span of musical sounds encompassed by the twelve different notes of the tempered scale, but also development beyond this range of sounds made virtually limitless by the advent of electronic devices. In this context, the art of Stravinsky and that of the Schoenberg school came to be, not dialectical alternatives with the possibility of composing their differences, but seemingly antagonistic and irreconcilable systems. As has already been said, the split which occurred in regard to form in European music at the post-romantic parting of the ways seemed incapable of being mended; the gap between the formal elements had grown so wide that a fusion seemed hopeless. It is true that Schoenberg, Berg, and other composers had shown a willingness to arrive at a *modus vivendi* where a synthesis might be possible between the achievements of the polydiatonic system (i.e. the use of polymodal and polytonal elements and in general a far broader concept of tonality than the orthodox one) and the dodecaphonic system. The tonal 'polarization' of the twelve-note scale and the rehabilitation of the conventional diatonic entity within its proper orbit to be found in their works could be regarded as clear proof of their intentions in the matter. On the other hand, with the possible exception of Frank Martin's experiments, no decisive step had been taken until the 1950s by the chief exponents of the antagonistic 'polydiatonic' trend towards approaching the same goal from the opposite direction. In *The Rake's Progress* Stravinsky seemed to have moved away from it for good. Actually, as we have seen, *The Rake's Progress* marked the farthest point reached by Stravinsky's neoclassicism rather than its culmination; and having reached this point he appears to have taken precisely the decisive step in question to arrive at a common meeting ground. In another work[1] I ventured the opinion that it was difficult to imagine Stravinsky as moving in this direction; but in retrospect there are hints of this possibility in his earlier works. Mention has been made of these tell-tale hints in connection with the *Three Pieces* for string quartet (1914), *The Five Fingers* (1921), and also the Symphonies of 1940 and 1945. In the *Three Pieces* and *The Five Fingers* there were passages in which each instrumental part kept strictly within the limits of a fixed

[1] See Vlad, *Modernità e tradizione*, Ch. XXII: 'Convergenze.'

portion of the scale, producing figures built up exclusively from a specific series of notes. In the Symphonies on the other hand there are bass figures running freely up and down the entire compass, cutting across the musical discourse and loosening the rigidity of the tonal structure. These two devices, taken together, constitute the underlying principle of dodecaphonic serial writing. Thus there are advance warnings of a 'serial' phase in Stravinsky's music in works written long before 1950; and even the manner in which this phase began is in keeping with one aspect of Stravinsky's development already discussed. We saw how this was a kind of secret germination, in which certain elements matured unseen and then burst forth suddenly, so that anyone who had not been aware of the slow process of incubation was caught off his guard. Stravinsky's *volte-face* after *The Rake's Progress* was all the more disconcerting in that just previously he had given the impression that he was moving in a totally different direction. What really happened was that before concluding his neo-classical episode, he drew the logical consequences from it, gathering together its most typical features in a large-scale work which might be taken as the crowning glory of his neo-classicism. As Massimo Mila rightly says,

between the two wars Stravinsky was the personification of neo-classicism; in him it achieved a depth and a splendour not found in any of its other exponents. Now that the age of neo-classicism is over (and this is one of the few things that can be said with any certainty about the age in which we live) Stravinsky saw the red light in time and in the most astonishing turnabout he ever made, he has edged closer and closer to the opposite extreme of contemporary musical sensibility of which he was for so long the antithesis.[2]

These overtures to the other side were not made suddenly, but gradually, step by step. The first step was the Cantata for soprano, tenor, female chorus, and a small instrumental ensemble. Stravinsky

[2] Article on Stravinsky in the Roman weekly *L'Espresso*, Vol. II, No 39, 23 September 1956. Today, when Igor Stravinsky has bidden a last farewell to life as an artist and as a man and two decades after the first performance of *The Rake's Progress*, the general picture of contemporary music looks very different. In the introductory pages added to the present edition, especially where reference is made to twelve-note music's having passed its historical peak, and in the new chapters added at the end of the book, I have taken account of the repercussions which this change may well have, not of course on the absolute, intrinsic validity of Stravinsky's work, but at any rate on the indirect historical incidence of his activities as a composer. Consequently I should perhaps have suppressed, or at any rate amended, the sections of the present chapter that in the light of the critical outlook of today may seem to be no longer valid. The reason why I have not done so, but have confined myself to making a few minor modifications, is that I wanted the reader to be able to recapture the atmosphere in which at the time I witnessed Stravinsky's conversion to twelve-note music and the sensational effect it certainly had on the world of music when it happened.

conducted this work for the first time on 11 November 1952 at a concert given by the Los Angeles Chamber Symphony Society, to which the Cantata is dedicated. Stravinsky himself wrote the programme note, which read as follows:[3]

My Cantata for solo soprano, solo tenor and female chorus and instrumental quintet of 2 flutes, 2 oboes (the second interchangeable with English horn) and cello was composed between April 1951 and August 1952. After finishing *The Rake's Progress* I was persuaded by a strong desire to compose another work in which the problems of setting English words to music would reappear, but this time in a purer, non-dramatic form. I selected from popular anonymous lyrics of the fifteenth and sixteenth centuries, verses which attracted me not only for their great beauty and their compelling syllabification, but for their construction, which suggested musical construction.

Three of the poems are semi-sacred. The fourth, 'Westron Wind', is a love lyric; the Cantata is therefore, secular.

The musical construction to which Stravinsky refers is the canonic structure of the music and the series of devices in vogue at the time of the great Flemish composers and revised by Schoenberg in the form of serial devices. In the Cantata these devices are found particularly in the melodic line described as *cantus cancrizans*, consisting of a series of sounds alternatively presented in their original form, then inverted, then in crab form. But Stravinsky applies these devices to a musical text that is as diatonic as *The Rake's Progress*. In fact, the use of ancient modes gives the work a still more archaic flavour. Incidentally, the mode he seems to prefer in the Prelude and its repetitions is the Phrygian, on which he based large sections of his earlier works of a ritual character such as *The Wedding* and the *Mass*. He says himself that the formal shape of the Cantata is suggested by the literary text. The four verses of the moving 'Lyke-Wake Dirge' provide the model for a Prelude, two Interludes, and a Postlude. These pieces are written in a free strophic form, using the same musical phrase with only slight modifications. The tune is one of the most appealing Stravinsky ever wrote. Between this choral 'lament' and its repeat there is a ricercare for soprano, a second ricercare for tenor, and an Aria for soprano and tenor. The Aria is written in a free form like that of the 'Lyke-Wake Dirge'; but the construction of the two ricercari, especially the second, involves the application of the devices referred to above. In the first ricercare, 'The Maidens Came', a young girl expresses in song her self-abnegation and abandonment in the love of Christ. The music movingly expresses the nostalgia for earthly joys and the consolation

---

[3] It is also reproduced on the sleeve of the record made subsequently (Columbia ML 4899).

of faith in a realm of 'eternal song' – the kingdom of Christ. The second ricercare, sung by the tenor, is written on a strange text, in the form of a scriptural episode such as might have been sung by a medieval jongleur; and in it, Christ recounts in the first person the story of His life, the Passion, Resurrection, and Ascension. As regards form, this Sacred History consists of an introduction in which the *cantus cancrizans* is repeated over and over again, and nine canons, each of them followed by a purely instrumental ritornello. The Aria, on the other hand, is a secular love song, essentially homophonic in structure.

The direction followed by Stravinsky in the Cantata is continued even more definitely in the next work, the Septet for clarinet, horn, bassoon, piano, violin, viola, and cello. It was written between July 1952 and February 1953, and dedicated to the Dumbarton Oaks Research Library and Collection. In the Cantata only two movements were built up from a serial germ; the Septet is constructed entirely on this basis; moreover, there is only a single serial motif. This is consistent with the fundamental principle of serial writing, namely that a work should have structural unity in every part and every dimension. The musical figure around which the Septet is built is:

At the beginning of the first movement this figure is stated simultaneously by the clarinet, in the following rhythm:

and the bassoon, with the values of the notes doubled:

The horn plays the same figure inverted, with the values doubled, but coming on the weak beats of the bars. Then the violin too plays the inversion, keeping the original values:

Later on there are crab forms of the same figure, like the following, played at the end by the cello (transposed down a fifth):

In the Septet, especially in the second and third movements, Stravinsky tightens up the serial pattern and begins to disentagle the threads of the musical fabric from their diatonic function and to spread them over the chromatic scale – which is free, though still governed by areas of tonal attraction, as in this passage in the third movement, for bassoon solo:

or the following piano passage:

taken up by the clarinet:

Even in the expressionist width of the intervals of which they are composed, these melodic lines suggest a distinct kinship with the musical outlook of the Viennese dodecaphonic school. The way in which in the second movement the basic figure is presented from different angles so as to bring out the effect of the timbres is particularly reminiscent of Webern.[4] The theme of the Passacaglia

[4] For the peculiar attraction which the music of Webern (more than that of any other contemporary composer) had for Stravinsky at the time, see Chapter VII, footnote 1.

as a whole is presented in the four classic serial variants – original form (*Grundgestalt*), crab, inversion, and crab inversion. The first five notes are a transposition of the five-note figure in the first movement. To these five notes eleven more are added, so that the entire thematic row in the Passacaglia now consists of sixteen notes – though only eight are different notes. The serial aspect of this theme is presented in seven alternating timbres by different instruments before being stated in full by the piano and the cello. At the end of the eight canonic variations making up the Passacaglia, the theme recurs as a complex polyphonic seven-part web in its various mirror canon forms. While the horn plays the inversion, the viola plays the crab, the violin plays the crab inversion, while the piano, cello, bassoon, and clarinet play four rhythmic variations of the original form.

In the Gigue which ends the piece, Stravinsky demonstrates one after the other the aspects of the 'row' used for each separate instrument, just as he had done thirty years earlier in *The Five Fingers*. It is a series of eight different sounds which have the twofold function of defining the thematic intervals, but more important still, of circumscribing in each instance the compass within which each individual voice moves. In this movement, too, the theme appears in crab form and inversion, this being explicitly marked by the composer in the score. This theme is identical with the form taken by the 'Ur-Motif' of the Septet in the Passacaglia. It is used as a basis for four fugues, the second and fourth being double fugues. Each fugue is based on a different serial hypostasis of the subject. This differentiation of form has its counterpart in a differentiation of tone colour. The first and third figures are played by the three stringed instruments, the second and fourth by the woodwind and piano. Woodwind and strings combine only in the final cadence to each figure, when the strict dynamic construction governing the entire movement is somewhat slackened.

Craft maintains that the Septet represents the most drastic step taken by Stravinsky for thirty years, and is certainly the key to Stravinsky's mentality during recent years. Another significant point referred to by Craft is that during 1952 Stravinsky took every opportunity to study the works of Schoenberg. He was doubtless influenced by Schoenberg's Gigue from the Suite, op. 29, when he included the Gigue in the Septet.

That same year, 1953, when Stravinsky had finished the Septet he wrote the *Three Songs from William Shakespeare* for mezzo-soprano, flute, clarinet, and viola. These songs also belong to the new direction taken by Stravinsky's art, since the musical content of each of the songs is organically serial in structure. The first song 'Musick to heare' is a setting of Shakespeare's eighth sonnet, in praise of music. The series on which it is based:

consists of twelve sounds, on eight different notes.[5] Like some of Webern's series, its internal structure is also serial, i.e. it too is made up of cells bearing a reciprocal serial relationship to each other. Thus the figure formed by the fourth, fifth, and sixth notes of the series:

is purely and simply the figure formed by the first three notes in crab form, with the same melodic and metrical values:

The second song is a setting of Ariel's song from Act II of *The Tempest*: 'Full fadom five'. The series on which this is based is stated in the form of a double canon by diminution at the fifth and by double diminution at the octave. The use of intervals of fourths, fifths, and sevenths and the $f > p$ attack of the instruments, suggests the sound of bells, to which the poetry too refers onomatopoeically at the end:

[5] Craft (*Avec Stravinsky*, p. 149), analysing the structure of this passage, divides the series into two parts: a series consisting of the first six notes, all different, and another in which notes are repeated.

The third song, 'When daisies pied' sets the stanzas from the last act of *Love's Labour's Lost*. Its serial motif:

is derived from the motif of the second song. Massimo Mila calls this song 'perhaps the most beautiful composition Stravinsky has contributed to the repertoire of vocal chamber music'.[6]

The next phase in Stravinsky's new development is illustrated by the work entitled *In Memoriam Dylan Thomas, Dirge Canons* for tenor voice, string quartet, and four trombones. This is a short composition written in 1954 in memory of the poet Dylan Thomas, who died tragically in New York, where he was to meet Stravinsky and discuss the libretto for a new opera. As the sub-title indicates, the work consists of two dirge canons incorporating a song on words from Dylan Thomas's *Collected Poems*. Stravinsky uses the two groups of four instruments like an organ, played in two registers, the different timbres being heard alternately but never mixing. From the point of view of serial technique, the writing is even stricter than in the three previous works. All the musical material of the canons which constitute the Prelude and of those constituting the Postlude and the Song – in other words, the composition of the entire work in all its minutest details – is derived without exception from a chromatic nucleus of five different notes:

and of its serial variants – the inversion:

the crab form:

[6] *Revista musicale italiana*, Bocca, Vol. LVI, No. 3, July-Sept. 1954, p. 279.

and the crab inversion:

In certain passages the individual parts are linked together in such a .way that the rows taken together embrace the entire compass of twelve notes. Here then we have Stravinsky's first entirely chromatic piece. The absence of diatonic relationships even in a tonally polarized compass, and the tendency towards panchromatic integration, give the work the character of a final stage before Stravinsky burned his boats and adopted the twelve-note system outright. The final step was taken in the *Canticum Sacrum ad honorem Sancti Marci Nominis*, written in 1955 and performed for the first time on 13 September 1956 in St. Mark's, Venice, on the occasion of the Nineteenth International Festival of Contemporary Music. The work is dedicated 'Urbi Venetiae in laude Sancti sui Presidis Beati Marci Apostolis', and the dedication is sung by the tenor and baritone accompanied by two trombones, as a sort of prelude to the work. To my mind, the *Canticum* is the most comprehensive and essential synthesis of elements it is possible to imagine at this particular stage in the evolution of European music. The multitude of ingredients which go into this 'summa' is staggering; but because of the homogeneity achieved by the fusion of elements and the very size of the work, which Mila describes as 'meagre, spare, and rugged; humble with a studied poverty' – and indeed about three-fifths of the work seems positively threadbare – very few of its qualities can be appreciated at first sight or on first hearing; they need to be heard again and again before they yield up their secrets.

From the point of view of form, this work embraces features which span the entire panorama of European musical history and gathers them all into one vast *omnium gatherum* – from Gregorian chant to Webern's spacious intervals; from the medieval organum and faburden to serialism; from the Byzantine modes to polymodality, polytonality, and atonality; from the old-fashioned diatonic to the modern poly-diatonic style and out-and-out chromaticism; from phrases which recall the archaic effect of the hocket and inflexions reminiscent of the Venice School of the Renaissance to the tightly-drawn dodeca-phonic curves; from the baroque solidity of harmonic masses to the contrapuntal *pointillisme* of the ultra-moderns; from an ensemble in the style of the old Venetian school to an instrumental disposition which betrays an acquaintance with Webern's Variations for orchestra. The *Canticum* is scored for organ, three trumpets, bass trumpet, two trombones, bass trombone, and contrabass trombone, violas, and double basses; in addition flute, two oboes, cor anglais, two bassoons, and double bassoon are used for the solo or concerted numbers.

It is highly significant that this synthesis should bear the hallmark of dodecaphony, thus showing once again the essential unifying power of the new system.

In connection with the *Canticum Sacrum* I used the word 'atonality'. I should perhaps add that I used it merely because it has come into common usage, not as in any way implying the negation of underlying links with tonality. I accept the word provided its meaning is restricted to describing the interplay of sound combinations beyond the scope of the classical tonal system. It is significant that both Schoenberg and Stravinsky reject the term 'atonality' if by 'atonality' we mean to deny the existence of any 'tonal' arrangement. Stravinsky says precisely this:[7]

We thus no longer find ourselves in the framework of classic tonality in the scholastic sense of the word. . . . Having reached this point, it is no less indispensable . . . to recognize the existence of certain poles of attraction. Diatonic tonality is only one means of orienting music towards these poles. The function of tonality is completely subordinated to the force of attraction of the pole of sonority. All music is nothing more than a succession of impulses that converge towards a definite point of repose. That is as true of Gregorian chant as it is of a Bach fugue, as true of Brahms's music as it is of Debussy's.
    This general law of attraction is satisfied in only a limited way by the traditional diatonic system, for that system possesses no absolute value. . . . But the fact remains that it is still impossible to lay down the rules that govern this new technique. Nor is this at all surprising. Harmony as it is taught today in the schools dictates rules that were not fixed until long after the publication of the works upon which they were based, rules which were unknown to the composers of these works. . . .
    So our chief concern is not so much what is known as tonality as what one might term the polar attraction of sound, of an interval, or even of a complex of tones. The sounding tone constitues in a way the essential axis of music. Musical form would be unimaginable in the absence of elements of attraction which make up every musical organism . . . the diatonic system has lived out its life cycle. . . . It was here that the gates opened upon what has been labelled with the abusive term: *atonality*. . . . The negating prefix *a* indicates a state of indifference in regard to the term, negating without entirely renouncing it. . . . If it were said that my music is atonal, that would be tantamount to saying that I had become deaf to tonality. Now it may well be that I remain for a considerable time within the bounds of the strict order of tonality, even though I may quite consciously break up this order for the purposes of establishing a new one. In that case I am not *atonal* but *antitonal*.

[7] *Poetics of Music*, pp. 35-38.

Stravinsky's answers to Robert Craft[8] follow on logically from his statements in the *Poetics*:

R.C.: 'In your own music, identity is established by melodic, rhythmic, and other means, but especially by tonality. Do you think you will ever abandon the tonal identification?'

I.S.: 'Possibly. We can still create a sense of return to exactly the same place without tonality: musical rhyme can accomplish the same thing as poetic rhyme. But form cannot exist without identity of some sort.'

R.C.: 'Do you think of the intervals in your series as tonal intervals; that is, do your intervals always exert tonal pull?'

I.S.: 'The intervals of my series are attracted by tonality; I compose vertically and that is in one sense at least, to compose tonally.'

Robert Gerhard, in an essay entitled 'Twelve-note technique in Stravinsky'[9] analyses the way in which tonal relationship is established within Stravinsky's series. Thus, in the series shown on page 190 of this text, Gerhard sees mainly a double hexachordal structure, which means that the notes constituting the first half of the series can be regarded as being arranged in a certain hexachordal order, while the notes in the second half of the series can be grouped in another hexachordal arrangement.

The nodal points of this type of series then consist of the first and last notes of these hexachords, i.e. notes 1-6 and 7-12 of the actual series. In the series quoted, the two hexachords are connected by a double relationship of a fifth. Between the first notes (A flat and E flat) and between the last notes (E and A) of the two hexachords there are intervals of a fifth, and the fifth more than any other interval tends to create poles of tonal attraction. In the series in question these relationships are extremely numerous owing to the fact that in addition to the hexachordal nodes there is also an interval of a fifth between notes 2 and 4 (G and D), 5 and 8 (F sharp and C sharp) and 7 and 9 (E flat and B flat). The whole series is thus literally steeped in relationships of fifths, and this relationship has a very definite tonal feeling. As Gerhard says:[10]

In the last analysis, the fascination of the Stravinskyan paradox – non-chromatic twelve-note music – lies perhaps in the fusion of opposites he achieves. He writes twelve-note music *in the spirit* of diatonicism, and diatonic music with a full experience of total chromaticism.

[8] *Conversations with Igor Stravinsky*, p. 24.
[9] *The Score*, June 1957, p. 38.
[10] ibid., p. 43.

To get back to the *Canticum*: the subject of the work too is
complex, but it has a spiritual unity, which derives from the
Apostolic virtues of the Saint whose name and evangelizing mission it
honours, as the sub-title and dedication indicate. (Indeed, it would
not be inappropriate to speak of an 'Apostolic cantata by Stravinsky',
as Lindlar does.) The aim of all the various literary themes, some of
them taken from the Gospel according to St. Mark, the rest from
the Song of Songs, the Epistles of St. John the Evangelist and the Book
of Psalms in the Latin version of the Vulgate, is to symbolize the
state of the Church Militant. Parallel with the underlying meaning
of the texts the architecture of the music is built up, both in its
broad outlines and in its more subtle inner structure. Craft compares
the general architectonic organization of the work to the Venetian
Basilica itself, saying that the five parts of the *Canticum Sacrum* are
each related to the other in the same way as the cupolas of St. Mark's
are related – the central one being the main one, with the others
arranged round it; the first and fifth are identical from the point of
view of structure and musical content, the second and fourth are
related, in spite of their differences of style and form, inasmuch as
both are for vocal solo.

The theme of the first and last movements is Christ's commandment, 'Go ye and teach all nations'. The middle movements are

conceived along the lines of the structure of the teaching Church. The second
symbolizes the founding of the Church of the Old Testament. The inspiration
of the third (the central cupola of Stravinsky's architecture, as already pointed
out) is the trinity of virtues, which assumes the role of theological superstructure and by means of the excerpts from the Scripture underlines the
continuity of the Old and New Testaments. The fourth part, following upon
the last of the virtues – *Fides*, is linked to this by a quotation from the Gospel
concerning the gift of Faith, and to emphasize the close connection, it is
derived from the same musical material. If the 'virtutes' can be called the
architectonic culmination of the *Canticum*, Faith is its central axis: *Cogito*
and *Credo*. It is possible also to find connections between the musical form
and the textual subject-matter in so far as this depends on a sort of understanding as to certain stylistic attributes and leaves itself open to the danger of
far-fetched parallels. The first part pronounces God's commandment, the last
part its fulfilment, and the music here is a reply or supplement to the first. It
is not an accident that the final movement consists of the *cancrizans* form of the
first, since this does at any rate establish the fact that it is its counterpart.[11]

Of the architecture of the middle part Lindlar says:[12]

In its division into five parts, the Responsorium, like the movements on either
side of it, which are also in five sections, is like a kind of mirror reduction

[11] See Craft-Piovesan-Vlad: *Le Musiche religiose di Igor Strawinsky* (Lombroso: Venice, 1956), p. 23.   [12] op. cit., p. 76.

of the five-part division of the whole work. The numerical symbolism in the
arrangement in 3, 5, 7, and 12 is no less significant than the inter-relationship
in meaning between the main movements of the *Canticum* : I and V as the
musical embodiment of the commandment; II and III as the dual nature of
love, earthly love, and heavenly love, as in the 1952 Cantata; III and IV as
the unity of Faith in society and in the individual.

In spite of the dangers of 'far-fetched parallels' I should like to
try to explain what the non-committal 'at any rate' in the above
quotation from Craft-Piovesan-Vlad implies. First of all, the re-
versal of time which the music of the first piece undergoes in the
fifth can also be correlated with the grammatical form of the texts.
in the first ('Euntes in mundum universum, praedicate evangelium
omni creaturae'), the imperative has a future implication; in the last
('Illi autem profecti, praedicaverunt ubique') this future has become
past. On a higher level of symbolism, the relationship may be
referred to the word of God given back to God. Further, through
the reversibility of time implied metaphorically by the *cancrizans*
treatment which the musical argument of the first piece is given in
the fifth piece, the music seems to reach towards a reality greater
not only than itself but greater than the span it encompasses, namely
the span of our experience of life. Thus once again we are confronted
with something more than our own three-dimensional space concept,
without having on this occasion to refer to the Swedenborgian idea
which so fascinated Schoenberg.[13] The theological intuition of the
'Perennial Philosophy' crystallized the concept of time which returns
to God, and the concept of the finality of the Divine Order that
hinted at the repudiation of the chronology of cause and effect.
Through one of the greatest achievements of the human mind, in
the last few years the antonomastic rational science of mathematics
has reached similar conclusions, conceiving hyperspace (or more
than four-dimensional space) as a region in which the passage of
time, merging into fields of spiritual forces, changes around, so that
past becomes future, future becomes past, and effects precede their
causes.

This digression was not intended to support the claim that the
relationship between music and metaphysical reality was consciously
in Stravinsky's mind when he wrote the works under discussion, in
the sense in which this relationship was part of Schoenberg's poetics;
nor is it suggested that the relationship was on anything but a purely

[13] The influence of Swedenborg's theosophy on Schoenberg, especially in
regard to the concept of space other than three-dimensional space, and the
non-differentiation of the spatial and temporal co-ordinates is discussed by the
author in *Modernità e tradizione*, Chapter XIII and elsewhere.

formal level. The reason why I felt I should outline my ideas on the subject is because I am anxious to bring to light anything calculated to justify the geometrical approach to musical composition, which in spite of much that is bogus, has for decades been making itself felt and becoming more and more inevitably the only possible course for most of the composers who have made or are at present making contemporary musical history. I am thinking not only of Bach's achievements, nor of what Busoni, Skriabin, Schoenberg, Berg, Webern and Stravinsky have done in the recent past and what Dallapiccola and the younger *avant-garde* composers are doing today; I am thinking also of people like Hindemith, who, although in the other camp, so to speak, gives us in the *Ludus Tonalis* one of the most outstanding examples of this method of composition. It could hardly be argued that the motivation of this technique is a sort of aesthetic masochism, the composer shutting himself off voluntarily and without any good reason from the substance of his work. Nor can it be assumed that the last fifty years have instituted a practice based simply and solely on an intellectual whim. On the contrary, it is hard to escape the conclusion that this tendency, which on examination we find has always been favoured in music, is growing stronger in music itself and is spreading to the other arts – today the sister arts more than ever approximate to the condition of music. This is happening at the very time when in the face of pragmatism and materialism even pure science is undergoing a metaphysical conversion. The obvious conclusion is that there are inexplicable factors at work bringing about a parallel situation all round. One conclusion I cannot endorse is that music has the power to reveal, genuinely and directly, a transcendent reality. I recognize that music may have ontological implications, but it cannot be regarded as a key to metaphysical knowledge, let alone enter upon any realm but that of our sense of perception, as I have already said apropos of Schoenberg's concept of tonal space.[14]

The relationship between music and transcendentalism can be established on a purely symbolic level, or at best it admits of indirect correlations. What music does possess, however, apart from the power of allowing man to see himself reflected in it, is the power (known to the priesthood of all religious rites from time immemorial) of making man forget himself, thus pre-disposing him to metaphysical contemplation. It is in this sense, as we have already seen,

[14] Vlad, *Modernità e tradizione*, p. 189.

that in the *Poetics of Music* Stravinsky defines the fundamental significance of music and its essential aim as embracing the twofold task of promoting 'a form of communion with our fellow man and with the Supreme Being', whereas in *Chronicle of My Life* he is up in arms against any attempt to bring together the divine order and the human order. What has been said above will explain later on the apparent contradiction between Stravinsky's attacks on 'art as a religion' and his conception of music as a means of communication with the Supreme Being. What he rightly condemns is making the possible metaphysical implications the avowed subject of a musical work, since only too often the result is a musical composition totally lacking in real musical meaning, and instead we get arbitrary and meaningless metaphysics. The art of musical sounds must be first of all an art of sounds in the physical sense before it can be warmed by the 'rays of Music, the eternal sun' as Busoni put it.

The compositions by Stravinsky which prompted the above are actually altogether down-to-earth pieces. The crab device does not in any way weaken the immediate significance of the passage thus treated, which gives every appearance of creative spontaneity. Thus Mila is right in saying that each such passage 'is the exact reverse of the other, the same thing looked at in a mirror, but together they constitute a completely meaningful melodic pattern; this is true whenever Stravinsky uses these canonic devices'. Craft too is right in saying that when we think of the ungainly mechanical quality of the rhythm in the majority of compositions which derive from the crab device, Stravinsky's success is all the more impressive, in that he creates rhythms which can run just as easily in the one direction as in another.

Structurally the piece is divided into three choral parts, supported by brass, strings, bassoons, and organ, with two interludes for organ and bassoons. Massimo Mila has discerned another meaning in the peculiar character of the individual phases, a metaphorical meaning, the outcome of a

concrete musical intuition . . . which gives the first and fifth pieces a profundity of meaning over and above the deliberate intentions of the composer . . . through the alternate repetition of two phrases, one choral and instrumental, the other played on the organ; the latter emphasizes the spiritual consolation inherent in the preaching of the Gospel, while the former ('Euntes in mundum universum praedicate evangelium') reveals with unconscious sincerity the fanaticism implicit in all proselytism. The fierce dissonant clashes of the wind instruments and the crude rhythm of the repeated chords depict preaching as a downright act of aggression, invasion, and occupation of men's consciences.

To achieve this sense of force, Stravinsky makes use of the dissonant
clashes which, as he himself admits, he had used in the past to
produce startlingly sensational effects. Since obvious differentiation
between dissonance and consonance is possible only in a diatonic
or polydiatonic style, Stravinsky at this point reverts to the use of
the polytonal devices characteristic of the early major works of his
so-called Russian period. Hence there are very good reasons why
this piece should sound like an echo of his past. The soothing
sweetness of the interludes, on the other hand, is achieved through
monomodal five-part writing, reminiscent of the watertight compart-
mentalism referred to at the beginning of this chapter in connection
with the *Three Pieces* for string quartet. In fact every one of the
five strands of the contrapuntal fabric is written in a definite portion
of the tessitura confined to five notes in the case of the highest
voice, four notes in the next highest, three in the third, two in the
fourth, and six different notes in the bass part. The three middle
sections of the *Canticum* are different from the movements at either
end in that they are written entirely on a series of twelve different
notes. Robert Craft[15] gives a detailed and minute serial analysis of
these pieces. I will not repeat it all here. All I will say is that it is
perfectly clear from this analysis that Stravinsky strove to attain a
synthesis between some of the more radical features of serial music
and tonality, and that there were evident signs of this synthesis even
in his early experiments along these lines.

The three middle movements are built up on two closely inter-
related series.

The first:

provides the structural basis for the second piece 'Surge Aquilo',
while the second:

[15] Craft-Piovesan-Vlad, op. cit.

supplies the material for the third movement ('Ad tres virtutes
hortationes') and the fourth ('Brevis motus cantilenae'). As can be
seen, the last four notes of the series reproduced in the first example
coincide with the series from the fifth to the second note, inclusive,
of the crab form of the series quoted in the second example; moreover there are two further corresponding serial intervals in both
series; the first and the last intervals are a minor and major second
respectively. The second piece, in the form of a two-part song, like
a baroque 'Sacra Sinfonia' according to Craft's description, is a tenor
solo with a few strands of counterpoint often merging into a single
strand, and played by the flute, cor anglais and harp, with three
double basses joining in for a few notes. The character of the piece
is described by Craft as lyrical, both poetically and musically. The
ecstasy of the yearning for God and His Kingdom turning away
from all romantic temptation, produces a strictly stylized dialogue.
In spite of this assertion, it should be pointed out that the rigorous
stylization of the piece does not prevent Stravinsky from achieving
at the same time some definite atmospheric effects, for instance the
spontaneous effect of the delicate fluttering of the flute to the
words '. . . veni auster et perfla. . . .' The series is established right
from the first bar in the form of three four-note chords derived from
the *cancrizans*:

Immediately afterwards the tenor states the series melodically in its
original form, and is soon joined by the cor anglais in counterpoint,
unfolding the series in crab inversion:

Next the tenor sings half the melody *cancrizans* and half in crab inversion, then the whole thing *cancrizans*. The rest of the piece consists entirely of analogous canonic phrases interspersed with variant repeats of the original harmonic motif. It is worth noting that in the first statement of the melody by the tenor the original series recalls two phrases from *Oedipus Rex* and the main motif of the finale of *The Rake's Progress*. On the whole it can be said that while in various instances such as:

the instrumentation has a distinct look of one of Webern's scores, the continuity of the vocal line is enough to eliminate any flavour of Webern from the general musical pattern. Webern (the Cantata op. 31 and the Variations op. 30 in particular) is very definitely suggested in the four-part canon (three parts sung by the choir and the fourth played by the trumpets) which makes up the third movement 'Caritas' after an initial purely instrumental introduction. Craft says that the final movement of Webern's Cantata op. 31 is particularly relevant because of the obvious influence it exerted on the composition of this canon. The wide intervals and the rhythmic approach are features characteristic of Webern, as is also the way in which Stravinsky has conceived the metrical articulation of each line in accordance with the independence of the canonic movement, which is that to be observed in performance, the joining of the four lines in the score by means of a bar-line being intended only for the convenience of the conductor.

But even here it must be said, as Craft himself says, that Webern's influence is exerted at the level of technical composition, but disappears as we proceed from the visible to the aural impression, thus proving once again, if proof were needed, that twelve-note technique does not necessarily dictate one particular style. Together with the pieces called 'Caritas' two other movements, 'Spes' and 'Fides', form a little three-part Cantata in the middle of the work, consisting of a dialogue between chorus and soloists interpolated between two choral canons. *Spes* is a sort of antiphonal chant in five phrases divided up among the tenor and baritone soloists and the two groups of female voices in the choir. In *Fides* 'the tribute to Faith prepares the ground for the drama of the succeeding episode for baritone and chorus, the soloist calling for the gift of faith in support of his unbelief' : 'Credo, Domine, adjuva incredulitatem meam'. Here Stravinsky's music is filled with an emotion as profound as it is restrained. The composer has concentrated wholly on that most dramatic and essential human theme, the painful choice between faith and doubt. The emotional significance of the passage is illustrated by the tremendous opening phrase sung by the baritone, unaccompanied by any of the instruments, in a free rhythm 'quasi rubato, con discrezione e non forte' :

This phrase is based on the crab form of the second series, transposed up a major second. It is an excellent example of the intensity of expression which can be attained when the extreme concentration and compactness of the melodic structure, enforced by the rules of serial writing which forbid the repetition of notes, is matched by a genuine, spontaneous creative urge. In this instance, every note has the greatest significance, every interval releases the utmost expressive intensity of which it is potentially capable. This piece marks perhaps one of the highest peaks of Stravinsky's creativeness and probably ranks as one of the great landmarks of dodecaphonic music – indeed of modern music in general.

Shortly after the *Canticum Sacrum ad honorem Sancti Marci Nominis*, Stravinsky transcribed Bach's chorale variations on the Christmas organ piece *Vom Himmel hoch da komm ich her* for choir and orchestra. Robert Craft, to whom the transcription is dedicated, says that Stravinsky wrote it to introduce the public to the least known of Bach's great contrapuntal works, which include the Goldberg Variations, the *Musical Offering* and the *Art of Fugue*. Bach was especially fond of the theme of these Variations; in addition to harmonizing it in the collection of Chorales, he used it again and again for his intricate contrapuntal compositions. The most important work based on it was written in 1746-7 and was later revised twice. It is included in the Bach-gesellschaft volume containing the organ works. The original manuscript bears the indication 'Per Canones à 2 clav. et Pedal'. In addition to the practical reason why Stravinsky transcribed the work, as pointed out by Craft, it seems to me that there is a more significant reason, bound up either with the particular stage of Stravinsky's music development or with the formal trends seen in his contemporary works, and particularly in the *Canticum Sacrum*. A strong indication of the relationship between the transcription of the Chorale Variations and the *Canticum*, which was written only a few months earlier, is the great similarity in orchestration. The only difference between the two works is that the transcription has a second flute, and the organ, bass trumpet, and double bass trombone are left out. Stravinsky evidently intended the two works to be performed together, and in fact he included the Variations in the programme of the concert at Venice, where the *Canticum* was performed for the very first time.

After so many alleged 'returns to Bach' this explicit approach to one of Bach's greatest works is particularly significant. The Chorale Variations are not a mere transcription[16] in the sense of a mere 'translation' of musical ideas from one set of timbres to another.

---

[16] In the course of his long career, Stravinsky has also made a number of transciptions in the strict sense of the word. Apart from those already mentioned here, several are worth noting; they came about mostly in connection with particular occasions or to meet practical needs: orchestration of Grieg's *Kobold* (1909); orchestration of Beethoven and Mussorgsky (*Song of the Flea*) (1910); arrangement of Tchaikovsky's ballet *The Sleeping Beauty* (1921) and *Pas de deux* (Bluebird) for chamber orchestra. Apart from the last-named none of the transcriptions mentioned have been published.

Nor is this work another example of 'music to the second power' such as he had often composed in the past, taking over ready-made musical ideas and subjecting them to a real process of 'phagocytosis' till they lost their original distinctive traits and took on the features of his own musical personality. To cite Craft again, Stravinsky's re-casting of Bach's chorale variations is unparalleled from the morphological standpoint.

No transcriber of his stature has attempted in the same degree to re-write what is not only a finished classical masterpiece, but also a monument of masterly counterpoint, and to do so stylistically, just as an architect re-moulding an older style re-fashions the entire style, which in the case of the musical composition in question means in part the content also; for while the new counterpoint derives from Bach's original, it introduces sounds extraneous to the harmonic style of the work itself. Moreover, Stravinsky's approach is definitely more dramatic than the abstract polyphony of the original, so that the character of the Bach-Stravinsky piece is different from that of Bach's composition. But even so, Stravinsky's attitude strikes one as more respectful towards Bach than the dead hand of reverence. He reveals himself, making no claims in the name of Bach; and far from merging the two composers, the transcription of *Vom Himmel hoch* appears as a new manifestation and a new musical revelation of both. It is a revelation at the highest spiritual level music can reach.[17]

Although the transcription of *Vom Himmel hoch* is in a sense out of keeping with this particular phase of Stravinsky's creative work, it reflects in more ways than one the composer's recent searchings. For evidence of this we have only to think of the isolated notes which Stravinsky has added to Bach's canon in the third Variation. They conceal yet another instance of Stravinsky's present predilection for Webern.

In contrast to this, the *Greetings Prelude: for the Eightieth Birthday of Pierre Monteux*[18] is linked with the aphoristic trend which for a time was very much in vogue among the composers of the Viennese school. It is a composition consisting of only thirty-two bars and lasting forty-five seconds. The characteristic structural

[17] *Translator's note:* This passage is translated from the Italian; the original English version was not available.
[18] The score published in 1956 by Boosey & Hawkes, London gives the date of composition of this piece as 1955. In *Stravinsky. A Complete Catalogue of His Published Works* (Boosey & Hawkes, June 1957) the date is given as 1956, and the title too is slightly changed: *Greetings Prelude.* Presumably the former date is the correct one, since Pierre Monteux' eightieth birthday was in 1955 – he was born on 4 April 1875. (There is a similar discrepancy in the dates as shown on the score and in the Boosey & Hawkes catalogue in the case of the *Canticum Sacrum.*) The date of the *Prelude* is confirmed, moreover, in *Themes and Episodes*, (p. 54), where Stravinsky says that the work 'Intended as a kind of singing telegram for the eightieth birthday of Pierre Monteux . . . was performed on that occasion, April 4, 1955, by Charles Munch and the Boston Symphony Orchestra.'

features, namely the application of certain typical serial devices to
diatonic material, place the *Greetings Prelude* in a category already
formed by works like Schoenberg's Suite for Strings and *Kol Nidre*,
Dallapiccola's *Sonatina canonica* and *Tartiniana*. In the *Greetings
Prelude*, the diatonic material is built up from the well-known tune
sung on the American continent to the birthday greeting 'Happy
birthday to you'. The 'differential' motifs which make up the short
theme are separated and expounded in accordance with Webern's
procedure of capillary differentiation of tone-colour. The row of
intervals making up the theme likewise goes through the regular
processes of serial variation; for example, between bars 16 and 20, the
second violins play the series retrograde.

   While he was engaged in composing the *Canticum Sacrum*, Stravinsky had photostat copies made of Gesualdo's *Sacrae cantiones*, published in Naples in 1603. In the last of the songs, 'Illumina nos', 'a
sette voci', the *sextus* and *bassus* parts are missing – most of the
part music of that time being kept only in the form of separate parts
and not in 'full score' form; and Stravinsky felt the urge to complete
the song by supplying new parts of his own.[19] He suggested the work
to the Venice Festival for performance at the concert at which his
Canticum Sacrum was to be played for the first time. But the Festival
authorities turned down the offer, on the grounds that Venice would
have nothing to do with a Neapolitan![20] Stravinsky therefore post-
poned the project and did not complete it until 1957, immediately
after finishing the ballet *Agon*, which he had been working on since
1954.

   In *Agon*, Stravinsky mostly follows the main lines of his recent
development. The musical world awaited this work with unusual
interest, if only because in it Stravinsky was returning, after an
interval of ten years (his previous work in choreographic form being
Orpheus, written in 1947) to the genre in which in the past he had
been regarded as most successful, namely the ballet. During those
ten years, Stravinsky had written music with a more and more
ascetic look, more introvert, more elevated and further removed
from any immediate relation with external phenomena. As regards

[19] Massimo Mila (*L'Espresso*, 17 November 1957, p. 3) very shrewdly establishes a link between Stravinsky's recent return to expressionism and his
admiration for Gesualdo, who was one of the most notable forerunners of the
musical expressionism of today.
[20] That at any rate is the reason cited in the preface to the score by
'Stravinsky's Californian Eckermann', as Lindlar calls Robert Craft. (In *A
Personal Preface* Craft describes himself as 'a kind of musical amanuensis to
Stravinsky'.)

form, he had carried out his gradual, methodical evolution towards the twelve-note system, as we have already seen; and it must be remembered that in that first decade, the twelve-note system had seemed to lead in practice to the conclusion that if there was not actually an incompatibility between the new technique and ballet music as such, the system was at any rate distinctly unsuitable for musical compositions designed to sustain and give life to choreographic action. Some critics, like Adorno, produced a 'theory of ballet music', bracketing it with Stravinsky's typical ballets and dubbing it a category antithetical to serial music. The masterly example of twelve-note ballet produced by Schoenberg as far back as 1932 – *The Dance of the Golden Calf* (the central section of Act II of *Moses and Aaron*) – should have been enough to show up the fallacy of any such allegation of incompatibility between twelve-note music and ballet. The trouble was, however, that until 1951 this Schoenberg masterpiece was completely unknown. And even today, the popular notion that dodecaphonic music is not a suitable medium for the dance has not altogether died out. Thus many people assumed that in *Agon* Stravinsky would retrace his steps. The very title of the work suggested a return to the period of Stravinsky's enthusiasm for Graeco-Roman subjects. In point of fact it would be quite wrong to regard *Agon* as forming the third part of a sort of mythological trilogy along with the neo-classical ballets *Apollo Musagetes* and *Orpheus*. The title '*Agon*' does not refer to any mythological subject, but denotes simply an abstract choreographic 'contest'.

The first performance of this 'contest' was given in concert form in Los Angeles on 17 July 1957, the eve of Stravinsky's seventy-fifth birthday. It was repeated in Italy on 21 October, in the presence of the composer, at the Accademia Filarmonica Romana. The first stage performance was given by Georges Balanchine on 1 December 1957 in New York with choreography compared by Stravinsky to one of Mondrian's abstractions. It would be equally incorrect to maintain that *Agon* has nothing in common with the series of neo-classical ballets from *Apollo Musagetes* via *A Card Game*, *Danses Concertantes*, and *Scènes de Ballet* to *Orpheus*. *Agon* is linked in more than one sense to these and other works of Stravinsky's so-called neo-classical period. There is no question of a return to neo-classicism, however, in the sense of straying from the path which had led Stravinsky to twelve-note music. The fact that we do find neo-classical elements in *Agon* simply means that certain aspects of his neo-

classicism, which for practical purposes had come to an end with
The Rake's Progress, were taken over by the composer in the new
technique he has now adopted, and constitute a further device to add
to those already embodied in the *Canticum Sacrum*. This is probably
what Robert Craft had in mind when he wrote[21] that *Agon* 'discovers
Stravinsky anew and gives a new unity to all his work'. However this
may be, in its fundamental stylistic structure, *Agon* certainly does not
represent a dead end or a turnabout in relation to the recent phase of
his evolution; in a sense it is a resumé of the various stages.

The work was begun in December 1953, i.e. before he wrote *In
Memoriam Dylan Thomas* and the *Canticum Sacrum*. After completing about two-fifths of the ballet, he stopped work on it to undertake the other two compositions. *Agon* was conceived in a diatonic,
modal style; but when Stravinsky started working on it again in
1956,[22] he already had behind him the experience of writing in the
twelve-note manner which we find in the middle section of the
Canticum, and he found it impossible to go back and continue *Agon*
on the formal plane on which he had begun it. The situation was
not unlike what had happened when he settled down to finish *The
Nightingale* after interrupting it to compose *Petrushka* and *The Rite
of Spring*. As we saw, in *The Nightingale* Stravinsky decided to
continue the composition in the new manner, without attempting
to adjust the idiom used in the earlier part to it. All he did on that
occasion was to give the work as a whole a homogeneous framework by repeating the 'Song of the Fisherman' at the end of each
part. Using a similar device of 'strategic repetition' in *Agon*, at the
end of the ballet, Stravinsky repeats the introductory Fanfare (the
piece written as long ago as 1953 and intended originally to be
played by three trombones) and the Prelude to the second part, in
the manner of two Interludes. But the relationship between this
seemingly diatonic framework and the serially organized material
which it frames is not one of mere juxtaposition. In the case of the
older parts of *The Nightingale*, Stravinsky must have felt that it was
impossible to equate them with the experience gained in writing
The Rite of Spring; they must either be left as they were or suppressed. Actually, after taking them as they stood into the stage
version he suppressed them (with the exception of the 'Song of the

[21] 'A Personal Preface', *The Score*, p. 13.
[22] The precise dates on which the individual parts of *Agon* were composed
are given by Craft in '*Ein Ballett für zwölf Tänzer*', *Melos*, October 1957,
p. 284 et seq.

Fisherman') in his later version of *The Nightingale* as a symphonic poem. In the case of the initial pieces written for *Agon*, he recast them in such a way that without changing their original diatonic-modal flavour he was able to link them organically with the new works he was writing in accordance with his personal approach to the use of serial twelve-note technique.

Craft tells us that the Fanfare, which Stravinsky first thought of in 1953, was enlarged and revised in the following year and then changed again when the whole work was finished. The main difference lies in the instrumentation; in the first revised version the trumpets were only accompanied by the harp, and in the second section, instead of a mandolin, there was a guitar. While the changes are largely instrumental it seems likely that Stravinsky also changed something of the intrinsic structure of the pieces in question. Where he did not do so it is a fair assumption that he considered the musical ideas, as originally conceived, to be capable of inducing a musical language which would merge organically into the dodeca-phonic pattern of the various pieces he had it in mind to compose. Stravinsky fashioned this language so that it presented a sort of epitome and synthesis of the stages of his development from the consciously archaic diatonic manner of the Cantata to the dodeca-phonic serial writing of the *Canticum Sacrum*.

The Fanfare, or Pas de quatre (when the curtain goes up four male dancers are lined up in a row, up-stage, with their backs to the audience) is definitely modal at the beginning. The literary subject of the Cantata was in the English tradition, but here from the very start, the peculiar method of orchestration is distinctly French, recalling the dance music at the Court of Burgundy and at the Parisian Court of Louis XIII and Louis XIV. In fact, Craft tells us that all the pieces in *Agon* were designed on the basis of examples given in a French manual of dancing instruction dating from the middle of the seventeenth century; and Stravinsky says that one of the illustrations in this manual, showing two trumpeters playing the accompaniment of a *bransle simple* gave him the idea of using this combination for his own *Bransle simple*.

By analogy with the so-called 'hautes et basses danses', fourteenth- and fifteenth-century literary works referred to 'musique haute et basse' and 'hauts et bas instruments'. The 'high' and 'low' designated the groups of accompanying instruments and these groups could consist of stringed or wind instruments or combinations such as lute, harp, and drum. In *Agon* this group consists of mandolin, harp, piano, and percussion, and the whole orchestral structure of the work reveals a concern for balanced groups of timbres. In the Pas de quatre this concern enhances the peculiar structure of the piece, which is divided into three sections, each with its special quality of timbre. In the first section the trumpets and horns are accompanied by piano, strings, and harp; in the second section, the flourish in the brass is offset by the harp, mandolin, cellos and double basses. The melodic figure on which the musical discourse of the first section is based:

appears here in an inverted variant.

In the first section, in addition to the notes, B, A, C, and D of the melodic figure, we get four other notes: G, F, E, and F sharp. In the second section C sharp and G sharp are added to these. The remaining two notes – B flat and D sharp – needed to make up the chromatic entity appear in the third section, played by the flutes, clarinets, trombones, and harps. Here (bars 26-30 of the score) Stravinsky seems to be setting forth as it were in paradigm form the feasible relationship between the polydiatonic style characteristic of him and out-and-out chromaticism.

Actually, in this section the chromatic sum of the musical design is found by adding together the diatonic differentials. Each individual instrument gravitates round a different 'pole' or tonal centre: the flutes round G; the harp round B flat; the first tenor trombone is in B while the second fluctuates between C and D flat; the clarinets play G minor and A major respectively. The passages for the clarinets, trombones, and harp consist of series of intervals, in original form and *cancrizans*. Before the end of the piece, the diatonic motif in the example quoted above undergoes a chromatic change:

which paves the way for the chromaticism of the second piece, Double Pas-de-quatre, danced by eight dancers.

This piece is divided into two parts and has the vital, exciting quality of the Rossini-like passages in *A Card Game*. In the first part, the woodwind and strings gradually introduce the twelve different notes in the following order:

One after another, the close chromatic intervals recall the basic chromatic motif of *In Memoriam Dylan Thomas*. At a given moment a motif is introduced, accompanied by a fluttering effect in the flutes and trumpets:

If we suppose that the note D has the function of a pedal throughout the piece, this motif can be related to the hexachordal cluster:

This very series of six different notes is used in the second part of the Double Pas-de-quatre. It is first stated by the flutes, in transposition:

A solo violin plays the inversion:

The flutes end the piece with a figure fashioned out of the crab inversion:

In the Triple Pas-de-quatre, danced by the eight female dancers and four males, i.e. the entire cast, the principal motifs of the Double Pas-de-quatre are presented mostly in their mirror variants. Stravinsky himself describes this piece as an 'imitation' of the other.

As in the preceding pieces, we find that in the Prelude, which is a sort of introduction to the first Pas-de-trois, we get a kind of lightening of the archaic flavour of the diatonic material by chromatic treatment. First of all the timpani and a single bassoon play a reiterated B flat and D flat respectively. Solo flutes and cellos then repeat a pattern consisting of the notes C – which the trumpet keeps repeating – and D, F, G, B. Then gongs and bassoon introduce the G flat. After a few bars the trumpet plays the E and A, and the bassoon and gong complete the chromatic scheme by playing the E flat. Within this formal framework there is a slow march in 3/4 time in which, as in the initial Fanfare, Craft finds curious and unexpected analogies with the atmosphere of *El Retablo de Maese Pedro*, although he does not suggest that Stravinsky is influenced by Falla. But even if such an influence really could be traced, it would merely mean a further widening of the span of Stravinsky's synthesis, which positively does not exclude any aspect of musical life, past or present.

In the first Pas-de-trois for male and female dancer, Stravinsky definitely steps out of the diatonic into the dodecaphonic realm. This Pas-de-trois consists of three different dances. The first, Saraband-Step, is danced by the male dancer. Instrumentally, the music consists of a solo for violin accompanied by xylophone and three trombones (except for two very short phrases for the cello). The second dance is a Gaillarde for two female dancers, in the form of a canon, followed by the inversion of the canon, played by the harp and mandolin supported freely by the flute and accompanied by the piano, timpani, viola, three cellos, and two solo double basses. The combination produces some exquisite chiaroscuro effects. In the opinion of Massimo Mila[23] the Gaillarde, 'so sensuous and so attractive with the Don Juanesque embellishments of the mandolin . . . is the most sensuous piece in *Agon*'.

Although he points out the difference in outlook between works like the Gaillarde and the later dodecaphonic pieces, Mila agrees that 'the disparities in structural technique do not imply any internal disparity . . .' Hence 'there is no real incongruity between the first part of *Agon* and the other two. The entire work belongs essentially to the later Stravinsky . . . who has discovered the means of expression required in serial technique'.[24]

The Coda, for one male and two female dancers, is based on the following note-row:

The chromatic look of this series and the number of intervals of a second bear a marked resemblance to the succession quoted on page 201. It is stated in inversion form in the first six bars. The harp and solo cello divide up the statement of the series between them, over a pedal held by the trumpets and mandolin, and play two notes at a time, the intervals of a second changing to alternate ninths and octaves. The inversion is repeated no less than nine times as the accompaniment to a new violin solo. The flutes and the mandolin execute a pattern derived from the original form of the series, while the crab and crab inversion are based on the four chords of the final cadence. First an Interlude, which is a varied repeat of the Prelude, leads on to the second Pas-de-trois for two male dancers and one female. This section is divided into the three Bransles already mentioned – Bransle simple (two dancers); Bransle gay (ballerina); and Bransle de Poitou (two male dancers and one female). The first Bransle is a strict canon treatment of the row of six notes:

---

[23] *L'Espresso*, Rome, 27 October 1957, p. 15.
[24] ibid.

The second too is based on a hexachordal series:

which is related to the series quoted in the second example on page 201 by its intervals of fourths and fifths. The main points of interest in this piece, however, are the curious polyrhythmic effect resulting from the contrapuntal relationship between the ostinato figure in 3/8 played throughout the piece by the castanets, and the asymmetrical patterns in 7/16 and 5/16 played by the flutes and bassoons. The third Bransle is structurally the most complex part of the whole work. The dodecaphonic series on which this Bransle is based:

is made up of the sum of the series of six notes shown in the first example and a second group of six notes which is nothing more than a permutation and transposition one tone down of the hexachordal series of the second Bransle. Furthermore, this latter six-note group is identical with the 'flattened' crab variation of the six-note series on which the Septet (cf. the first example on page 178) is based. Stravinsky uses the series quoted in the example above, either in its complete dodecaphonic form, and its mirror variants, or in its hexachordal dichotomy, i.e. regarding the two sets of six notes as independent series. In addition, he also uses the device of permutation. Thus, for example, in the passage between bar 347 and bar 351, the violas and cellos play a figure consisting of the first three notes of each hexachord followed by the second three notes of each hexachord to produce the following dodecaphonic cluster:

A further reprise of the Prelude as an Interlude leads on to a Pas-de-deux for male and female dancers, divided into an Adagio, two Variations, a Refrain, Coda, and Stretta. The ballet ends with four Duos (for male and female dancers) and four Trios (for one male and two female dancers) followed without interruption by a final repeat of the Fanfare. I do not propose to analyse in detail the structure of this part of the work. All that need be said is that it is based for the most part on another series in which the favourite interval is a major or augmented minor second:

though the Variations and the Refrain for male dancer use only an eight-note series:

The dodecaphonic serial writing becomes more and more strict, so much so that in the Adagio we find definite instances of the influence of Webern's Symphony, and in the four Duos there are unmistakable reminiscences of Webern's Quartet, op. 28. In the Duos, the music seems to have been reduced to a structural pattern pure and simple, a conventional catalogue of abstract serial modules. The violas and cellos begin with a statement of the series as shown in the example quoted immediately above, in crab inversion, with inexpressive pizzicato effects and a uniform rhythmic beat:

They then play the original form of the same series. The trombones, livening up the rhythm only slightly with a few syncopations, play

the crab variant, which is immediately taken up by the strings. These again reduce the rhythm to a dead level, and continue, with the same dull, inexorable metronomic movement, to churn out the notes of the inversion. The trombones make an attempt to bring some rhythmic life to the repeat of the crab inversion, but the repeat of the inversion by the strings immediately cancels out every trace of differentiation of metre. In the whole piece there is no counterpoint, no harmony to give a second dimension to the abstract line formed by the succession of the twelve notes, the twelve musical 'dots' plotted in accordance with the four main formulas of serial writing.

In the light of the utterly monodic nature of the piece, the very title 'four Duos' seems paradoxical, unless we try to imagine the uniformity of the musical thread as the abstract symbol of the unity of the individual couples. Passages like these invite the sort of criticism that Adorno[25] levelled at some of Webern's works, where he feels that the composer has given up the idea of 'composing' in the sense of a personal creative effort and has simply indulged in the mechanical, impersonal jotting down of lifeless serial formulas. On the other hand, these passages may remind some listeners of certain late works of Beethoven,[26] where we find the most daring of form and content side by side with the frequent use of more conventional formulas, which in their context have an extraordinary privative function – we feel that they are used to rid the score of every vestige of the dramatic, making it almost apathetic and giving it a sense of the sublime and of liberation from all earthly passion. Craft feels that Stravinsky might have written the same words on his score as Beethoven wrote on the Lento of the Quartet in A Minor, the comparison referring more than anything else to the composer's inner need which had led him to submit to a special creative pattern, overcoming the impulses more natural to him in order to carry out a task beyond the range of his own subjective feelings.

[25] op. cit., p. 73.
[26] Adorno draws a parallel between the function of the conventional elements in late Beethoven and the twelve-note system. ibid., pp. 78-80.

XXI Threni: Stravinsky's first Completely Twelve-Note Work

The end of the final chapter of the original edition of this book reads as follows: 'There is no telling what will be the latest development in Stravinsky's personal manner of applying dodecaphonic technique. But we can agree with Craft that "whatever Stravinsky does will be of the utmost importance for every composer who uses serial technique, and will help to put the hall-mark on their achievements".[1] He will undoubtedly continue to employ in the service of musical unity the incomparable power of synthesis which has long been recognized. Indeed as long ago as 1932, that very perspicacious critic H. H. Stuckenschmidt called one of his essays "Stravinsky or the Fusion of the Infusible". If this was an apt title for the works written in the first third of the century, it is decidedly more to the point when applied to the works of the most recent period of Stravinsky's career. Information supplied to the author of this book by Stravinsky himself as to his future plans suggests that the orbit within which his power of synthesis operates is likely to expand even further, structurally as well as musically and poetically. We shall see the proof of this when Stravinsky finishes the work begun in Italy in the summer of 1957, and almost completed by January 1958, Threni – id est Lamentationes Jeremiae Prophetae. This work was conceived as a Leçon de Ténèbres and carries on and develops in a grammatical sense the tendency firmly and vigorously established in his previous works, particularly the Canticum Sacrum and Agon. At the same time, the spiritual theme of Threni is still further evidence of Stravinsky's peculiarly religious nature.'

This prophecy was amply fulfilled. The Lamentationes were written in the spring of 1958; the score bears the date 21 March. The work was commissioned by the Norddeutscher Rundfunk, Hamburg, to which it is dedicated. It was given its first performance in Venice on 23 September 1958 in the hall of the Scuola Grande di

[1] 'A Personal Preface', The Score, p. 13.

San Rocco during the Twenty-first International Festival of Contemporary Music, at a concert in memory of the Director of the Festival, the late Alessandro Piovesan. In Stravinsky's career as an artist, *Threni* represents a culminating point, and it is important both spiritually and stylistically. It is without any doubt the most ambitious and structurally the most complex of all his religious works. In *Conversations with Igor Stravinsky* (p. 123) Craft leads Stravinsky on to make a statement as to his aspirations regarding the 'Lamentations' as a religious work. The statement is so significant in relation to what has already been said here about Stravinsky and religious music that I should like to quote the passage in its entirety.

R.C. 'Your *Mass*, *Canticum Sacrum* and *Threni* are the strongest challenges in two hundred years to the decline of the Church as a musical institution.'

I.S. 'I wish they were effective challenges. I had hoped my *Mass* would be used liturgically, but I have no such aspiration for the *Threni*, which is why I call it not *Tenebrae Service*, but *Lamentations*.

'Whether or not the Church was the wisest patron – though I think it was; we commit fewer musical sins in Church – it was rich in musical forms. How much poorer we are without the sacred musical services, without the Masses, the Passions, the round-the-calendar cantatas of the Protestants, the motets and Sacred Concerts, and Vespers and so many others. These are not merely defunct forms but parts of the musical spirit in disuse.

'The Church knew what the Psalmist knew: music praises God. Music is as well or better able to praise Him than the building of the church and all its decoration; it is the Church's greatest ornament. Glory, glory, glory; the music of Orlando Lassus's motet praises God, and this particular "glory" does not exist in secular music. And not only glory, though I think of it first because the glory of the Laudate, the joy of the Doxology, are all but extinct, but prayer and penitence and many others cannot be secularized. The spirit disappears with the form. I am not comparing "emotional range" or "variety" in sacred and secular music. The music of the nineteenth and twentieth centuries – it is all secular – is "expressively" and "emotionally" beyond anything in the music of the earlier centuries: the *Angst* in *Lulu*, for instance (gory, gory, gory), or the tension, the perpetuation of the moment of epitasis, in Schoenberg's music. I say, simply, that without the Church, "left to our own devices", we are poorer by many musical forms.

'When I call the nineteenth century "secular" I mean by it to distinguish between religious religious music and secular religious music. The latter is inspired by humanity in general, by art, by *Übermensch*, by goodness, and by goodness knows what. Religious music without religion is almost always vulgar. It can also be dull. There is dull church music from Hucbald to Haydn, but not vulgar church music. (Of course there is vulgar church music now, but it is not really of or for the church. I hope, too, that my sacred music is a protest against the Platonic tradition, which has been the Church's tradition through Plotinus and Erigena, of music as anti-moral. Of course Lucifer had music. Ezekiel refers to his "tabrets and pipes" and Isaiah to the "noise of his viols". But Lucifer took his music with him from Paradise, and even in Hell, as Bosch shows music is able to represent Paradise and become the "bride of the cosmos".

'It has been corrupted by musicians, is the Church's answer, the Church whose musical history is a series of attacks against polyphony, the true musical expression of Western Christendom, until music retires from it in the eighteenth century or confounds it with the theatre. The corrupting musicians Bosch means are probably Josquin and Ockeghem, the corrupting artifacts the polyphonic marvels of Josquin, Ockeghem, Compère, Brumel.'

R.C. 'Must one be a believer to compose in these forms?'

I.S. 'Certainly, and not merely a believer in "symbolic figures", but in the Person of the Lord, the Person of the Devil, and the Miracles of the Church.'

'The music which comes from Paradise and is able to represent Paradise and become the bride of the Cosmos' : thus, in connection with *Threni*, Stravinsky has set forth in an absolutely explicit and downright manner the ontological concept of music we have seen emerging slowly and gradually in his earlier compositions and writings. Is it a pure coincidence that in a formal sense too, *Threni* represents the end of the road as far as his development is concerned, with the unqualified, wholesale adoption of twelve-note technique? The question has still more point if we bear in mind the metaphysical implications of the dodecaphonic theory, and I should be the last to say no, having striven for years to throw light on these implications, though with all due circumspection and in full awareness of the limits and dangers of such attempts. Whatever the truth of the matter, *Threni* marks a step forward in advance of the *Canticum*, where we saw – as in *Agon* too – that the twelve-note passages were lumped together with non-dodecaphonic passages constructed on serial principles or built up quite freely. In addition, the dodecaphonic-serial forms could be referred to a number of basic schemes, whereas in *Threni* the whole framework is based from beginning to end on a single twelve-note cluster which is discernible as early as bar 18, the first eighteen bars being in the nature of an introductory statement :

In the opening phrase (bars 1-5) the woodwinds and strings trace figures based mainly on the harsh, taut intervals of augmented octave, minor ninth (bars 1 and 2), and major seventh (bar 5), and in marked contrast with this we get the cold, open fifths of bars 3 and 4, while the accents, acciaccaturas and pauses give the whole passage a plastic, almost tangible expressive force, like a series of groans and deep sighs. Thus the formal exposition coincides with the artistic exposition of the work. This opening phrase implies the intimate junction of the following succession of twelve different notes:

They are, of course, two variants of the same series, the second
inverted. However, when I analysed the work from the proofs which
Stravinsky sent me so that I could write the programme note for
Threni for the Venice Festival, I found it impossible to make out
which of the versions of the series should be regarded as the original,
for the simple reason that they appear simultaneously from the
outset. Stravinsky explained to me later that the first thematic idea
for the entire work had no connection with either of the two series
quoted, but consisted of the phrase (bars 6-18) in which the soprano
soloist announces the beginning of the *Lamentations of the Prophet
Jeremiah*. The serial pattern implicit in this phrase is:

Stravinsky bases the entire work on this series, so that it can really
be called the 'original series'. This explanation on the part of
Stravinsky is important, in my opinion, not so much in regard to
the identification of the series (in fact Stravinsky suggested that I
should stress the mutual relationship between the various basic
forms of the serial cluster rather than the question of which came
first) as indicating the spontaneity and the thematic concreteness of
the musical idea on which the work is built up. At any rate, if we
take the series quoted above as being the original form, the two
mentioned first will be the crab (C_1) and crab inversion (CI_7),
respectively,[2] transposed a tritone. While the soprano sings the motif
embodying the original series, the alto soloist also presents the
beginning of the Lamentation on a melodic line based on the inversion of the row:

[2] The subscript numbers following the symbols of the various serial forms
refer to the number of notes of the (descending) chromatic scale in the
interval of the transposition.

At the same time the instruments interweave the crab (C_1), the crab transposed down a minor third (C_4), the crab inversion (CI) and the crab inversion transposed down a major sixth (CI_{10}).

The series quoted, and their transpositions by a third and a tritone, play an extremely important part in the construction of the musical fabric of the whole work, even though, as we shall see, Stravinsky not only makes liberal use of other transpositions of the original series and its variants, but distils from it also quite a number of different serial patterns obtained by a process of permutation.

An examination, however perfunctory, of the tonal potentialities inherent in the 'raw material' used by Stravinsky for the composition of *Threni* at once throws light on the peculiar method by which he conceives twelve-note writing tonally. For example, if we look first of all at the original series itself and its possible combinations with the other forms derived from it, we find that the group of notes resulting from the superimposition of the first five notes on the first five notes of the inversion (cf. the first vocal entry) contains no notes other than those which (using the enharmonic equivalents, of course) belong to the tonality of G sharp minor (melodic minor ascending). From the sixth to the eleventh notes, the original series comprises six notes proper to the scale of C major, while the scale is complete if we add to these six notes the segment of the inversion from the fifth to the ninth notes. If we study the harmonic effect of the superimposition of the O, I, C_4 and CI_{10} forms, we find that apart from the D sharp which is common to all four forms of the series, and the A (sixth note of O and I and third note of C_4 and CI_{10}), the two-note chords A sharp-G sharp, B-G, F-C sharp, E-D, C-F sharp, recur constantly in both the O-I and the C_4-CI_{10} combinations. Furthermore, the four-note chord F (or E sharp)-G sharp-B flat (or A sharp)-C sharp is sounded by both the fourth and fifth notes of the individual series:

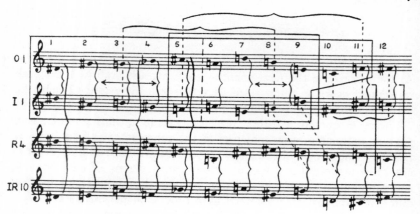

All these and indeed many other elements resulting from various superimpositions which I do not propose to investigate at this point, though it would certainly be most revealing to analyse them, could very well be thought of as nuclei of a closely-woven, solid tonal fabric. It must not be imagined, of course, that Stravinsky uses these elements naïvely, to produce a harmonic texture and tonal relationship akin to the devices handed down by the eighteenth- and nineteenth-century composers. Far from it – even more than in his previous works, the synthesis he achieves with simple ingredients is quite complex. In this respect, the stylistic thread which we have pointed out time after time as running through all this work is still there – and so is the diatonic flavour culled from the elements he is synthesizing. What is new, as far as Stravinsky is concerned, is the fact that these elements are no longer tonally heterogeneous, but are given a unity by the serialism. Indeed, one wonders whether Stravinsky does not provide a more satisfactory answer than either Berg or even Schoenberg to the question asked in the latter's *Harmonielehre*, namely whether the manner in which the new sounds are inter-related does not constitute in fact the tonality of a twelve-note series. Who knows but that this may turn out to be the special contribution which Stravinsky, with his special personal characteristics and musical sensibility, has to make to the history of twelve-note music. However this may be, these few analytical notes may help to explain how we are to understand Stravinsky's statement quoted in Chapter XX to the effect that the intervals of his series 'are attracted by tonality' and that he composes vertically, since he hears 'harmonically, as he has always done'. When we listen to

Threni, which is after all a one hundred per cent. dodecaphonic, serial work, we get the feeling of a composition governed by the tonal and modal sensibility characteristic of all Stravinsky's works from his early years of maturity onwards. Thus starting with the Introduction, the form, the expression, and the ideas it contains are presented with the utmost lucidity. The extreme complexity of the writing is transformed into a plastic simplicity of utterance, and the incredible subtlety of the formal structure appears as a model of architectonic clarity. At the same time, the very personal rhythmic devices and accents, and the unique manner of playing on the transpositions and concatenations of serial formulas – not so as to get rid of tonal relations but rather to achieve a novel and still more subtle tonal polarization of the chromatic scale – stamp every page with Stravinsky's unmistakable hallmark. This applies even to the passages that look so like Webern in the printed score, and to those based on devices ranging from the serial extrapolation technique used with conspicuous success by Alban Berg in *Lulu* to serial segmentation and permutation introduced by Schoenberg as far back as 1933 in the *Three Songs*, op. 48, but only now being developed properly by the younger post-Webern *avant-garde* composers.

Stravinsky assimilates all these devices and manipulates them, enriching them in a way which it is impossible to define without a minute analysis altogether beyond the purpose and the scope of this book. The important point is to recognize the extraordinary nobility and the admirably dignified quality of the entire work.

For the singing and playing of the *Lamentations*, Stravinsky has used vocal and instrumental forces on a more ambitious scale than in his previous works for orchestra and chorus. The vocal requirements consist of a large mixed choir and six soloists (soprano, contralto, first and second tenors, first and second basses) supplemented from time to time by other voices (second contralto and third bass) taken from the choir. The orchestral ensemble differs from the ordinary symphony orchestra in that there are no bassoons or trumpets, but instead there are less orthodox instruments such as alto clarinet, bugle, and sarrusophone.[3] Apart from these there are two flutes, two oboes, cor anglais, two clarinets, bass clarinet, four horns, three trombones, tuba, pianoforte, harp, celeste, gong, timpani, and strings. Stravinsky's use of all these instrumental resources

---

[3] For the performance in Venice the sarrusophone part was divided between two contra-bassoons. The part proved to be too difficult for the sarrusophone players engaged by the Hamburg orchestra.

creates a tremendous variety of both homogeneous and contrasting timbres, without at any time using all of them together to achieve a shattering 'tutti' effect. Here again is an instance of the sobriety with which he puts into the mouth of the Prophet, in the deserted streets of Jerusalem, bitter sighs and groans of the lamentation for the people of Israel held captive by Nebuchadnezzar.

The *Lamentations of Jeremiah* are of course a separate book of the Old Testament, coming after the prophecies. The whole book consists of five poems, or more precisely, 'Elegies' – the term used in the Vulgate text set by Stravinsky. The *Lamentations* form part of both the ritual of the Jewish synagogue and the services of the Catholic Church, where they are sung on certain occasions during Holy Week such as the 'Tenebrae' on Maundy Thursday and Good Friday, and the Easter Saturday Matins. The Church does not use the Elegies in their entirety, and similarly, fragments only have been used by the various composers who have set the *Lamentations* – Palestrina, Pierre de la Rue, Claudin de Sermisy, Carpentras, Lassus, Morales, Victoria, Ingegneri, Nanino, Couperin, and others. But whereas the Church uses fragments of all five Elegies, Stravinsky has set to music fragments of only the first, third, and fifth in the Latin text of the Vulgate – hence the subtitles of the three parts of the work. On the other hand, he has followed the Church ecclesiastical usage by keeping one structural feature of the original text, namely the Hebrew letters which link the *Lamentations* with the alphabetical acrostic: each strophe begins with one of the twenty-two letters of the Hebrew alphabet, from Aleph to Thau (except for the third Elegy, where the same letters are repeated three times, and the fifth, which omits them). The purpose of these letters in ancient times was to provide an eminently easy way of ensuring that the texts had not been tampered with in the process of transmission, orally or in writing; but even among the Jews, it began to be looked on as a test of the poet's skill to be able to take this utilitarian device and incorporate it into his poem.

From the first Elegy ('Jerusalem humiliata et derelicta') Stravinsky has chosen several groups of short verses each designated by a letter of the Hebrew alphabet: Group 1 (Aleph); group 2 (Beth) – omitting the last four verses; group 5 (He), likewise omitting the last two verses; group 11 (Caph), omitting the first four verses; and group 20 (Res). The names of the Hebrew letters are sung by the choir in a brief interjection, the repeat in a variant breaking up the composition so that the individual sections correspond to the various sets of verses. Thus the five sets of verses have their counterpart in the five sections of the musical composition. The first, third and fifth are parallel, having the same musical structure. At the beginning the text is recited *sotto voce* by the whole choir, supported by long instrumental pedals. It is then sung by the first tenor soloist, with bugle accompaniment and a counterpoint of women's voices supported by the strings playing tremolo. The second and fourth sections (Diphona I and II) are in two-part counterpoint (first and second tenors, solo) *a cappella*. The musical form of the second part also (De Elegia tertia) is composed strictly in accordance with the text, and like the latter, it is sub-divided into three parts: 1. 'Querimonia', 2. 'Sensus spei', 3. 'Solacium'. Each part has as many sections as it contains sets of verses, set to music. In the text each set of verses is divided into three sub-groups, the Hebrew letter being repeated before each. Consequently, each section of the music likewise consists of three parts, separated by the interjection of the appropriate letter of the Hebrew alphabet. In 'Querimonia', the interpolation of the letter consists each time of one or two bars sung by the female voices of the choir, accompanied by three trombones, the verses being sung by the male voices only. After each of the three interjections on Aleph, the second basso profundo sings a melodic passage – 'Monodia'. After each of the three interpolations on Beth, the first tenor and the second bass sing a two-part canon. The first tenor and the first and second basses sing a three-part canon after each of the interjections on Vau. Finally, the first and second tenors and the first and second basses follow up each choral interpolation on Zain with a double four-part canon. In the second part, 'Sensus spei', the expression of hope, the declaiming of the Hebrew letters by the soloists and choir alternately, with the support of different instrumental groups, produces a series of pedals in triplets on twelve different notes reproducing the crab in version of the fundamental note-row transposed a minor third down. Over these pedals, soloists and choir take turns singing the verses Heth, Teth, Lamed, Nun, Samech, Ain, Tsade, and Coph, producing other serial forms. Thus the series comes to govern even the spatial and temporal arrangement of the patterns derived from it, and to some extent even the shape of the transpositions, infusing life into a typically serial form which is utterly independent of traditional polyphony, let alone sonata form. In other words, this piece is, if not the first, at any rate a significant example of the new forms emerging in strict, organic adherence to the spirit of serial technique.

The third part, 'Solacium', the expression of solace, is parallel in form with the first part, 'Querimonia': each of the nine inter-jections – three on Res(h), three on Sin and three on Thau – is followed by a different canonic counterpoint. Here too, as in the third Elegy, we find a penchant for the use of serial forms in permutation and segmentation of the most varied kind. One passage of unusual interest as far as the permutation device is concerned is that on the words 'Audisti opprobrium meum Domine' following the first interpolation on Sin:

Here the first tenor sings a melody which contains the notes of the crab inversion (CI₇) of the basic row 1-3-5-7-9-11-12-10-8-6-4-2 (i.e. missing out every other note in a forward direction and continuing in the same way from the end back to the beginning). At the same time the first bass unfolds the inversion of this permutation pattern, while the horns, and on the last two notes the strings, divide up among them with a kind of pointilliste effect a series deduced from the original *cancrizans*, in the following order: 1-4-7-10-2-5-8-11-3-7-9-12 (i.e. skipping two notes each time and repeating the performance twice in the same direction).

The sets of verses which Stravinsky has set to music from the fifth Elegy, the title of which – 'Oratio Jeremiae Prophetae' – is sung as a sort of introduction by the two bass soloists – are nos. 1, 19, and 21. This Elegy differs from the others, as already mentioned, in that the text is not broken up by the Hebrew characters. Neverthe-less, here too Stravinsky establishes a certain parallelism of structure with the first Elegy by giving the instruments alone the interjections which come before the first and second sets of verses, the words being divided between the choir, speaking *sotto voce*, and the soloists singing. Then all the voices, solo and chorus, join in singing the words 'Converte nos, Domine, et convertemur, innova dies nostros, sicut a principio', to the accompaniment of the horns. To begin with (bars 405-411) the four parts of the chorus, joined one after the other by the four solo voices, are accompanied by the first and third horns (except for an occasional plucking of the harp), forming a fabric of six individual strands implying six serial forms (CI_{10} and CI_5 played by the horns or harp, and O_1, C_1, I_1 and CI_7 in the vocal parts). From bar 412 to bar 417, where the second and fourth horns enter, two further strands are added to the web of sound, bringing it up to eight separate parts. Thus we get the simultaneous presentation of the series I_1, C_4, O_{10} and CI_7 by the horns and C_1, O_1, CI_1 and I_7 by the voices, all the notes of these series, especially the sung notes, being divided up among the various voices in an intricate pattern of criss-crossing. As far as structural complexity and polyphonic cohesion are concerned, this passage is the climax of the whole work. But far from being the peak of expressive intensity, it is actually the most relaxed, a moment of sublime dynamic calm. Stravinsky here carries to its ultimate conclusion the possibility, pointed out in connection with the analysis of the structure of *Threni*, of achieving tonal polarization of the twelve-note scale by adding together the diatonic implications of the various series. Thus the work ends on a note of solemn, humble prayer, which the instruments bring to a close after the words 'sicut a principio' with a 'perfect' consonance, as if to symbolize arrival at the final resting-place where all turbulence of spirit is soothed and dispersed.

One further remark is called for. It has to do with Stravinsky's orchestration, and is connected with what was said in Chapter VII concerning the curiously chamber-music-like conception of instrumental writing which crept into Stravinsky's work in the period following the composition of *The Rite of Spring*. In that connection I wrote: 'Before refashioning (the Wagnerian orchestra), Stravinsky seems to have felt the need to take it to pieces completely and fit it together again bit by bit.' Once Stravinsky had achieved this and returned to the use of the regular orchestra with *Oedipus Rex*, his instrumental writing 'bears the mark of his experience with "individualized" groups and with the analytical approach' (see p. 103) used in the chamber works written after *The Rite of Spring*. But though he introduced innovations in the use of instruments and his orchestration was frequently unorthodox (as in the *Symphony of Psalms*, where the violins and violas are replaced by two pianos), he did not tamper with the traditional relationship of the instruments of the orchestra. This is quite evident from the very look of the scores, where the various instruments appear for the most part in the sequence ordinarily adopted since the early days of classical symphonic music. Even in *Threni*, this general order is observed in many instances, though there are considerable departures from it in certain passages. In the 'Sensus spei' piece, for example (bar 217), where the first pedal, on the word 'Lamed', starts on E, the arrangement of the various vocal and instrumental parts in the score is changed completely, and instead of the usual sequence we get odd and unexpected juxtapositions of voices and instruments. The flute and first and second horn parts are next to the choral staves; the first tenor is bracketed with the alto and bass clarinets; the second bass is placed alongside the piano and the timpani. This grouping obviously has a formal significance; it seems fairly clear that the aim is to indicate even on paper the peculiar disposition of the musical strands by groups of timbres with which Stravinsky achieves novel orchestral and vocal effects. This picking out of small groups of selected tone colour from the orchestral mass is still more noticeable in a work which Stravinsky began even before the first performance of the *Lamentations of Jeremiah*. I discussed this work with him personally in Venice during the rehearsals of *Threni* in September 1958. He then thought of entitling the work 'Concerto for Pianoforte and Groups of Instruments'. But eventually (as we shall see in the next chapter) he decided to call it *Movements*.

Stravinsky wrote a short piece in memory of Prince Max Egon zu Fürstenberg, the generous patron of the Donaueschingen Festival. Each of the three concerts included in the 1959 Festival began with a 'tombeau' composed by Pierre Boulez, Wolfgang Fortner, and Igor Stravinsky respectively. Stravinsky's piece, which is called *Epitaphium für das Grabmal des Prinzen Max Egon zu Fürstenberg*, is something new in musical aphorism : it is only seven bars long and lasts about fifty seconds. The music consists of a twelve-note series in linear exposition (except in the sixth bar, where the exposition is double). The piece is written for three instruments : a harp, which plays the first, third, fifth, and seventh bars, and flute and clarinet playing a duet in the remaining bars. The atmosphere of the piece is that of priestly ritual.

Incidentally, this trend towards a structural reorganization of the orchestral body on Stravinsky's part coincides with a similar outlook among the *avant-garde* followers of Webern, cf. Boulez's work *Doubles* and Stockhausen's piece for three orchestras (in actual fact three orchestral groups). Let us refrain from raising the question of precedent or of influences in this connection. Craft somewhere mentions an episode which seems to me to hit the nail on the head. It seems that some time ago, Aaron Copland said that Stravinsky had influenced three succeeding generations of American composers. He now feels that 'three' should read 'four', and the fourth applies also to Europe. The reason why Stravinsky has been a source of inspiration for so many musicians is of course because he himself drank deep from every new source. His capacity for assimilation was part and parcel of his capacity for development. It is rare to find so receptive an outlook in an artist of seventy-five, an artist who yet remained faithful to his own style. Stravinsky undergoes influences, absorbs influences, and transmits influences. Further proof that the adoption of serial technique on Stravinsky's part was not a mere passive gesture, which shows how far his experience in his earlier works helped to crystallize the theory of total serial writing, is to be found in Antoine Goléa's book on Boulez : [4]

... Only three composers could serve as a guide to Boulez in his attempts at systematization of rhythm and the integration within the world of sound of a world of rhythm constructed on a proportionate scale : Debussy, Stravinsky and Webern and especially the first two; for in Webern, the crystal purity of the musical language, and the height of logical thinking he achieved in his compositions had no counterpart on the rhythmical side beyond a few desultory sketches; whereas in Stravinsky in his *The Rite of Spring* days, musical structure and rhythmic structure merged completely.

Boulez confirms Goléa's astute observation on the very next page, mentioning Stravinsky's scores as his invariable *vade mecum*, both before and after his discovery of Webern, who 'opened up vistas as Debussy and Stravinsky could never have done, in the way of intensity of expression and timbre'.

Thus it becomes clearer every day that figures like Debussy, Stravinsky, Schoenberg, Berg, and Webern, far from being mutually exclusive, were needed in their different ways to forge what we see today as the new universal language of music in its various dimensions and its varied aspects. The seemingly inevitable division and segregation into watertight compartments of the different outlooks and movements which appeared as if they were leading twentieth-century music along different paths is disappearing; indeed, in retrospect the apparent antagonism seems like a figment of the imagination

[4] *Rencontres avec Pierre Boulez*, Julliard: Paris, 1958, p. 47.

rather than concrete fact. We now see that there was interchange, impalpable but nevertheless fruitful, constantly going on between the artistic experiments of different schools apparently divergent and often ostensibly arch-enemies. Of all the great composers of the twentieth century, Stravinsky has been essentially the most accessible, the least hide-bound and dogmatic; and this too has contributed to making the mutual relationship between him and the other streams of contemporary music one of the most stimulating and fruitful influences ever exerted by any composer throughout the whole history of Western music.

XXII Works written by Stravinsky
between 1959 and 1966

The first work to be considered in this chapter is *Movements*, a composition for piano and orchestra already referred to briefly on p. 220. Stravinsky himself gives some valuable information on *Movements* in *Memories and Commentaries*. He states (p. 106) that in this work he has discovered 'serial combinations' new to him, and that he realized in the process of writing it that he is becoming 'not less but more and more of a serial composer'. He considers *Movements* 'the most advanced music from the point of view of construction' he has composed so far. And with a slight suggestion of self-satisfaction he asserts that 'No theorist could determine the spelling of the note order in, for example, the flute solo near the beginning, or the derivation of the three F's announcing the last movement simply by knowing the original order, however unique the combinatorial properties of this particular series.'

One of the earliest analyses of the work, an article by Andreas Briner which appeared in the June 1960 issue of *Melos* under the title of 'Guillaume de Machaut 1958/59 or Stravinsky's *Movements for piano and orchestra*', gives the series as follows:[1]

Briner goes on to say that structurally the series consists of four groups of three notes, each of which undergoes frequent permutations and combinations with other serial structures as the work proceeds. Actually, we have only to examine the first two bars of *Movements* to realize that the serial order as given by Briner appears

[1] It may be pointed out, incidentally, that the series in question is similar to one used some fourteen years ago by the present author and by Luigi Dallapiccola, and discussed in *La Storia della Dodecafonia* (pp. 248 and 307).

there in a form already slightly altered, or perhaps rather, not yet complete. The D appears not between the E and the E flat but later, between the A and the C, while the last two notes of the series are inverted.[2] If we now turn to the series on which the third episode ('Ad tres virtutes hortationes') of the *Canticum Sacrum* is based (see the last example on page 190), we find that by bringing forward the third note from the end of the series shown there (D), so that it comes between the E and the D sharp, we get a series similar to that used in *Movements*, i.e. likewise composed of the same four groups of three notes each. This discovery would seem to be important as a preliminary indication of the substantial unity to be found even at the structural level (i.e. in the nature of the fundamental series used) in practically all the compositions belonging to this period of Stravinsky's activity. The work reaches its highest point of structural complexity in the final movement where, as Stravinsky again points out, five orders are rotated instead of four, with six alternates for each of the five, while at the same time, the six work in all directions as though through a crystal. In the past Stravinsky had favoured a kind of circular permutation in which diatonic figures rotate around one another by successive displacement of the initial strong accent from one note to the next. The rotation he now speaks of presumably refers to a procedure which from this point on is characteristic of his particular way of using twelve-note technique in his larger compositions. To achieve greater variety not only in the musical figures used in the works but in the actual sound material from which the musical imagery is fashioned, he does not confine himself to taking one fundamental series at a time together with his usual mirror variants plus the relative transpositions, but frequently splits the series into segments which are used independently; furthermore, within these segments he operates a particular type of circular permutation, i.e. taking each single succession of notes, starting not only with the first note but with the succeeding notes as well. Thus, for example, in addition to a hexachordal succession (which is in general that preferred by Stravinsky, and for convenience let us indicate the notes by the figures 1-2-3-4-5-6), we also find in these works the successions 2-3-4-5-6-1, 3-4-5-6-1-2, 4-5-6-1-2-3, 5-6-1-2-3-4, 6-1-2-3-4-5. Adding together the various permutations of the individual segments that make up the complete series obviously produces an

---

[2] E. W. White (op. cit., p. 465), gives as the original form of the series in *Movements* a version in which the first two notes also of the series indicated by Briner are inverted and the D is the sixth note.

extreme variety of dodecaphonic clusters. Going on to superimpose various serial forms in more or less compact layers, Stravinsky derives other structural elements by splitting up these layers vertically or diagonally. The fact that the serial alternatives resulting from this procedure are so numerous does indeed make it very difficult to analyse the structure of these works, although we certainly need not take literally Stravinsky's assertion cited above that no theorist could unravel some of the particularly intricate knots of his latest works. It is important to note at this point that the very extensive use of serial permutations in late Stravinsky was counterbalanced by very sparing use of transpositions. He often prefers to use the note that began the original series as the starting note of mirror forms and permutations. The tonal polarization thus created at the outset is especially evident in his later vocal works, whereas in the instrumental works the centripetal tonal forces are curbed or actually neutralized. This is to be observed above all in *Movements*, as we shall see later on. In this work, incidentally, the rhythmic language is the most advanced Stravinsky has employed so far; and this too gives a hint of serialism which is further reflected in the instrumental timbre of the various sections.

As the title indicates, the piece consists of a number of movements – five to be precise. Between each different movement is a very short interlude, which at the same time acts as a means of bridging over the changes in tempo from one movement to the next. Stravinsky's own view is that the most significant development to be found in *Movements* is the tendency towards *antitonality*', and he says he is amazed at this himself, in view of the fact that in *Threni* simple triadic references occur in every bar. The fact has already been mentioned (see p. 184) that in the *Poetics of Music* Stravinsky coined the term 'antitonal', which far from implying a negation of tonality emphasizes its existence as a force that cannot be eliminated, but only neutralized at best; and in further clarification of his ideas on the subject he cited the example of an aeronaut who as he flies overcomes the force of gravity, but does not become thereby 'antigravitational'. Thus, if in *Movements* Stravinsky now discerns an antitonal tendency, it means that in this work he has actually achieved what in the passage just cited he had planned theoretically, hypothetically, namely to write a piece in which the tonal forces would be constantly defeated or eluded, a piece, so to speak, poised in the air, 'qui ne pèse, ni pose'. The effect of *Movements* on the listener is that of a very strange work indeed, one which transcends not only all sense of earthly gravity, but every contingent existential motive of an expressive nature.[3]

In structural complexity, *Movements* not only outdoes any work composed by Stravinsky previously but goes on where Webern's art leaves off, representing Stravinsky's closest approach to the younger post-Webern *avant-garde*. Yet even here, Stravinsky somehow succeeds in offsetting the forward-looking drive with a broadening of the range of retrospective assimilation characteristic of his music. In fact, he admits himself that the polyrhythmic combinations in *Movements* have parallels in ancient works such as the second (three-voice) 'Agnus Dei' in the *Missa l'Homme armé* of Josquin des Prés, in Baude Cordier's *Pour le deffault du dieu Bacchus*, and in fragments from the Cyprus Codex. Certain rhythmic peculiarities take us back to Guillaume de Machaut and in general to the tradition of the fourteenth-century isorhythmic motet. Thus Stravinsky renews and pursues still further his miracles of reconstruction, reflecting the authentic style of periods and schools which now embrace the entire range of Western musical tradition.

In that same year (1959) Stravinsky wrote two short works on a funeral theme: *Epitaphium für das Grabmal des Prinzen Max Egon zu Fürstenberg* and *Double Canon Raoul Dufy in Memoriam*. Mention has already been made of the *Epitaphium*. It may be added that in *Memories and Commentaries* (p. 106) he speaks of it as 'a kind of Hymn, like Purcell's *Funeral Music for Queen Mary*'. The analogy refers presumably to the ideal nature of the subject, since from the strictly musical point of view the work may perhaps suggest Webern, but certainly not Purcell. The piece was in fact written for performance in a programme along with Webern's *Five Sacred Songs* (op. 15), where the combination of flute and clarinet is used. This gave Stravinsky the idea of making use of the instruments at hand instead of the two flutes he had had in mind originally. In an analysis of the piece he writes: 'There are four antiphonal strophes for the harp, and four for the wind duet, and each strophe is a complete order of the series[4] – harp: O, I, R, RI; winds: O, RI, R, I.' There is no contradiction between this statement and the fact already mentioned, that the harp has four bars and the wood-

---

[3] In this respect it seems significant that the choreography conceived by Georges Balanchine to the music of *Movements*, danced by the New York City Ballet in April 1963 appeared to *The Times*'s correspondent 'an essay in suspended motion' (quoted by E. W. White, op. cit., p. 468).

[4] The original form of this series is C sharp, A sharp, D sharp, E, C, B, F sharp, F, D, G, G sharp A.

wind only three. Clearly, Stravinsky identifies each single dodeca-phonically complete figure with an antiphonal strophe, the superimposition of two serial forms in the next-to-last bar giving rise, in his mind, to a double strophe. He goes on to say: 'The constructive problem that first attracted me in the two-part counter-point of the first phrase was the harmonic use of minor seconds.' The consequent prevalence of harmonic intervals of a second throughout the piece gives it an asperity and an astringent flavour, tempered, it is true, by the soft-edged timbre of the instruments which Stravinsky uses in his avowed intention that the sonorities should throughout be veiled ('I want the whole piece to be very muffled').

More cantabile in character and more direct in its expressiveness is the Double Canon for string quartet, in memory of the painter Raoul Dufy. Each instrument has a purely melodic line, without any double stopping. This in itself would suggest the quasi-vocal nature of the work. The lucidity of the discourse and the apparent simplicity of the musical imagery conceal a complex and extremely strict construction. The two violins execute the first canon by play-ing twice over, a major second apart, a series of twelve notes and their retrograde inversion. The viola and cello superimpose on this canon another canon into which the retrograde pattern of the original series is woven. The series consists of a juxtaposition of motifs somewhat analogous both to the serial motif of *In Memoriam Dylan Thomas* and to the famous theme based on the name BACH.

In 1960, Stravinsky published an orchestral work entitled *Monu-mentum pro Gesualdo di Venosa ad CD annum: Three Madrigals recomposed for Instruments*. It is a tribute commemorating the four-hundredth anniversary of the birth of a man whom Stravinsky re-gards as 'one of the most personal and most original musicians ever born to my art'.[5] As far back as 1954 he had been so fascinated by the incredibly bold art of Gesualdo, a composer far in advance of his age, that he had the idea of writing 'instrumental translations' of Gesualdo's madrigals. At the outset the project seemed unrealizable, and he abandoned it, only returning to it in February 1960, by which time he had acquired a more thorough knowledge of Gesualdo's music and a more intimate acquaintance with his style. However, we find earlier creative evidence of Stravinsky's interest in Gesualdo's music as far back as 1957, when he completed the sacred song 'Illumina nos'. This was the last of a set of twenty *Sacrae cantiones*

[5] *Expositions and Developments*, p. 106.

which the Prince of Venosa had printed in Naples in 1603, publishing
– according to the practice of the time – not the complete score but
the separate parts alone. Exceptionally for Gesualdo, the number of
parts in 'Illumina nos' was seven, possibly because of the 'Septiformi
Paracliti gratia' mentioned in the text.[6] Of the seven parts only five
are available today; the *sextus* and the *bassus* are lost. Stravinsky
re-wrote the two missing parts, in the spirit of Gesualdo's music,
naturally, but without pretending that he was producing a 'copy'
of what the original must have looked like. In fact we have no call
to quarrel with Stravinsky when he says 'I am in it as well as
Gesualdo'.[7]

In September 1959 Stravinsky also supplied the missing parts of
the second and twelfth items from the same set; and the following
year the three pieces were published together under the title of *Tres
Sacrae Cantiones by Carlo Gesualdo di Venosa (1560-1613) completed
by Igor Stravinsky for the 400th Anniversary of Gesualdo's Birth*.
The problems which Stravinsky had to solve were less complex in
the last two pieces, entitled 'Da pacem, Domine' and 'Assumpta est
Maria' respectively. They are two six-part notets in canon form,
four parts only being available. In both instances the shape of the
sextus was dictated by explicit rules governing the canon in relation
to one of the existing parts. Thus in 'Da pacem, Domine' the *tenor*
bears the marking 'in diapente canon' (i.e. in canon at the fifth),
whereas in 'Assumpta est Maria' a canon is called for 'in diapason'
(i.e. at the fourth). In either case the problem of completing the
composition involved no more than the choice of the proper interval
at which to introduce the imitating voices. Then all that had to be
done was to supply the missing bass parts.

When the task of completing the *Sacrae cantiones* was finished,
Stravinsky again turned to the project abandoned in 1954 and wrote
the *Monumentum*. The work was given its first performance in
September 1960 during the twenty-third Festival of the International
Society for Contemporary Music in Venice; it consists of three
madrigals of Gesualdo 'recomposed' for instruments : 'Asciugate i
begli occhi' (No. 14 in Book V); 'Ma tu, cagion di quella' (No. 18 in
Book V), and 'Beltà poi che t'assenti' (No. 2 in Book VI). As already
stated, these were not transcriptions in the ordinary sense but

---

[6] Stravinsky too had this idea, and he brought it out by making the first
simultaneous entry of all seven parts coincide with the word 'septiformi'; he
also explicitly drew attention to this 'very dramatic symbolization of the
text' (see *Conversations with Igor Stravinsky*, p. 34).
[7] ibid., p. 33.

'recompositions' in the sense that Stravinsky did not simply transcribe the three vocal pieces for the instruments of a regular symphony orchestra, but reworked the musical substance of the compositions from scratch. The character of Gesualdo's composition is completely transformed by the timbre and articulation of the brass and the double-reed instruments, so that, for example, the first of the three madrigals takes on the character of an 'instrumental *canzone*' in the real sense. The register shifts and the rotation of timbres in a series of groups are affected, especially in the third madrigal, by procedures akin to the medieval hocket.

In that same year, 1960, Stravinsky started work on a composition for Paul Sacher who, as the reader may recall, had previously commissioned from him the Concerto in D for String Orchestra. The work was completed on 31 January 1961, and bears the title *A Sermon, a Narrative and a Prayer*. It is written for alto and tenor soloists, speaker, chorus, and orchestra. The texts consist of fragments of the Epistles and the Acts of the Apostles in the Authorized Version of the Bible, plus a prayer from *Four Birds from Noah's Ark*, by the Elizabethan poet Thomas Dekker. This 'New Testament cantata' was conceived by Stravinsky, avowedly, as a pendant to the 'Biblical cantata' *Threni*.[8] Certain peculiarities in the writing link *A Sermon, a Narrative and a Prayer* with the outlook of *Threni* and differentiate it sharply from that of *Movements*. In the latter work, as we have seen, Stravinsky strove constantly to avoid any tonal polarization of the sound patterns. Now, in *A Sermon, a Narrative and a Prayer*, he returns to the contrapuntal style of the canons in *Threni*. He himself uses the term 'a kind of *triadic* atonality'[9] in reference to his peculiar way of developing non-tonal – indeed strictly twelve-note – structures while continuing to use, or again using triads and other chords similar to those characteristic of the tonal system. Outwardly, this return towards tonality might seem to be motivated by the inherent demands of choral writing. Actually, it is also, and in fact mainly, prompted by a more profound inner need for expression. This need, and certain manifest thematic similarities, link the cantata with the *Double Canon Raoul Dufy in Memoriam* of 1959 and the *In Memoriam Dylan Thomas* of 1954. For the cantata too seems as if conceived under the inspiration of the mystery of death, and the final section is explicitly an 'in memoriam', dedicated to the

---

[8] See the letter sent by Stravinsky to Paul Sacher on 7 August 1961, quoted in *Melos* (April 1962), p. 124.
[9] *Expositions and Developments*, p.107.

memory of the Rev. James McLane who died in 1960. The thematic similarities referred to derive from the close parallelism in the structure of the musical material handled in the three works. This material consists predominantly of shifting permutations of a series of five notes within an interval of a major third sounding consecutively or simultaneously. In support of the above contention, let us look first of all at the fundamental series used in *A Sermon, a Narrative and a Prayer*:

This can be deduced from what the first and second violins and the alto flute play in the first six bars of the work, while the flute, one of the clarinets, and a solo violin weave various serial fragments around it. Two groups (each comprising five adjacent notes) are ranged round a central group consisting of the two notes B flat and B natural. Let us now look back at the fundamental series used in the *Double Canon Raoul Dufy in Memoriam* and already mentioned. It is stated as follows:

If we compare the two series, we find that the first group of five notes of the above example comprises – though in a different order – the same notes as the second five-note group of the row used in *A Sermon*. There is a similar relationship between the other five-note groups of the two series and also between the two-note groups, with the difference that in the *Double Canon* series the position of the two-note group is not central.[10] If we now think back to *In*

---

[10] It may be noted that the series as used in *A Sermon* admits of a different analytical breakdown from that indicated at the outset, thus offering a further analogy with the structure of the *Double Canon* series. This possibility is based on the fact that notes 3 to 7 (i.e. C-D-D flat-B flat-B natural) constitute a group of five adjacent sounds, while the initial E flat and E natural form a group of two adjacent notes, so that the structural partition of this row into an asymmetrical group of two notes followed by two contiguous groups of five notes can be regarded as parallel in part with that of the series used in the *Double Canon*. Among other particular structural features of the series in *A Sermon* (used by Stravinsky for internal 'rhyming' in the music), let us merely recall the similarity between the patterns formed by the notes 3-4-5-6 (C-D-D flat-B flat) and 9-10-11-12 (G-A-A flat-F) respectively.

Memoriam Dylan Thomas we find that the fundamental structural nucleus of this work (reproduced on p. 182) contains the same five notes as the first group of the series used in *A Sermon* and the second group of the *Double Canon* series.

The musical patterns resulting from the various ways of arranging the five notes included in such groups are eminently chromatic in character, and in this respect it is significant that in *Memories and Commentaries* (p. 115), Stravinsky specifically discusses the connexion between pathos and chromaticism. The quality of pathos in the cantata is that of a work in which the ultimate experience of human life is distilled. The texts of the three subdivisions of the work throw light on its gradual progression. The text of the first section consists of St. Paul's aphorisms on hope and faith. This 'Sermon' is divided into eight short sections in which chorus and tenor solo alternate on an orchestral backdrop where the instruments are never used all at the same time. It is followed by a 'Narrative' in which the speaker and the solo singers without the chorus but with a dramatic accompaniment by the orchestra, narrate the episode of the stoning of St. Stephen from the *Acts of the Apostles*. The last part is a fervent 'Prayer' by one who awaits the hour when he will be 'cut off before night' and in the meantime invokes God's blessing so that he may be 'one of those singers who shall cry to Thee Alleluia'. There is a mournful solo for the contralto and a strict rhythmic three-part canon. Then comes the final 'Alleluia' chorus, in which serial constellations arrange themselves into diatonic halos silhouetted against the dark pendulum-like ostinatos of the three tam-tams, the double basses, piano, and harp. For a moment we seem to see the Stravinsky of the *Symphony of Psalms*, though here the direct, staggeringly impressive power of the *Symphony* has been decanted, tamed, sublimated.

'And our Lord is a consuming fire': St. Paul's words set in the first part of the cantata are echoed in the verses on the fire of divine love which comprise the fourth part of the last of the *Four Quartets* of T. S. Eliot. On these verses, in February 1962 Stravinsky composed an Anthem, which he dedicated to the eminent poet. The term 'Anthem' is applied in the Anglican liturgy to vocal works imitative in style and motet-like in character, on English paraphrases of Biblical texts. Stravinsky uses the term in this precise sense, and even the T. S. Eliot fragment, though not a 'paraphrase', is clearly inspired by passages from the Holy Scriptures. Some commentators on the poet interpret the image of the 'dove descending' and 'break-

ing the air' as having a dual symbolic meaning, signifying at once
the pentecostal tongues of flame and the enemy bomber (the last of
the *Four Quartets* was published in 1942, during the war). Even if
there were any justification for such an interpretation, Stravinsky
certainly did not pay any heed to it, but composed his *Anthem* in
the light of the basic spiritual theme of the poetry. The structural
simplification, or better, stripping to the bone, which we find in the
cantata is here carried still further. Whereas in *Movements* Stravinsky defied the theorists to determine the spelling of the note order
of certain extremely complex passages, in the Anthem the actual
structural skeleton, like every other aspect of the music, is at once
crystal clear. The four voices of the choir simply develop the four
orders of a series, not even making use of all the possible transpositions and proceeding always from the first or last notes of the
original form.[11] The 3/4 rhythm undergoes no change whatever.
There is no displacement of the metric accents. The piece takes
shape through the repetition, practically without variation, of a
two-part canon followed by a four-part canon. Outward show of
any kind is clearly ruled out from the start. Absolute essentiality is
equated with absolute simplicity.

Between the end of 1961 and early 1962 Stravinsky wrote *Eight
Instrumental Miniatures* – a re-thinking in orchestral terms of the
'Eight very easy melodies on five notes' for piano which he had
published forty years earlier under the title of *The Five Fingers*. In
Chapter XI above, when these little piano pieces were discussed, it
was pointed out that they anticipated certain procedures which
Stravinsky was to adopt in a recent work – the Septet. This anticipation may perhaps be the key to one of the reasons which led the
composer to undertake the task of re-fashioning the eight melodies
for piano. The ostensible occasion for the work was a commission
from the Monday Evening Concerts in Los Angeles (which paid for
the transcription of the first four pieces – they were played there
for the first time on 26 March 1962) and the Canadian Broadcasting
Company in Toronto, which commissioned the other three pieces,
so that the entire series of *Eight Miniatures* were performed in
Toronto on 29 April of the same year. In *Eight Instrumental Minia-*

[11] Incidentally, this series too:

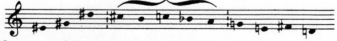

has a five-note nucleus similar to those already mentioned.

tures, the intrinsic structure of the melodies remains essentially unchanged. All that happens is that in the course of their reincarnation in different tone-colours there are shifts of register and key, some filling-out and a few additions and canon elaborations. On the other hand, the original sequence of the pieces is altered. Only the first, fifth, and eighth of the melodies stay where they were. The second melody becomes the eighth *Miniature*, the third becomes No. 4, the fourth No. 7, the sixth No. 3, and the seventh No. 2. The suite of *Eight Miniatures* thus runs as follows: Andantino (for oboes, bassoons and horn); Vivace (a tarantella-like piece for wind instruments); Lento; Allegretto (orchestrated almost like a peal of bells); Moderato (for flutes, clarinet, horn and strings); Allegro (Tempo di marcia); Larghetto (more or less a Sicilienne); and the final piece Tempo di tango ('pesante'), which he had orchestrated earlier. This '*Tihuna Blues*' tango, as he called it, had been given its first performance in December 1961 at Mexico City.

On 14 June 1962, the day before Stravinsky's eightieth birthday, the Columbia Broadcasting System televised his first work conceived and written expressly for television. The music was commissioned by the American Federation of Television and Radio Artists for *Noah and the Flood*, a 'danced drama' with choreography by Georges Balanchine. Stravinsky preferred to call his composition *The Flood*, describing it as a biblical allegory based on Noah and the Ark. He explains why he deleted Noah's name from the title of the work: 'Because Noah is mere history. As a genuine antediluvian he is a great curiosity, of course, but a side-show curiosity. And even as "eternal man", the second Adam, the – to Augustinians – Old Testament Christ image, he is less important than the Eternal Catastrophe. *The Flood* is also *The Bomb*.'[12]

'The Bomb' is obviously the atom bomb. Once again, as in *The Rite of Spring*, *mutatis mutandis*, Stravinsky has recourse to ancient symbols to depict the tragic image of impending doom that hangs over modern man, the sword of Damocles of final catastrophe. The allegorical explanation leaves no shred of doubt as to the theme and the composer's intentions. To use a somewhat hackneyed phrase, Stravinsky may be said to have conceived *The Flood* purely and simply as a message of peace to mankind. That being so, it had to be immediately comprehensible to the widest public imaginable today. He himself modestly asserts that he 'tried hard to keep *The Flood* very simple as music', since the work had been commissioned

[12] *Expositions and Developments*, p. 127.

for television after all, and he 'could not regard this commission
cynically'.[13] In sketching out the work he duly bore in mind the
requirements of television also in the sense that the pictorial and
musical actuality derives from the rapid succession of images on
the television screen. Stravinsky actually put forward the view that
the accessibility he had aimed at because he was dealing with the
television medium might conceivably make *The Flood* the first
musical work in the serial idiom to achieve real popularity with a
vast uninitiated public – more or less in the same way as *Peter and
the Wolf!* Whether he put forward this optimistic notion as a joke
or because he really hoped it was true, I do not know. What is
certain is that neither the first televised performance nor the first
performance on the stage was sufficiently successful to encourage
any such hopes. In fact, the television programme sponsored by the
Columbia Broadcasting System was a resounding flop, while the first
stage production – by the Hamburg State Opera in the spring of 1963,
at Hamburg, at the Zagreb Festival, and at the Scala in Milan – had
only a modest and by no means unanimous *succès d'estime* in all
three places. It should be said, however, that in each instance much
of the blame for the apathy of the public was due to factors that
had nothing to do with the musical performance, let alone with the
intrinsic substance of the music itself. As regards the television performance, the brilliant talents of Georges Balanchine could not
disguise the weaknesses of a ragged television production and the
general context of the programme, which was sponsored by a
manufacturer of shampoos and interrupted constantly by 'commercials'. The performance at the Hamburg Opera too, although
altogether more dignified and in the hands of a stage director of great
prestige (Gunther Rennert) was open to serious criticism. Stravinsky
admitted as much in private; he told me personally that Rennert's
production was too operatic for a work which was definitely not
an opera. He had conceived it as a 'musical play', a 'dance piece in
character, a story told by dance as well as by narration'.[14] The
Working Notes for 'The Flood' included in *Dialogues and a Diary*
(pp. 89-98) throw further light of a most revealing kind not only
on the way in which Stravinsky envisaged the performance of the
work, but on the imagery and symbolism he wished to portray in it
and also on the actual gestation of the composition. Among other
things he says he had been unable to imagine the work transferred

on to the operatic stage because of the 'musical speed' which was typically cinematographic. But the entire passage warrants quotation, since it contains a number of most valuable observations on the possibility of a type of opera written specifically for television: 'Television', he writes, 'should someday succeed in sponsoring a new, in the sense of more concentrated, musicodramatic form . . . Visually it offers every advantage over stage opera, but the saving of musical time interests me more than anything visual. This new musical economy was the one specific of the medium which guided my conception of *The Flood*. Because the succession of visualizations can be instantaneous, the composer may dispense with the afflatus of overtures, connecting episodes, curtain music. I have used only one or two notes to punctuate each stage in *The Creation* . . .' The text of *The Flood*, chosen and arranged by Robert Craft and derived from the Old Testament story of the Creation and from fifteenth-century English miracle plays of the Chester and York cycles, presents a quick synthetic sketch of the early chapters of the Bible. The music is similarly concise, consisting of a kind of aphoristic, laconic discourse presented in forms reproduced, as it were, in miniature. The duration of the musical part of the work is just over twenty minutes.

A short instrumental Prelude depicts the primeval Chaos. A *Te Deum*,[15] reminiscent of a Byzantine hymn, and the repetition of this at the end, constitute the framework of the stage action, which takes as its starting-point the separation of the dry land from the waters and makes reference successively to the creation of living things and of man, the fall of Lucifer, the works of Satan, the banishment from Paradise, and finally the story of Noah and the Flood. The distinction between 'celestials' and 'terrestrials' is drastically achieved: the former sing, the latter merely speak. The invisible role of God is assigned to two basses who sing in a strict, archaic counterpoint, the Trinity being completed by an instrumental voice closely united with them. The manner and the tempo in which they sing never change – an intentional symbol of the divine immutability. Satan, on the other hand, is interpreted by a single tenor voice, which according to Stravinsky should be somewhat ambivalent,

---

[15] In connection with this *Te Deum* (which he himself describes jokingly as 'not Gregorian but Igorian chant') Stravinsky had originally imagined Seraphim, Russian style, framed like icons so as to form a triangular altar; and he comments: 'This iconostasis should resemble a real Byzantine altar with the Chiasma or X Symbol on top. The piece begins and ends with the Church.'

slightly 'paederastic' in timbre; and he sings a melodic line at once sophisticated and fatuous in its frivolous syncopated rhythms.

Not only is the work as a whole conceived as an allegory; allegorical meanings can also be discerned in the various individual parts. Take for example the seven instrumental bars with which the Prelude opens. Here the multitude of symbolic references combined with the direct allusiveness of the imagery tempt the commentator to agree with the description given by the German critic Klaus Wagner: 'a terse cryptogram of the Creation in sound'.[16] The upbeat before the first bar consists of a widely separated fifth. The notes which make it up (C and G) are as it were projected to either end of a musical spectrum which is still empty. In a flash the void is filled by five other fifths (B flat-F; A flat-E flat; F sharp-C sharp, or enharmonically G flat-D flat, E-B, and D-A) forming a chromatic block of twelve different sounds, representing chaos. The device of depicting chaos in music, and the nothingness preceding it, by means of bare fifths and fourths, as Stravinsky does, is conventional in the extreme. Indeed, he makes it clear that he has deliberately adopted a form of expression based on a positively hoary tradition: 'My representation of Chaos is not so different from Haydn's.'[17] But like the later Beethoven, so the later Stravinsky can transform hackneyed conventions into the most extraordinary musical phenomena, can start with commonplaces and reach the stars. And if we look closely, many of the striking things in this work turn out to be quite modest in scale and quite unpretentious in character. Consider for example how Stravinsky succeeds in fashioning from the 'chaotic' and therefore virtually amorphous chromatic block in the first bar the lapidary, pregnant structures on which he bases the entire work. By 'virtually amorphous' I mean that this block of sound actually has inherent in it a very precise structure. This is not so much because it is made up of a series of fifths[18] as because of its peculiar

---

[16] *Melos* (June 1965), p. 203. Such an interpretation is in fact justified if not actually suggested by the composer himself when he states that 'Whereas the music of *Petroushka* attempts to create resemblances, *The Flood* music is, structurally speaking, all symbolic.' (*Dialogues and a Diary*, p. 90.)
[17] *Expositions and Developments*, p. 124.
[18] E. E. White maintains that the note-row in fifths implicit in this 'chord of Chaos' is the one used by Britten in *The Turn of the Screw* (*Stravinsky, the Composer and his Works*, p. 480, note 2). It is true that the series in question does use fifths in its internal structure; but the analogy between the two serial forms stops there, and it is certainly impossible to say they are the same. It should be noted that twelve-note clusters of this type, i.e. in a form that can be referred to the circle of fifths, are among the least differentiated, most primitive serial forms. And it may be precisely for that reason that Stravinsky made use of this type of cluster to fashion his musical symbol

registration, the seven lower notes belonging entirely to the scale D flat major while the seven upper notes are identical with the seven notes of the scale of D major. The pair of notes F sharp (or G flat) and C sharp (or D flat) are common to both keys. Situated in the centre of the chord, the interval of a fifth formed by these two notes acts as a structural hinge for the music, governing the tonal relationships within the twelve-note cluster arranged round it. In their turn the two diatonic sequences of seven notes act as 'modal situations', as diatonic matrices of all the twelve-note patterns in the work. At the end of the first bar and through the next four bars the individual structural elements appear to emerge from the chaos and confusion as each short crescendo comes to an end. At the sixth bar (perhaps at this point there is an implied reference to the chronological symbol of the creation of man) there appears a serial figure which is to fulfil a vital function in the subsequent weaving of the musical fabric:

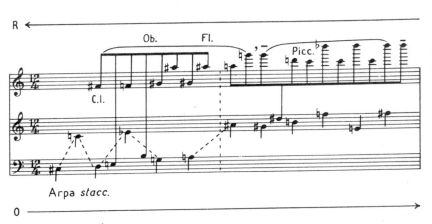

If we look closely at the above quotation we find that the figure in question is derived from a combination of the twelve-note series played by the harp, and its retrograde form played by the wood-

representing nothingness, Chaos from which then emerges the musical fabric symbolizing in turn the cosmic order. To be more accurate, Stravinsky uses this group of fifths not as an organized series but as a mere twelve-note agglomerate whose latent potential for construction became evident when he began the 'serial construction' of the *Te Deum*. This explains the antithesis he says he conceived (as we shall see) between serialism and chaos. Similarly it is possible to relate the beginning of *The Flood* to the first few pages of Haydn's *Creation*, to the opening of Beethoven's Ninth Symphony, and above all to the favourite opening devices used by Bruckner, who seemed, by the way he slowly built up his symphonic fabric from masses of bare fifths, to evoke with every opening of a symphony the birth of music itself.

wind with note values halved.[19] The relationship between this series and the diatonic components of the original complete chord in the first bar is seen clearly if we observe that in the first six crotchets of the example quoted the notes in the lower register (the bottom stave) belong to the scale of D major, while those in the two upper staves belong (enharmonically in some cases) to the scale D flat major. The series, moreover, is confined within an interval bounded by a C sharp (D flat) and an F sharp which, as has already been said, represents the kernel of the musical material used by Stravinsky as the basis for this work. The serial derivation technique applied here with such ingenuity and subtlety recalls, *mutatis mutandis*, the technique used by Berg in *Lulu*, though it is not suggested that any actual analogy can be drawn between the themes generated by the different series. As a matter of fact, the Stravinsky series in question can be regarded as quite typical of his twelve-note manner. If we recall the group of three notes (C sharp-C-D) at the beginning of the row, and the parallel group (F-E-F sharp) at the end, we see that half the series is the same as that of *Movements*. The central segment, consisting of the notes G-A-A sharp-G sharp-B, is of the five-note type for which Stravinsky has had a predilection from *In Memoriam Dylan Thomas* onwards. As the work proceeds this series remains closely bound up with the figure of man and his destiny. Transposed a fifth and in combination with its inversion, it represents the two aspects of the voice of God in the act of creation of 'man in our image'. In the double form seen in the sixth bar, where it is transposed down an octave, the same serial pattern depicts the expulsion from Paradise. In the exact original form, preceded by a repetition of the other five opening bars of the *Prelude*, it denotes the end of the *Flood* and the beginning anew of the world ('. . . a world begins to be . . .'); and a final reprise concludes the work. This concluding passage, instead of being associated with Chaos, refers to original sin, thus completing the musical equation between the negation of the material order and the negation of the moral order. The single bar into which Stravinsky condenses the allegory of Eden and the curse of original sin is, he says 'the largest and most complete-in-itself I have ever composed . . . the dramatic climax of the whole work' (ibid., p. 93). The subsequent reprise of the 'Jacob's ladder music' is invested with the symbolic function of

---

[19] In *Dialogues and a Diary*, Stravinsky talks of the ascending pattern of this serial form as a 'musical Jacob's ladder'. His posthumous comradeship with Schoenberg thus receives a symbolic seal.

leading to 'primal light' – the *Urlicht* reminiscent of Mahler. He goes on to say of this bar: 'I have allotted but fifteen seconds of music for this change from the lowest to the highest, but the music should be able to accomplish it. Music is a non-temporal magic carpet' (ibid.). The seventh bar, like a 'Demiurgic symbol of the day of rest' – to cite once again Klaus Wagner's hermeneutical commentary – ends this aphoristic orchestral 'Genesis' with a static chord comprising the seven notes of the scale of D flat major. In combination with the complementary chord of D, this harmonic entity plays an important cadential function throughout the entire episode, generating a relationship comparable to the traditional relationship between tonic and dominant. In this connection it is significant that Stravinsky began to compose *The Flood*, as he himself states, by establishing a comprehensive plan of the cadences to be used, while at the same time, at the visual level, he was conceiving an interplay of flashes of lightning designed to bring out as vividly as possible the highlights of the scenic action. Thus he realized the necessity for really effective musical cadences which would act as definite punctuation marks calculated to 'give the listener a sure sense of location, topographical location in the music'.[20]

The D flat chord mentioned above is the starting-point for the Te Deum with which Stravinsky begins his serial construction proper, expressly attributing to it the symbolic function of representing order as opposed to Chaos. 'This "chaos" may also be thought of as the antithesis of "serial".'[21] The Byzantine character of the Te Deum, already mentioned, and the diatonic and modal flavour of the melodic strands of which it is made up, are so marked that a listener not forewarned might have the impression that Stravinsky had returned to the manner of tonal compositions such as *The Wedding* and had momentarily abandoned the strict application of the rules of the twelve-note system. Actually, as I have said, it is here that Stravinsky launches the serial construction peculiar to *The Flood*. The tenors begin, tracing a retrograde inversion of the series as stated in the sixth bar; the altos, imitated by the sopranos, sing a melodic line based on the original form transposed a fifth; while the horn accompanies the choir, playing a melodic line of which the serial scheme:

[20] op. cit., p. 124.
[21] ibid., p. 125.

is the result of so arranging the notes of the two scales D and D flat as to form six intervals of a whole tone and four similar groups of four notes. Outwardly, and viewed as a whole, *The Flood* fits quite logically into the picture of Stravinsky's past experimentation. He pursues and develops, and adapts to the peculiar requirements of the television medium, premises stated nearly half a century earlier in *Renard* and the *The Soldier's Tale*. The descriptions of these works: 'a Burlesque in song and dance', 'to be read, played, and danced', fit *The Flood* perfectly too, so long as we bear in mind that the formal synthesis which Stravinsky achieves in the two earlier works is here broadened in scope, so that *The Flood* partakes of a whole series of genres – ballet, spoken drama, incidental music, melodrama, stage cantata, and *opera in musica*. Formally speaking, the description given by Stravinsky – 'biblical allegory' – is sufficiently vague to take in all the various aspects of this many-sided work.

The above brief analysis will perhaps suffice to indicate that the spiritual and stylistic plane on which *The Flood* stands is far removed from that of Prokofiev's popular composition. But though it contains passages where the music is anything but simple and easily accessible (whatever Stravinsky may think) *The Flood* seems to me to possess a great and immediate power of suggestion, chiefly because of the extraordinary clarity and plasticity of formal construction which Stravinsky sought and genuinely achieved. Without ever descending to the level of background music of an illustrative and merely functional kind, the music invariably fits the stage situation: it manages to suggest the insidious writhing of the serpent; the crude wooden gestures of the boat-builders (in the choreographic episode 'The Building of the Ark'); the variegated, milling horde of animals (in the melodrama 'The Catalogue of Animals'); the petulant quarrel between Noah and his wife (in the piece entitled 'The Comedy'); and the rising and subsequent ebbing of the flood waters. The piece specifically called 'The Flood' (here again designed with choreographic treatment in mind) is an example of how Stravinsky, instead of avoiding direct relationships between the shape of his music and the imagery to which it is related, deliberately establishes them either symbolically or by way of 'sound effects' of a concrete nature and hence immediately accessible. At the symbolical level, the rising and the subsequent ebbing of the waters is reflected in the 'mirror construction' of the piece, which (like one of the episodes in the *Canticum Sacrum*) turns back when it reaches the middle and retraces its steps.

That Stravinsky actually felt the need to have recourse to sound effects in the literal sense is confirmed in a subsequent passage of the *Working Notes* (*Dialogues and a Diary*, p. 95): 'I.S. thinks the music for Noah's 'the earth is overflowed with flood' might be supplemented by an electronic effect suggesting atmospheric disturbances, or by a pure noise, like a sinus tone'.[22] The notion of using electronic noises or sounds of any kind was not put into actual practice in *The Flood*, but the passage in question seems to me interesting as furnishing the first evidence Stravinsky has given us that he would be prepared to use even electronic effects. Hitherto he had never mentioned such an eventuality, even though after criticizing the use made of the potentialities of electronic music (*Conversations with Igor Stravinsky*, p. 111-12) he later advocated the use of electronic mechanisms in the music of the future, together with exploitation of 'mirror acoustic effects' and 'electronically produced sound, mixed or used adjunctively with traditional instrumental sound' (*Memories and Commentaries*, p. 125).

In spite of all this, Stravinsky denies all descriptive intention of a visual nature, affirming (in the *Diary*): 'The music imitates not waves and winds, but time. The interruptions in the violin/flute line say: "No, it isn't over". As the skin of the sun is fire, so here the violins and flutes are the skin drawn over the body of the sound. This "La Mer" has no "de l'aube à midi" but only a time experience of something that is terrible and that lasts'. These affirmations of Stravinsky's need not, however, prevent others detecting direct physical suggestions in this piece. Massimo Mila describes suggestions of this sort in the following terms:[23] 'The rain falling in sheets during the flood . . . sculptured indelibly by Stravinsky through the whining, fitful repetitions of the series filled in by the other instruments in a tremolo of violins and flutes: it is a real deluge, torrential rain – the Flood, in short. The series does not inhibit thematic treatment; the structure is

---

[22] With regard to the erroneous comparison of a sine tone to a pure noise (sine tones represent the very essence of tone, being devoid of harmonics and hence surely the very opposite of noise), Craft must have misconstrued Stravinsky's thought; he probably meant not a noise, but simply a sound.

[23] Massimo Mila, 'Il Diluvio di Strawinsky', *L'Espresso* (Rome, 17 July 1963), p. 30.

no obstacle to expression, indeed to realistic expression. These few short pages alone would suffice to prove the perennial vitality of Stravinsky's genius.'

Yet another proof of this vitality was to be given immediately afterwards by Stravinsky in *Abraham and Isaac*, a 'Sacred Ballad' for baritone and chamber orchestra. Begun in 1962 following a visit to Israel, and completed in 1963, the work is 'dedicated to the people of the State of Israel' as a token of gratitude for the hospitality he enjoyed during his tour. The first performance was given in August 1964 at Caesarea during the Israeli Music Festival. In a letter to the organizers of the Festival, Stravinsky states that one of his reasons for writing *Abraham and Isaac* was because he was attracted by the theme and 'the Hebrew language as sound'. The text he set to music is the Hebrew version of Chapter 22 of Genesis, verses 1-19. As in the case of the Latin text of *Oedipus Rex*, Stravinsky here gives explicit instructions that 'no translation of the Hebrew should ever be attempted as the syllables, both as accentuation and timbre, are a precisely fixed and principal element of the music'. In the letter quoted above, he says that the verbal and the musical accentuation coincide here – a very rare occurrence in his music.

The musical images, spare and concise as a drypoint engraving, follow one another and are linked together in a musical discourse in which narrative and dialogue alternate. The vocal writing oscillates between syllabic scansion and melismatic chant which suggests in a subtle way the oriental atmosphere and the remoteness in time of the biblical episode to which the text refers. Like all the music belonging to this most recent period of Stravinsky's work, *Abraham and Isaac* again bears witness to the personal, flexible manner in which the composer makes use of the resources of twelve-note serial technique, without any formalism or pedantry. As he says himself in the explanatory letter quoted above, the musical basis of the composition is a series of twelve sounds which in the course of the work is split up into smaller units.[24] This series, stated by the violas and the first bassoon in the first five bars:[25]

[24]The main parts of this letter are quoted (in German translation) by Peter Gradenwitz in an article entitled 'Zwölf Töne für Abraham von Igor Strawinsky' in *Melos* (November 1964), p. 364. Later Stravinsky reproduced the text in one of the *Program Notes* (*Themes and Episodes*, pp. 55-6).
[25] In the vocal score the eighth note of the series is given as C sharp instead of D sharp, owing to an error of printing or transcription.

is of the same type as that described in connexion with *A Sermon, A Narrative and a Prayer* and the *Double Canon Raoul Dufy in Memoriam*. It consists of a group of two chromatically adjacent sounds and two groups of five notes within the interval of a major third. On the other hand, there is a suggestion of the serial material of *The Flood* in its latent tonal dichotomy: the first part can be regarded as belonging to the key of C sharp major or G sharp major (with the F double sharp at the beginning as leading note), while the second part (from the fifth note onwards) is virtually centred round the D. But one of the characteristic features of this series is the symmetrical arrangement of the various intervals.

Although the work is designed all in one piece, without any interruption, it displays throughout an architectural though flexible structure. It begins with a short instrumental introduction, in which the series constituting the theme of the work is stated in both melodic and harmonic form. The first part begins, tranquillo and cantabile in character. The baritone solo is accompanied by instruments in two-part and later three-part counterpoint, with only occasional harmonic punctuation. This part comprises the verses describing how God, wishing to tempt Abraham, calls him and bids him go into the land of Moriah and there sacrifice his only son, Isaac, for a burnt offering upon one of the mountains He will indicate. Abraham departs with Isaac, after cleaving the wood for the burnt offering, taking along also two young men. This first part culminates in a fermata on the word *Haelohim* (God). A short recitative-like section contains that part of the text which describes how, on the third day, Abraham lifts up his eyes and sees the place of which God has told him. He makes his way there, accompanied by Isaac, bidding the two young men who have come with them await his return. This is followed by an orchestral interlude which starts out as a short *cadenza quasi rubato*, for solo flute framed by chords in the strings, and develops gradually into a series of solemn, mysterious harmonic sequences assigned mainly to instruments of low-pitched, dark register and timbre: tuba, trombones, bassoons, bass clarinet, cor anglais, cellos, and double basses. Next comes a part marked 'meno mosso' which constitutes the longest section of the Ballad. The voice part, dramatic and in places agitated, prevails here, by reason of the almost expressionist tension of its wide intervals, over the orchestral part, which supports and sets it off and effectually punctuates the musical discourse. This section includes the whole of the episode of the sacrifice, which is prevented at the crucial moment by the intervention of the Angel of the Lord; the blessing; and the divine promise to multiply the seed of Abraham, who had obeyed the voice of the Lord and had not withheld his only son. A short andante coda, the text of which describes the return of Abraham and his companions to Beer-sheba, concludes the Ballad, 'tranquillo' and with nothing in the nature of a rhetorical peroration.

In the five most recent works with which I was able to become acquainted[26] before adding the present chapter, Stravinsky once again turns to the funeral theme which, together with his growing predilection for hieratic religious subjects, is an invariable feature of the spiritual landscape of his last creative phase. The works in question are the orchestral *Variations 'Aldous Huxley in Memoriam'*; the *Elegy for J.F.K.* (in two versions: for mezzo soprano and three clarinets, and for baritone and three clarinets); the *Introitus* for male chorus and seven instruments 'T. S. Eliot in Memoriam'; the *Requiem Canticles* for contralto and bass soloists, chorus and orchestra, and finally *The Owl and the Pussy-cat*, for voice and piano. The *Variations* for orchestra were written between 1963 and 1964, and first performed in Chicago on 17 April 1965. In Europe they were twice performed during 1965. At the end of May 1965 the work was performed in Warsaw on the occasion of Stravinsky's first visit to Poland after forty years of absence from what he made a point of describing during his visit as the country of origin of his family. Then in October 1965 the *Variations* were given during the *Festwochen* in Berlin. Public and critics alike, both in Warsaw and in Berlin, were puzzled by the work, which is as difficult to comprehend as *Movements*, if not more so. There is, in fact, a distinct cleavage between the many vocal works and the relatively few purely instrumental compositions of Stravinsky's late period: whereas the former tend towards greater and greater clarity of expression and a

---

[26] I have still not been able to hear or read the score of the *Fanfare for a New Theater* composed in 1964 and dedicated 'to Lincoln and George', i.e. Lincoln Kirstein and George Balanchine. The first performance of this piece for two trumpets took place at the New York State Theater in the Lincoln Center, New York on 19 April 1964.

more and more marked imaginative and expressive quality, the latter give evidence of a trend towards an increasingly subtle complexity of structure with a total detachment from any external influence, and towards a state of sublimation which makes it impossible to relate the music to earthly themes.

In the *Variations*, the structural polymorphy appears to be pushed to the point beyond which it virtually turns into its opposite and becomes amorphous. It is in this sense that we must interpret statements such as that of the Polish critic Tadeusz Kaczynski:[27] 'the autonomous nature of the individual parts and the formal atomization of the work go so far as almost to reach the point – according to the law of polarity – where chance prevails.' We have already seen how in *The Flood* Stravinsky makes use of a dialectical *volte-face* of this nature in depicting the amorphous state of Chaos by means of an ingeniously intricate pattern made up of the entire series of twelve notes. In the *Variations*, the instrumental arrangement would appear to indicate the composer's intention to produce sound clusters of the utmost density and at the same time so dissociated as to acquire an almost disembodied lightness. Typical in this respect are three variations which constitute the architectural framework of the entire work. The first is stated by twelve solo violins, while the other two employ respectively four violins, six violas, and two double basses, and eleven woodwind plus a horn, i.e. always twelve instruments. These are treated as solo instruments and at the same time combined in iridescent auras of sound. Kaczynski writes: 'Never did a composer so advanced in years write so modern a work . . . None of Stravinsky's previous compositions is as *avant-garde* as the *Variations* . . . the pinnacle of Stravinsky's entire twelve-note period' and 'the beginning of a new period of creativity.'[28] To Kaczynski's statement that an analysis of the score showed the *Variations* to be altogether different from any of Stravinsky's other compositions, even the next most recent ones belonging to his twelve-note period, the composer replied with fine irony: 'Yes, the *Variations* are different . . . because the technical approach is different. It is, after all, a purely contrapuntal work. Music of this type was written in the fifteenth century. Thus it is ancient music, far older than you imagine.'

On 11 March 1965, in anticipation of the world première of the

[27] Tadeusz Kaczynski, 'Igor Strawinsky acht Tage in Warschau', in *Melos* (September 1965), p. 319.
[28] ibid.

work, Stravinsky dictated a presentation in which the precedent invoked is still more recent: '*Veränderungen* – alterations or mutations, Bach's word for the Goldberg Variations – could be used to describe my *Variations* as well, except that I have altered or diversified a series, instead of a theme or subject. In fact, I do not have a theme, in the textbook sense, whereas Bach's theme (for comparison) is a complete aria.'

In *Themes and Episodes* (p. 60) Stravinsky quotes the pitch series on which the variations are based:

'The bipartite division is basic', he writes, each of the two groups of six notes comprising it being both fragments of the entire twelve-note series and unities, and hence invertible or reversible. Apart from the division thus pointed out by the composer himself, it seems to me that other possible structural articulations of the series can be derived from the modal disposition of the notes that comprise the series. It may be noticed that the initial group of five notes and the succeeding four notes have a distinctly diatonic flavour, whereas the last three notes form a chromatic succession. It may also be observed that the first five notes come within the orbit of the tonic A minor chord, while the eight notes from the fourth to the twelfth of the row virtually imply the scale of G sharp minor, harmonic or melodic, in both forms, ascending and descending. If Stravinsky's innate tonal sense is no longer superficially evident, it continues to operate at a deeper level, informing the very structural roots, the very germinal core of a work that strikes the listener as one of the furthest removed of all Stravinsky's compositions from tradition and from the eminently tonal music of his earlier periods. The relative simplicity of the infrastructure of the basic series in question does not, however, produce a corresponding simplicity in the macro-structure of the greater part of the *Variations*. This is because the sum, the integration of these serial elements emerges as extremely complex, and characterized by the polymorphism already mentioned.

Stravinsky goes on to say (ibid., p. 61): 'The density of the twelve-part variations is the main innovation in the work. One might think of these constructions as musical mobiles. in that the patterns within them will seem to change perspective with repeated hearings.

They are relieved and offset by music of a contrasting starkness and even, notably in the first variation, by *Klangfarben* monody – which is also variation.'

Rhythm assumes a particularly important role in this work. 'Some of us think that the role of rhythm is larger today than ever before, but however that may be, in the absence of harmonic modulation it must play a considerable part in the delineation of form. And more than ever before, the composer must be certain of building rhythmic unity into a variety. In my *Variations*, tempo is a variable and pulsation a constant.'

Analysis of the three principal variations referred to shows that they are organized on the basis of a definite rhythmic matrix of successions of groups of twelve metrical units divided in the proportion $4/8+3/8+5/8$. The eye is at once caught by the resemblance between this serial arrangement of the rhythm, and the subdivision of the twelve-note series into two diatonic groups of five and four notes respectively and one chromatic group of three notes. We do not know how far this permutational relation between the two series, which have to do with different parameters of the work, is intentional and consciously carried through. However, Stravinsky's assertion seems very significant in this connection: 'The question of length (duration) is inseparable from that of depth and/or height (content).'

Turning to examine the way in which the rhythmic series fulfils its function in what Stravinsky calls 'the delineation of form', we see that this series occurs four times in each of the three principal variations, that is twelve times altogether. In each of these variations, each of the twelve different parts which make it up present a rhythmic articulation different from that of the other eleven. Each single part, however, preserves its own articulation throughout the three variations, while the pitch of the notes concerned changes. One is reminded of the devices of 'dragma' and 'talea' in the isorhythmic motets of the Ars Nova and late Middle Ages. It was perhaps of this aspect of his *Variations* that Stravinsky was thinking when he made the remark quoted above that his music was in some sense 'ancient'.

The three variations which make up the core of this work and which we have examined in greater detail, because of their unusual formal interest, are surrounded by other diversely constructed variations which act respectively as introduction, intermezzo, and finale. The formal aspect of the work can be summed up as follows: an opening harmonic sequence derived from the 'Klangfarben monody' of which Stravinsky talks constitutes the introduction to what we have considered the first principal Variation. An intermezzo for flutes, oboe, and bassoons (and thus less dense than the Variation but more dense than the prelude) leads to the second principal Variation. Between this and the third Variation in twelve parts comes the intermezzo, constructed on an ampler scale out of five short variations. The first of these begins as a three-part variation for woodwind to which trumpets and strings are successively added; the second is a three-part invention for trombone supported by two dynamically contrasted chords in rapid alternation; the third contrapuntally weaves the cor anglais, the clarinets, a bassoon, a horn, and the strings; the fourth is characterized by staccato trombone chords; the fifth is a fugato for strings punctuated by pianoforte. The third principal Variation is followed by a postlude which is related to the prelude. This eleventh part of the work leads to a final cadence made up of five chords which use only eleven notes of the basic series. The twelfth note (a G sharp) is reserved for the last bar of the Variations, thus completing the dodecaphonic constellation which has governed the work from beginning to end in every detail.

In this work, the contrast between its duration (the *Variations* last less than five minutes) and the number of musical events which occur therein, means that there is a great concentration of intellectual and audible material to perceive and understand. It is here that Stravinsky sees the principal reason why the *Variations* are difficult to approach. In the note which we have already quoted he addresses the public directly, evidently foreseeing a negative reaction.

'But whether full, partly full or empty, the musical statements of the *Variations* are concise, I prefer to think, rather than short. They are whatever one thinks, a radical contrast to the prolix manner of speech of most of the late last-century music which is the pabulum of our regular concert life; and there lies the difficulty, mine with you no less than yours with me . . .'

I think that Stravinsky is mistaken if he really thinks that the work's difficulty lies only in its aphoristic conciseness. I do not mean to say that the advice he gives to his hearers is useless. Quite the contrary. It is very valuable and sufficiently interesting to be cited here. 'I do not know how to guide listeners other than to advise them to listen not once but repeatedly . . . I may say that they should not look for the boundary lines of the individual variations, but try instead to hear the piece as a whole. And a second thought;

I *can* recommend one guide, the orchestra itself. The use of families and individuals in contrast is a principal projective element of the form, especially of its symmetries and reversibles. The leading solo roles are those of the flutes, bassoons and trombones; and perhaps my economy is inconsistent in that trumpet and horn families have in comparison so little to do; I needed only a spot of red, however, and a spot of blue. I might add that the orchestral *dramatis personae* is unusual in that four rather than the standard five string parts are required (there is only one division of violins) and that each must be of equal weight. Percussion instruments are not used, but their position is occupied by the piano and harp which appear as a couple (married).'

I do not believe, however, that analytical notes of this kind are enough to help the listener to appreciate the spiritual appeal of the work. Indeed it is proper to the spiritual level of the work that it remains difficult of access even to someone who can understand the musical patterns. It is a typical 'third-period' work (to use the old terminology of Beethoven criticism), and the 'separation from earthly things' of third-period works transforms their whole content. This becomes so to speak ordered from within, taking on a crystal-line structure which renders it transparent to everything immaterial and transcendental. Works of this kind can be described as a sort of 'spiritual exercise in music' divorced from any ritual or explicitly religious statement. Stravinsky's spirituality manifests itself in the *Variations* in an absolutely pure form.

Completely different in character, and thus confirming what was said above in regard to the distinct difference of approach between the orchestral works and the vocal works of Stravinsky's latest period, is the *Elegy for J.F.K.*, which was given its first performance in Los Angeles on 6 April 1964 and was repeated at Philharmonic Hall, New York, on 6 December 1964, in connection with the events commemorating the first anniversary of the tragic death of President Kennedy. Here there is no piling up of highly complex serial struc-tures rendered still more dense, nor on the other hand is there any elision of discursive links or any attempt to rarefy the expressive atmosphere. The voice and the three clarinets (an ensemble for which Stravinsky has always had a predilection) describe with quiet composure, but with an inner, consuming intensity of expression, melodic patterns which fuse in a transparent texture of sound and an immediately palpable eloquence. Stravinsky's score intones the words of a poetic text by W. H. Auden, which though not actually written with reference to the assassination of the young American President, is admirably suited to the expression of the sentiments and reflections which this tragic event, indeed in general the death of any 'just man', should arouse in the minds and hearts of men. Stravinsky follows every nuance of the text with infinite delicacy, underlining musically every comma, every caesura, every phrase, and in general throwing the extrinsic form of the text into musical relief and thus at the same time enhancing and transfiguring its intrinsic poetic meaning.

The serial shape of the piece is of the utmost transparency. The alto clarinet states the theme in a succession of twelve notes which the solo voice imitates, inverting its retrograde form:

These are the only serial forms, and they are used, either *recte* or *cancrizans*, throughout the entire piece, without being transposed or modified in any other way. If we examine their internal structure and the way in which they are interrelated, we find that there is a modal flavour about them; that the sounds in the middle of the series (F and B) coincide; that the first and last intervals of each series (major second and tritone) are identical; and that there is a symmetrical arrangement of the intervals resulting from the super-imposition of the two series, the first and last consisting of two intervals of a fifth which fulfil a cadential function similar to the part played by like intervals of a fifth in *The Flood*. In the *Elegy*, five flexible cadences separate the verses of the poem. The G sharp, the first and last note, respectively, of the two series shown above, becomes the pivot of each individual cadence, the true pole of the tonal forces which govern the development of the work. It is an admirable example, within its brief compass, of the 'recitar cantando' which was regarded in the past as the ideal method of effectively associating speech and song.

Along the same lines as the *Elegy*, but on a broader scale, is the

Introitus[29] composed by Stravinsky as a tribute to the memory of
T. S. Eliot, who died on 4 January 1965. Stravinsky felt a spiritual
affinity with the poet based on the similarity of their religious leanings,
and, as we have seen, had previously set one of Eliot's poems to music
in the *Anthem*.

The *Introitus* is a setting of words from the Requiem Mass. It uses a
divided male chorus (tenors and basses) singing or declaiming alternately, and a small instrumental ensemble. The latter comprises two
solo melodic instruments (viola and double bass) – though they are
not employed in a strictly melodic fashion – and a group of percussion or plucked instruments: piano, harp, tam-tam and timpani
(two parts) – used, conversely, in a cantabile manner as well as for
rhythmic and colour effects. Stravinsky says (*Themes and Episodes*,
p. 63) that the only instrumental novelty in the *Introitus* is 'the
incidence of the complete series in a group of timpani *coperti* . . .
and the main function of the viola and string bass is to support and
clarify the tuning of these funeral drums'. On the other hand, here
again, as in the *Elegy*, the instruments emerge in their own right so
to speak, punctuating the strophic arrangement of the composition
and separating the different verses of the text. Stravinsky achieves
the dramatic effect of the 'Requiem aeternam' by reverting to the
use of the rhythmic device of constantly shifting accents and
asymmetrical phrasing. After the first verse has been sung by the
chorus, it is repeated, but declaimed this time, up to the words
'dona ei, Domine'. Then comes an instrumental interlude by the
viola and double bass, after which the basses in the choir intone the 'Te
decet hymnus'. Next, tenors and basses recite the verse 'Exaudi
orationem meam', and then repeat the 'Requiem aeternam' all together, in unison, on a simple melodic line. 'The four melodic
versions of the pitch orders are sung as a *cantus firmus* in the form
of a processional, which is a little ritual the poet might have liked.'
(ibid.) The last vocal phrase ends with the melody on which the

---

[29] Indications of the intrinsic affinity between the two works are to be
found in the shape of the series on which their respective structures are
based:

Elegy series:
Introitus series:

words 'The Heavens are silent' are sung in the *Elegy for J.F.K.* Of this extremely simple melodic phrase, consisting of two diatonically adjacent notes of the same length, Stravinsky says (ibid., p. 58) that it is 'a melodic-rhythmic stutter characteristic of my speech from *Les Noces* to the *Concerto in D*, and earlier and later as well – a lifelong affliction, in fact'. Auden's words now give meaning to this 'lifelong affliction'. For all his faith, declared so often, in the presence of the 'silence of the Heavens', Stravinsky's eloquence degenerates into a stutter and is stifled until an act of vital will-power takes him out of his slough of despond. Despond and escape from despond : would it be unduly arbitrary to discern in this dialectical theme a touch of Beethoven in Stravinsky? What his music does not manifest is the struggle to achieve this victory on the emotional level. Hence one might think that his preferences would lead him towards late Beethoven, where the battle is over and done with, fought and won. And sure enough, in *Thoughts of an Octogenarian* (*Dialogues and a Diary*, p. 24) Stravinsky sings the praises of Beethoven's Great Fugue – 'I love it beyond any other'.

It seems that as early as 1963 or 1964 Stravinsky was playing with the idea of composing a true Requiem in which an outlet would be found for that funeral vein, the different manifestations of which we have seen stage by stage throughout the long curve of his creative career. In an article in *Tempo* (Winter 1966/7, page 14) Eric Walter White suggests that the news of the death of T. S. Eliot led Stravinsky to put off once more the full realization of this project and give it partial expression in the *Introitus* which we have discussed above. The *Requiem* at last followed the *Introitus* almost without a gap (between the two works there is only the briefest of intercalations, an orchestral *Canon* on a theme from *Firebird* lasting less than half a minute). The *Requiem* is one of the longest works of Stravinsky's last period, a quarter of an hour in duration; it thus resembles his *Mass* in size. He called the work not 'Requiem Mass' but *Requiem Canticles*, thus marking the distinction between this and similar works of the eighteenth and nineteenth centuries. In fact the title 'Requiem Mass' would have been incorrect, since the sections of the Ordinary are lacking, while the actual text, the Proper of the Requiem Mass, has been used by Stravinsky in an incomplete form.

The work, dedicated 'to the memory of Helen Buchanan Seeger', had its first performance on 8 October 1966, under the direction of Robert Craft. To the critics present, among whom was White, the music appeared, except perhaps at the beginning, neither dodeca-phonic nor atonal. Far from being surprising, this impression only confirms what was said above about the distinction which has been established between the vocal and instrumental works of Stravinsky's last creative period. Like his other late compositions which involve singing, the *Requiem Canticles* present a clear, flexible, and concise formal articulation, while the internal structures seem to have a generally diatonic/modal savour, and a tonal polarity which is easily recognizable, even if it cannot easily be defined or fitted into normal analytical schemes. But we only have to examine carefully the orchestral *Prelude* with which the work begins to find immedi-ate proof that such a character is not due to Stravinsky's abandon-ment of serial writing, but is on the contrary further evidence of his personal method of pursuing what one may call the tonal in-vestigation of serial space, an investigation, initiated by the Viennese serialists themselves, which in Stravinsky leads at one time to the recovery of traditional or even archaic techniques, at another to the evolution and employment of entirely new procedures.

In the *Prelude* of the *Requiem Canticles* the body of strings are employed throughout in the percussive trembling of 'Tutte semi-crome eguale, =250' (in Stravinsky's somewhat approximate Italian). This regular, *ostinato* pulsation is given a feeling of dramatic, nervous anguish by frequent changes of rhythmic articulation ex-pressed in irregular bars of 5/16 or 7/16. The notes which embody this tremor – like a heart throbbing with fear before the supreme day dawns of wrath and judgement – are inscribed within a har-monic network which can be set out schematically as follows:

This schema shows clearly that the harmonic configuration of the movement can be referred to a pattern of twelve notes and one of its retrograde forms. This pattern is divided into two diatonic/tonal fields, one comprising the notes F-C-B-A-D (with the addition of an A sharp and a G in a solo violin part), the other the notes C sharp-D sharp-G sharp-F sharp-E (with the eventual reappearance of the G, which in some places moves from the beginning to the end of this second serial segment to connect with the retrograde form of the series). The passage from the first to the second tonal field of the series generates a kind of cadential tension in the first part of the *Prelude* which in the second part is resolved by the passage in the opposite direction. Above this harmonic-rhythmic ground a first violin solo traces out, in sighing tones, the melodic profile of the second hexachord, retrograde and transposed a tritone. A second violin joins the first (with rhythmically displaced notes), and, in the second part of the *Prelude*, a solo viola, cello, and double bass complete the usual quintet, always playing figures which can be referred to a part of one or other of the dodecaphonic forms into which the fundamental series is transformed, and reflecting in this way its modal dichotomy.

Stravinsky's inclination to use permutations of series became so marked in the successive parts of *Requiem Canticles* that one commentator speaks of two distinct series as being the most surprising technical point of the work (Claudio Spies, 'Some Notes on Stravinsky's Requiem Settings' in *Perspectives of New Music*, vol. V, No. 5, Princeton, Spring-Summer 1967, p. 108, and later in the volume quoted in note 11, p. 277). The second series would appear to derive from a particular handling of the retrograde form of the first series implicit in the second part of the serial scheme of the Prelude quoted above :

Initial series (retrograde) :

Spies backs up his contention by reproducing some working tables copied from Stravinsky's letters. It seems clear from the musical example given above, however, that there are two unrelated series with a central nucleus in common, but with one fundamental difference (not pointed out by Spies in his strictly grammatical analysis), namely that whereas the initial series splits up into diatonic segments, the second is of a chromatic type similar to those we have seen in Stravinsky's earlier serial compositions. The first five notes fit chromatically within a major third, the next four within a minor third, and the last three within a major second. Possibly Stravinsky felt the need to offer this chromatic alternative to the diatonicism of the work so as to differentiate the parts where the subjective expressive tension is acute from those in which an objective mood prevails. The chromatic series fulfils its function in the pleading of the *Exaudi*, in the expressionist lacerations of the *Rex tremendae*, in the anguish and torture of the *Lacrimosa*. The diatonic series is seen in action in the implacable, non-human pulsation of the *Prelude*, the violent mass scene of the *Dies irae*, and the majestic *Tuba mirum*. Elsewhere the various series and fragments of series alternate or combine in different ways.

The harmonic structure of the *Prelude*, with its central symmetry, reflects in its turn the symmetrical arrangement of the whole work. At its centre is a purely instrumental *Interlude* (the first movement composed by Stravinsky) before which are placed three vocal pieces preceded by the *Prelude* and after which are another three vocal pieces followed by a *Postlude* also for solo instruments.

In the first vocal movement, *Exaudi*, the choir sings the words of the last verse of the psalm which ends the Introit of the Requiem Mass: 'Exaudi orationem meam, ad te omnis caro veniet.' The homophonic simplicity of the choral part recalls the climate of the *Agnus Dei* of Stravinsky's Mass. In this extremely sober and concise context, the repetition of a few words and a few intervals is enough to confer on the apparent serenity of the movement an accent of intense, even if repressed, sorrow. With 'accenti in piano' the orchestra delicately accompanies, punctuates, and frames the unadorned choral writing.

The *Dies irae* follows. Here, unexpectedly and for a few moments only, Stravinsky's inborn violence breaks out. This violence goes to the very roots of his temperament and his art, and, like a spring charged with energy, has the potentiality of action even when it is checked or repressed as in so much of Stravinsky's music, giving it a latent tension even though tamed or inhibited. In the *Dies irae* this spring is released, and orchestra and choir 'explode like a rocket', in White's words. Piano, strings, and timpani twist the inverted form of the basic series in a violent fortissimo arabesque like a lightning flash, on the last notes of which the choir, supported by the brass, loudly cry the terror of the 'Dies irae', and then repeat the last word pianissimo, 'come eco', as if fear was suffocating the

voice of humanity. There is another flash of lightning on the piano
and strings and a new cry: 'dies illa'. After a third flash the vocal
line comes to an end: the rest of the two verses of the *Dies irae* are
articulated by the whole choir 'parlando sottovoce' under a hail of
notes from the piano which reels off forms of the series complete
and fragmentary, permutated and rotated, supported by the skeletal
sounds of the xylophone, the whistling of the four flutes, and the
interjections of the tenor trombones. When the piano, timpani, and
strings again take up the lightning flashes of the beginning, the choir
seems to have no more voice with which to answer, and only after
these instruments are unleashed a second time do the voices cry out
again and echo for the last time the pregnant rhythmic motive of
the 'Dies Irae'. In my opinion Stravinsky reaches in this movement
one of the peaks of his achievement, and not only of his recent
work. In all musical literature there is no other *Dies irae* in which
a like dramatic power is combined with such economy of means.

After the *Dies irae* Stravinsky set a verse of the *Tuba mirum*,
entrusting the voice part to the bass soloist in accordance with
traditional usage, and writing an accompaniment for two trumpets,
first trombone, and finally two bassoons. The movement is based
mainly on the inversion of the fundamental series and on its original
form distributed between soloist and instruments to create about
the vocal melisma a livid atmosphere in which re-echo the harsh
sounds of the trumpets in their bass register.

After these first three vocal movements there follows the orchestral
Interlude which forms the axis about which, as has already been
said, the whole work revolves, both structurally and temporally.
Written for flutes, bassoons, horns, and timpani, the *Interlude* takes
its character from an incisive rhythm analogous to that of the *Dies
irae*. Now the other three vocal pieces follow. Omitting the text
from 'Mors stupebit' to 'sit securus', Stravinsky set the first verse of
the *Rex tremendae* for the four parts of the choir treated alternately
contrapuntally and homophonically and accompanied by a trumpet
and trombone which move by intervals of an almost expressionist
variety. Into this sound landscape flutes and lower strings insert
rhythmic shudders of icy chords steadily repeated. Next comes the
Lacrimosa, set in full. The protagonist of this movement is the
solo contralto, together with the flutes, harp, and two double basses,
with brief interruptions by the strings and muted trombones. In the
voice part lamenting melismas and supplicatory chanting alternate.

The final respond of the Requiem Mass, *Libera me*, has also been set by Stravinsky in its entirety. The movement takes the form of a homophonic chorale, chanted in the style of a litany by four solo voices from the chorus against a shadowy background created by the rest of the chorus who recite the same text in psalm-singing style ('tutti parlando in piano'). The four horns accompany the voices with a sonority which White justly compares to that of a harmonium, evoking for him 'shades of Rossini' – evidently the Rossini of the *Petite messe solennelle*.[30] The subdued atmosphere of the movement, if not the musical figures, may remind one also of the *Messe des pauvres* of Erik Satie, made darker and more dramatic. The *Postlude* is divided into three sections, each of which comes to rest on a prolonged horn note which emerges from a chord for flutes, piano, and harp. In the wake of this note, the celesta, bells, and vibraphone, with regular periodic movement, begin processions of chords absolutely even in duration and intensity, perfectly anonymous because deprived of all individual harmonic tension and dissolved in the pure sonorous airs of a celestial carillon. The love of bells which Stravinsky always nourished here finds its mystical fulfilment.

The timbre of this last movement has suggested an approach to the Boulez of the *Improvisations sur Mallarmé*. White correctly describes such an association as superficial and finds in 'this carefully calculated chiming of verticals in some ways a serial parallel to the chorale at the end of Stravinsky's Symphonies of Wind Instruments'. Here, as in that chorale, all personal feeling is dissolved, absorbed into a sense of universal piety and solidarity in the face of looming night in which all earthly existence is destined to vanish. In the *Song*, placed at the centre of *In Memoriam Dylan Thomas* (one of the few pages of his work effectively and directly marked with an explicit expressive pathos), the composer clothed and gave musical effect to the poet's verses in which, rebelling against his own father's death, he sought the voice of protest of all mankind, exhorting them:

> 'Do not go gentle into that good night,
> Old age should burn and rave at close of day;
> Rage, rage against the dying of the light.'

When he set these yearning verses, Stravinsky evidently put on one side his tranquil religious faith, and also rejected the stoic resigna-

---

[30] As Claudio Spies points out in the article quoted above, Stravinsky had in fact originally written the horn parts for the harmonium – like certain other wind passages in the *Dies irae*, the *Tuba mirum*, the *Lacrimosa*, and the *Postlude*. But the changes were made before the orchestral rehearsals began.

tion which was able to confer a ritual dignity on his tragic Greek music. The *Requiem Canticles* are an intimate and dramatic work, but he did not wish them to be tragic. On the contrary, in the *Postlude* he seems to have resumed and sublimated the ultimate aim of all his work : to bring peace and comfort, expressing consolatory catharsis through a human experience whose most obvious symbol remains the figure of Oedipus, impotent plaything of a blind destiny, who, though not culpably responsible for the evil of this world, nevertheless shares in it and must expiate it, and cannot expect pardon as a deserved prize but only as inscrutable grace. To this grace the art of the latest Stravinsky seems to aspire, according to his conception of music, already quoted, as 'a form of communion with our fellow man – and with the Supreme Being' (see p. 155). But even if one were to consider Stravinsky's longing to participate in 'ontological reality' as illusory, and his declared faith the fruit of narcotic autosuggestion, the actual creative results of such spiritual premises should constitute the noblest reasons for enjoying the 'consolations musicae', if only on an aesthetic plane. Stravinsky's art remains valid, even as 'art for art's sake'.

It has been said – indeed it has been written (see Peter Heyworth's letters from Edinburgh in *Nuova Rivista Italiana*, September-October 1967, p. 596) – that Stravinsky was afraid he would never finish the *Requiem Canticles*. Once he did bring this most important work to a successful conclusion, in a moment of relaxation he set to music one of Edward Lear's Nonsense Songs : *The Owl and the Pussy-cat* – a 'musical charm' as Luciano Berio calls it in the introductory note for the concert on 11 September 1967 when the piece had its first performance at the 30th International Festival of Contemporary Music in Venice.

This delicious little song, dedicated to 'Vera' (Stravinsky's wife), is in two-part counterpoint : the voice part, and the piano part, doubled at the octave, which accompanies the voice in canon. The shape of the piece is the outcome of the melodic unfolding and the contrapuntal intertwining of the various forms of the following twelve-note row :

Thus the composition is written entirely in accordance with dodeca-phonic serial principles. Yet the lay listener hearing the song for the first time might well get the impression that Stravinsky had reverted to the spirit and the style of the vocal works of his Russian period of fifty years back. *The Owl and the Pussy-cat* actually does reflect something of the music of that period (especially the works with a child-like flavour in which he set to music those delightful Russian nonsense rhymes) viewed through the prism of Stravinsky's contemporary serial writing. How such a phenomenon could come about is easily comprehensible if we look closely at the structure of the row quoted above and then compare it with the intrinsic modal shape of his compositions of fifty or sixty years earlier. In the series he uses, a group of four notes making up a diminished seventh (notes 8, 9, 10 and 11) is surrounded by eight notes belonging to one of those modes of limited transpositions on which not only Stravinsky's little Russian pieces but even large-scale works like the *Scherzo Fantastique* and *Petrushka* are very largely based. (On page 7 I refer to bars in the *Scherzo Fantastique*, each of which is based exclusively on one of the three possible transpositions of the mode in question.) Thus Stravinsky's sensibility is once again seen to be one of the essential factors working from within to ensure the unity of his seemingly protean creativeness.

XXIII The Last Years

After *The Owl and the Pussy-cat* Stravinsky was to live another four years, but they were years in which the steady, unremitting deterioration of his health forced him to work less and less, and only spasmodically. And of the little he did compose, only a small part has been published, hardly more in fact that the instrumentation of two sacred songs, for voice and piano, from Hugo Wolf's *Spanisches Liederbuch*, dated May 1968. The songs are dedicated to Marilyn Horne, although in actual fact the first performance was given not by her but by the mezzo-soprano Christina Krooskos, who sang them on 6 September 1968 at the Los Angeles County Museum of Art. Robert Craft conducted the small instrumental ensemble consisting of three clarinets in A, two horns in F, and a quintet of solo strings. Early in October of the following year 1969, Dietrich Fischer-Dieskau was to have sung the two pieces, again under Craft's baton, during the *Berliner Festwochen*. But the singer fell ill at the last moment and was replaced by the Swedish mezzo Kerstin Meyer, who sang the first song: *Herr was trägt der Boden hier*, and the American soprano Catherine Gayer, who sang the second song: *Wunden trägst du*. Neither on this occasion nor on others, for example when the first performance was given in Rome on 22 January 1970, did the critics show any sign of having grasped the real significance and importance of this last and seemingly quite modest, unpretentious Stravinskyan score.

Some critics were puzzled by Stravinsky's unexpected espousal of Hugo Wolf. They did not understand that if Stravinsky was finally coming full circle in his assimilation of musical tradition by actually identifying himself, practically on his deathbed, with a champion of German late-romanticism (Wagner had already had some influence on him in his youthful Symphony, the early German romantics in *Capriccio*, and the Slav romantics – Chopin and Tchaikovsky in particular – paradoxically in some of his neo-classical compositions) he did so because he discovered affinities with Wolf as with the other musicians of the past towards whom he was creatively drawn.

Stravinsky discovered in the *Two Sacred Songs* something of himself,
something he seemed as it were to be recovering as if it had been
taken from him beforehand, as if his predecessor had been imitating
him. Those 'poignant "hairpin" diminuendos . . . in every bar' were
already to be found in the plaintive solo string passage at the beginning of the *Requiem Canticles*:

And the gesture of entreaty in this passage, where an interval is
repeated with a sob-like insistence before dissolving into a broader,
anguished melodic curve, is reflected in anticipation in the two
introductory bars of Wolf's second song:

Note how the melodic line in the second bar is kept chromatically
within an interval of a third, virtually foreshadowing a *modus
operandi* for which, as we have seen, Stravinsky showed a predilection from *In Memoriam Dylan Thomas* onwards. In the same bar
also, a rising major second and a falling minor second form a recur-
ring figure which serves as the basic cell of this song and, as has
been said, of the first song as well. Wolf – whether he was aware of

it or not is unimportant – made alternative use of three of the four
possible serial variants, although obviously this does not amount
to wholesale serialization of the entire melodic and harmonic texture,
but is merely reflected consequentially in the interval structure of
the melody. (However, the harmony as well coherently reflects the
interval structure of the original cell, by making preferential use of
major and minor sevenths, never diminished sevenths, in other words
by using the only intervals other than seconds that can be formed
with the notes of the melodic cell.) Thus, for example, the melodic
lines of each of the two introductory bars of the first song quoted
above are found to be inversions of the same cell. In bars 8, 9 and 10
of the song the melodic line can be seen as an inverse retrograde
form of the same cell followed by the one indicated above as the
original cell (see example on p. 263). This is the same as the cell on
which the series in *Movements* is based. (See example on p. 223.) The
melody in the second bar of the first song is identical with the
second group of three notes of the series in *Movements*. Three bars
later, the notes of Wolf's melody are identical with the succeeding
three notes of the same series in retrograde order, while in the
accompaniment the same form of the cell, transposed, is repeated
with two different harmonizations. The concluding phrase of the
first song quoted contains all the notes of the central segment of
the series in *Movements*, with the order changed (4-6-7-8-5-9). But
the same six notes also constitute the first half of the series in the
third piece of the *Canticum Sacrum* (see page 224), and a similar
melodic design emerges from the last five notes of the series in *Agon*
cited on page 204. Examples of this type of relationship could be
multiplied in connection with each individual bar of the two songs.
I will not dwell on the subject, but below is a conspectus from which
any reader interested in this type of structural analysis can discern
some of the many analogies between phrases of Wolf's *lieder* and
certain segments of the series on which *Agon*, *The Flood* and *Requiem
Canticles* are based:

Requiem Canticles is the work that presents the most numerous and closest links with these Wolf songs. In support of this statement, let us look once again at the *Requiem Canticles* series quoted in the example on p. 254. It will be seen that the groups of three notes B-A-A sharp (3-4-5) and D-C sharp-D sharp (6-7-8) correspond to two serial variants of the basic cell in the two Wolf songs. But the last three notes of the series (F sharp-E-G) form a motif which can also be related to the same cell if its intervals are expanded so that the minor second becomes a major second and the major second becomes a minor third. The identical situation occurs in the second of the Wolf songs, the first part of which (repeated at the end to complete the *da capo* form) ends with this very motif:

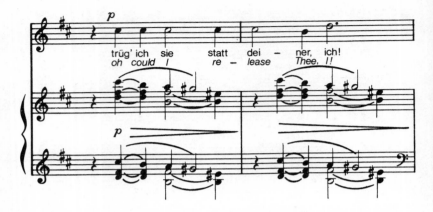

However, if we compare the first choral section of the *Requiem Canticles (Exaudi)* with *Herr, was trägt der Boden hier*, the result is quite astonishing. The entire melodic line of the sopranos in the *Exaudi* might almost be said to be contained already in the Wolf song. The melodic shape of the first bar:

is the exact inversion (within the same interval G-D sharp moreover) of the sixth bar from the end of the *lied* in question:

This is taken up after six instrumental bars and embodied in a short phrase by means of a connecting figure that emerges from the original cell, consisting of two different intervals of a second, the minor second undergoing a kind of supplicating, double oscillation in opposite directions, like the systole and diastole of a heart at the moment of final agony:

Ex – au – di   O – ra – ti – o – nem   me – – am

After one more instrumental bar, we have six further choral bars, and then a coda of three bars for the strings concludes the piece in a laconic manner reminiscent of Webern:

Ad te,   ad te,   om-nis ca – ro   ve – ni – et,   ve – ni – – et

The similarity between these final six bars and the final five bars of the Wolf song is quite obvious: we have two more or less parallel melodic lines that first proceed stepwise, then return on themselves (as if to evoke a noumenon – the name BACH) and then dip downwards to die away in an instrumental echo in Wolf, a vocal echo in Stravinsky. I would certainly not wish to hazard a guess as to the way in which this intricate network of links, conscious or unconscious, between Stravinsky and Wolf came about. What is certain is that in giving expression to his elective affinity with a composer like Wolf, with whom no one hitherto would ever have dreamed of bracketing him, Stravinsky has used every means of bridging the gap between Wolf and himself with discretion and at the same time with unerring effectiveness. His instrumentation was said to be 'deliberately sober, without intrusion of any sort' but it is typically Stravinskyan instrumentation; in fact the strict antiphonal distinction between wind and strings finds its exact counterpart in the similarly antiphonal instrumentation of *In Memoriam Dylan Thomas*. Thus we need only compare the first two bars of *Herr was trägt der Boden hier* with the corresponding bars as orchestrated by Stravinsky to detect another of the characteristic rules he followed in filling out the scores of the two compositions. He eliminates the harmonic doubling of the chords, and following his own predilection for essential austerity he makes the whole polyphonic texture more subtle and more penetrating. In other words, he does exactly the opposite of what is normally done by orchestrators of piano works or pieces for other solo instruments. They usually feel that they have to expand, thicken and pad out the musical substance. There is only one point, in the third bar of the second song, where Stravinsky does not proceed by 'lightening' the texture but actually prolongs a note (a middle G played by the first horn) and brings in the lower octave played by the second horn two crotchets earlier. These are minor adjuncts serving to create pivots around which he redesigns the harmonic framework, transforming the chords into melodic lines (chromatically drawn in the clarinets, more diatonically smooth and calm in the first violin and viola), differentiating the timbres, articulating and annotating Wolf's piano texture. Whenever Stravinsky does anything that involves modifying Wolf's musical structure it seems to be done with utter, affectionate delicacy giving an even more melting quality to what Stuckenschmidt describes as a *Mitleidshymnus* (hymn of compassion), although it might still more properly be described as a hymn of mutual compassion between Creator and creature, the supreme anthem of universal suffering as the price of life : the suffering of the human soul as it contemplates, yet cannot itself experience, Christ's bleeding, mortal wounds and suffering; the acceptance of martyrdom by the Saviour as the price 'of having loved so ardently' the soul of man, the price of 'achieving its salvation'. These themes, characteristic of a certain kind of Spanish Catholic poetry fusing spiritual chastity and sensuous passion, mystical exaltation and earthly torment, a burning love of life and a nostalgic yearning for sacrifice and death, and admirably rendered in the German translation of Paul Heyse and Emanuel Geibel, undoubtedly helped to make Stravinsky feel the two Wolf songs as 'his own'. Instinctively he must have felt them as a last, crowning witness to his own religious feelings and, I would say, to his own view of life and art as a combination and juxtaposition of a wild, primordial, dark sensuality with a constant striving towards the sublime and the transcendental. These dialectical contrasts, whether reflected in the pagan symbols of Dionysus and Apollo or in the Christian ethos, are brought into harmony by Stravinsky at the price of an unremitting effort (this is one of the fundamental constants of creativity) to achieve as it were a physical reduction of the metaphysical,[1] a concrete, tangible musical incarnation of the impalpable, intangible, elusive, inconceivable, inexpressible mystery of the Divine Being. In Stravinsky, as in Schoenberg, there exists side by side, although in symmetrically different proportions, an Aaron ready and willing to imagine and

---

[1] In *Thoughts of an Octogenarian* he writes: 'My "human measure" is not only possible, but also exact. It is, first of all, absolutely physical, and it is immediate.'

express and a Moses ready to place a taboo on imagination and expression. Let us then round off the sketch made by Stravinsky himself in relation to Schoenberg (see pages 278–9) by saying that although they started out from opposite poles, at a certain point of their lives these two supreme masters made a complete turnabout in their poetic outlook, turning in opposite directions, and in the end found themselves close together in achieving the highest creative goals reached by man in the musical field so far in the present century.

But I am straying too far towards a conclusion for which this discussion of Stravinsky is not yet ready. In reacting against what I felt to be a shortsighted underestimate of the significance of Stravinsky's last published works, I may have gone too far in the opposite direction. Nevertheless the factual data I have given, backed up with analysis, seem to me more than sufficient to demonstrate that Igor Stravinsky's instrumentation of the Two Sacred Songs of Hugo Wolf, far from being 'anonymous' and lacking his 'signature', is profoundly imbued with his style, pervaded with his sensibility, steeped in his spirit. It is not 'music to the second power' nor is it – or rather it is very much more than – a simple transcription or instrumentation. It is not a work which a Society of Authors would catalogue under the heading of 'original works', but is infinitely more original than so much music that is fully accepted in that category. In fact, it represents a unique example of its kind; and if for that reason only, it warranted this lengthy discussion. Moreover, as I have said, it is the last musical composition published by Stravinsky, and it is with painful reluctance that I see this as the end of his creative span, and tell myself that the wellspring of Stravinsky's creativeness is now forever dried up. But it is a consolation to cherish the hope, indeed the conviction, that musical thoughts of his will still be revealed as time goes on. For we know from his interviews and statements, from his dialogues with Craft and from Craft's diaries, that he never ceased thinking about music and writing down musical thoughts even during his illness, during his long sojourns in clinics and hospitals and right up to the moment of his death.

For instance Stravinsky himself described in an interview given to the *New York Review* a group of 'transcriptions from Bach's *Well-Tempered Clavier*' finished in the New York Hospital on 17 June 1969, just a day before his eighty-seventh birthday:[2]

[2] Quoted in *Melos*, XXXVII, No. 2, February 1970.

'I had planned to set four fugues – one each in two, three, four, and five voices – for solo winds (clarinets and bassoons), and to set their preludes for string orchestra. But the four-voiced fugue that I finally chose suited solo strings only, besides which I later doubled the instruments in the two-voiced fugue, for the sonority . . . The music has hardly been altered in the trans-ferral – certainly it has not acquired any technicolour or any stereo – but a character of performance *has* been imposed on it through the phrasing, articulation, and rhythmic alteration. The ornamentation is not florid, I might add, for while under- not over-embellishment is the commonplace of mis-performance today, I am still mindful of the complaint of Mrs. Delaney, the Handelian, concerning a performance of Corelli's *Christmas Concerto* in Dublin in 1750, that the final cadence, instead of being "clear and distinct ⌈was⌉ filled up with frippery and graces . . ." As for my "aim", if I must pretend to have one, I simply wished to make the music available in another instrumental form than the keyboard, which may also have been Mozart's "aim" in transcribing five fugues from the same collection for two violins, viola and bass.'

The first performance of these transcriptions was scheduled to take place during the same *Berliner Festwochen* concert in 1969 which also featured the instrumental versions of Wolf's Sacred Songs, but at the last moment the transcriptions of Bach's preludes and fugues were removed from the programme. Craft[3] has the following comment to make in his diary entry of 2 October 1969 : 'At the dress rehearsal this morning I decided, together with Nicolas Nabokov,[4] not to play I.S's new Bach transcriptions, too little if anything of I.S. being discernible in them as they stand now, virtually unedited.'

In spite of the assurances and the verbal explanations given to me by Nabokov concerning the reasons for this decision, I cannot help but feel that the justification for it is not any alleged short-coming in Stravinsky's transcriptions; it may prove rather to be the last link in the long chain of misunderstandings which was clearly destined to dog Stravinsky's creative steps from his earliest begin-nings to his latest brainchild. I have shown how much of Stravinsky is revealed by the instrumentation of Wolf's songs which one of the most famous critics dismissed as 'anonymous'. Obviously it is impossible to forecast with certainty that a change of heart will take place in the case of the transcriptions of the Bach pieces also. But the way in which Stravinsky himself spoke about them is sufficiently lucid and precise to leave reasonable room for hope that this will be so.

It is certainly to be hoped that these works will be published as

---

[3] *Stravinsky: Chronicle of a Friendship*, p. 370.
[4] Director of the *Berliner Festwochen*.

soon as possible so that we shall have an opportunity to study the original, or at any rate a version amended by Stravinsky himself and not by others, however well-meaning and disinterested they may be. After all, the Master would have had plenty of time to produce a revised version, if he had really felt it necessary, during the year and a half he still had left after the abortive performance of the work in Berlin – a year and a half in which, apart from periods of grave illness, there were weeks and even months during which he could not only work but even travel between one continent and another.

In February 1970, I sent him an invitation to attend the thirty-third *Maggio Musicale Fiorentino* in Florence, which was to be devoted to the period between the two world wars, in other words mainly to neo-classicism, so that there were many works by Stravinsky on the programme. In reply, he said he would like to be able to accept the invitation and would shortly be arriving in Europe; and he told me that he had decided to leave California permanently and to take a *pied-à-terre* in New York, but hoped later to find a house in or near Paris where he could spend most of his remaining days.[5] It remained a mere wish. On 30 March the composer moved into the new apartment on Fifth Avenue, New York, which he had acquired after abandoning his plan to take up residence in Paris. There Stravinsky spent the last six days of his life, which ended in the night of 6–7 April; and from there began the last voyage which was to bring him on 15 April 1971, at the conclusion of his life on earth, to his final resting-place in the peace of the island of San Michele in Venice, after an Orthodox Church funeral ceremony celebrated in the Basilica of SS. Giovanni e Paolo by the Armenian Archimandrite Malissianos, in the presence of a Catholic Bishop and ministers of the Evangelical and Anglican churches, symbolizing as it were the spiritual universality which Stravinsky's art had brought into being.

The 1967 English edition of this book ended as follows: 'Today, at over 84 years of age, Stravinsky is still vigorously active. His work is still a "work in progress". Let us therefore not write "Finis" at the conclusion of this chapter; let us leave the end of the book open, ready to receive further comments on such compositions as may well be forthcoming at any moment from one of the last musicians fashioned in the ancient mould.' This ending must, alas,

[5] The letter is reproduced in Quaderno No. 1 published by the Ente Autonomo Teatro Communale of Florence and devoted to the thirty-third *Maggio Musicale Fiorentino*.

now be changed, although the concluding phrase is still valid. Stravinsky has indeed been one of the last great composers to whom it was given to develop to the full the musical tradition based on the potentialities of the tempered scale system whose historical development has today undoubtedly reached its limit, as we have realized for a long time. This does not, however, mean the passing of the actual concept of a tradition that may or may not continue to be based on the use of the twelve notes equally distributed over the octave, but that still represents a continual stockpiling of 'works' – individualized sound structures capable of being handed down to posterity, of being associated in the mind, of making history. There are those today who, feeling themselves incapable of still producing valid and vital works, blame their own impotence on some alleged general, objective impossibility, and arrogantly inveigh against what the Germans call disparagingly '*Opus-Musik*'. Well, Stravinsky was certainly until the end of his days an '*Opus-Musiker*' in the sense of a musician who in spite of his keen interest in everything that was new in contemporary music, felt himself more and more deeply attached to tradition, to the point of expressing a strong nostalgia for the actual working conditions of Bach himself – the man who had virtually set in motion the evolutionary cycle which Stravinsky was bringing to an end. Thus in the 'Personal' chapter of the *Dialogues*,[6] setting down 'Thoughts of an Octogenarian' Stravinsky confesses:

'I was born out of time in the sense that by temperament and talent I would have been more suited for the life of a small Bach, living in anonymity and composing regularly for an established service and for God. I did weather the world I was born to, weathered it well, you will say, and I have survived – though not uncorrupted – the hucksterism of publishers, music festivals, recording companies, publicity, including my own ("Self-love is unquestionably the chief motive which leads anyone to speak, and more especially to write respecting himself." – Alfieri, *Memoirs*), conductors, critics (with whom my real argument is that the person who practises the vocation of music should not be judged by the person who has no vocation and does not understand musical practice, and to whom music must therefore be of infinitely less fundamental consequence), and all of the misunderstandings about performance the word concerts has come to mean. But the small Bach might have composed three times as much music.'

A few years later, while he was working on the *Requiem Canticles* for the first performance, to be given at Princeton University, the Master, now eighty-four years of age, spoke of the future that might be in store for him: 'I know only that in the *coronat opus* of my

---

[6] *Dialogues and a Diary*, p. 23.

later years, the Princeton Requiem (I say that now because I am working on it), I continue to believe in my taste buds and to follow the logic of my ear, quaint expressions which will seem even quainter when I add that I require as much hearing at the piano as ever before; and this, I am certain, is not because of age, is not a sign of dotage. I know, too, that I will never cross the gulf from well-tempered pitches to "sounds" and "noises" of contemporary music and will never abdicate the rule of my ears. But predictions are dangerous. *Basta!*' And in a footnote he adds:

'Pitch and interval relationships are for me the primary dimension, whereas for such younger colleagues as the Stockhausen followers (call them the *eau de Cologne*) the pitches may be less important than the shape of the room or the direction of the sound. I understand this switch of emphasis, however; after all, a new composer must win his spurs in new territory. What I cannot understand is the mind which chooses to leave the completion of its work to the megrims of performers; that and the manic-depressive fluctuations of a fashion that swings from total control to no control. from the serialization of all elements to chance.'[7]

Aesthetic considerations apart, it was his ethical approach to music, to art in general and to life itself, that Stravinsky could not leave to chance: Stravinsky, medieval/modern artist; Stravinsky, composer 'born out of time' yet embodying, and moving ahead of, his time; Stravinsky, man of the world *par excellence* and consummate musician; Stravinsky, incarnation of all that is paradoxical in our lives and guide in overcoming the tragically adverse circumstances of human life; Stravinsky, dateless up-to-date composer who looked beyond all fashion towards eternal values.

Today I am more reluctant than ever to write 'Finis' at the end of this book. There are still passages, fragments, and pieces by Stravinsky I would like to know about; there are compositions of his which everyone is supposed to know but which in actual fact still need to be studied, reflected upon, examined more thoroughly and analysed in a number of ways insufficiently realized and possibly not even guessed. This work on Stravinsky still remains, then, a 'work in progress'.

[7] *Themes and Episodes*, pp. 23-4.

Appendix: Stravinsky and Schoenberg

In contemporary music circles Stravinsky was for a long time regarded as the antithesis of all that Arnold Schoenberg stood for. Until quite recently critics have tended to identify these two outstanding figures with one or other of the main currents in contemporary music. Whether this is justified is debatable; nor perhaps is it correct to regard Schoenberg and Stravinsky as marking the extreme limits of earlier twentieth-century music. Webern applied the twelve-note method in a far more thorough-going manner than did Schoenberg, and both Milhaud and Hindemith at times used polyharmony and polytonality much more boldly and consequentially than ever Stravinsky did. Schoenberg and Stravinsky thus mark neither the outer boundaries of modern music nor its only lines of development. What they represent, rather, are two poles around and in relation to which all other musical trends and movements of the twentieth century fall into place. For a long time these two composers seemed to be the embodiment of two irreconcilable tendencies that had destroyed the unity of musical language. But since 1952 there have been many signs to suggest that their paths were ultimately convergent, and that the things they stood for will turn out to be complementary rather than antagonistic.

If we look back from the vantage-point of today, it becomes clear that the true creators of modern music contributed, although in different ways and degrees, to a common historical task. Their achievement was to break through the barriers of the traditional, overworked diatonic system based on the major and minor scales of seven notes, and to give musical composition the free and organic use of all the remaining sound material available within the range of the tempered scale system, in other words the use of all the chromatic possibilities of the twelve separate elements into which the octave had been equally divided since the time of Bach.

Schoenberg and the other composers who followed his example achieved this goal by carrying on the process of sensitizing and chromatically altering the diatonic functions already taken a long

way by Wagner, and finally brought traditional harmony to satura-
tion point, with the consequent destruction of its tonal barriers, and
the establishment of theoretical equality of the twelve different notes.
The other path to this goal in Western music during the first half
of the twentieth century was the transcending of these same traditional
limits by a novel synthesis of elements diatonic in character but tonally
heterogeneous. This is the approach of Stravinsky and the composers
whose paths ran parallel to his.

When the end of the First World War brought the exhaustion of
the expressionism which had acted as a catalyst, providing a justification on a subjective level for iconoclasm and revolutionary innovation
(expressionism in a broad sense affected Stravinsky too – the Stravinsky of the savage *Rite of Spring*), the *avant-garde* composers of the
time found a white-hot material in their possession which needed
to be fashioned and moulded; and both Stravinsky and Schoenberg,
and others, turned for a time to the use of traditional formal devices
for this purpose. The result was the neo-classical phase which now
seems to have been a feature of all music throughout Europe between
the two wars, with the exception of a few isolated figures like
Varèse. Where the paths of Stravinsky and Schoenberg diverged for
a fairly long period was in regard to infrastructural forms. Schoenberg conceived the consequential method of composing with twelve
notes. Stravinsky felt the need, before deciding to take the decisive
step towards the adoption of dodecaphony, for a long period of
empirical simplification, a return to a less complex exploitation of
tonal relations. This in the outcome enabled him at the same time
to effect that extraordinary creative assimilation of the Western
world's musical past which marked his personal brand of neo-
classicism. He seems to have realized instinctively that he could not
take the final step over the threshold of a tradition before he had
made it really his very own and had relived its fundamental values
in his own creative experience. The implication was that once this
process had been completed, he too would adopt the twelve-note
system.

When, between the end of 1957 and the beginning of 1958, I
handed the first edition of this book over to the printer, Stravinsky
was approaching the end of the journey, begun after *The Rake's
Progress*, that had brought him closer and closer to the goal of serial
dodecaphony. By the time he reached the last two milestones along
this road, represented by the *Canticum Sacrum* and *Agon*, he had
already entered a realm belonging in part at least to the world of

twelve-note music. In the *Septet* and the *Three Songs from William Shakespeare* he had applied certain procedures of a serial nature to diatonic material, and in the *Dirge Canons: In Memoriam Dylan Thomas* he had made use of fragmentary chromatic series; he subsequently based entire sections of the *Canticum* and *Agon* on whole clusters of twelve different notes. In view of this steady, methodical precedent, it was not unduly rash to prophesy that sooner or later he would decide to adopt the method of composing with twelve notes *in toto*, bending and adapting it, of course, to the peculiar needs of his personality and style.

I tried at the time to highlight points in support of the view that there was already a latent tendency, evident in the works immediately following *The Rake's Progress*, that in the long run was bound to prevail over any remaining hesitation about becoming a genuine convert to the serial method, a step which implied among other things the recognition that the path opened by Schoenberg was indeed the main road of twentieth-century music. Incidentally, I may say that my diffident prophecies as to the imminence of Stravinsky's conversion were at the time dismissed and ridiculed by quite a few critics who had not made a close study of the intrinsic evolution of his art; and they were taken aback when my predictions turned out to be fully justified. Even a shrewd scholar like Hans Keller writes that 'Stravinsky's absorption of Schoenberg's technique was arguably the profoundest surprise in the history of music'.[1] There were, of course, some who were ready to attribute Stravinsky's sensational *volte-face* to a supposedly unquenchable desire on his part to jump on the bandwagon, not to be left behind by a movement that seemed to have the monopoly of up-to-dateness, in this instance the young post-Webern *avant-garde*. But there are those also who maintain the very opposite. Eric Walter White, for example, in his *Stravinsky, the Composer and his Works*[2] refers to a joking statement by the composer that 'My instinct is to recompose . . . Whatever interests me, whatever I love, I wish to make my own (I am probably describing a rare form of kleptomania)',[3] and he observes that Stravinsky's habit of behaving like a 'thieving magpie' has never been directed at the work of any of his living contemporaries, but only at music of the past, belonging to history and constituting a part of our musical heritage. White observes very

[1] Hans Keller: *Stravinsky at Rehearsal*, Denis Dobson; London, 1962, p. 3.
[2] Faber & Faber, London 1966, p. 513.
[3] Stravinsky and Craft: *Memories and Commentaries*, p. 110.

pertinently that the composition closest to Rimsky-Korsakov, namely *The Firebird*, was not written by Stravinsky under the supervision of his teacher but after his death. White also points out that Stravinsky's approach to the 'Viennese troika' did not take place until Schoenberg had followed Berg and Webern to the grave. In fact, however, in the case of the Viennese dodecaphonists Stravinsky did not take possession of their works, but simply adopted a method advocated by them. On the other hand, the same point validates all the more White's statement that Stravinsky was preparing to become a twelve-note composer at the very time when dodecaphony was on the wane, in the sense that the limit of its historical incidence was being drawn and developments were being realised which tended to surpass it. Not only in the field of electronic music, not to mention *musique concrète*, but even in the field of instrumental and vocal music still based on the twelve notes of the tempered scale, the concept of serial music was being challenged and in many cases abandoned. Very soon Stravinsky would have found himself having to defend the serial elements, and by implication his recent creative work, against the young iconoclasts 'Who already regard "serial" as an indecent word.'[4] Hence his conversion to twelve-note music cannot really be attributed to casual extrinsic causes; we must try to discover and understand the reasons, inherent in his entire evolution, which seem to have led him to his latest position. I have to confess, however, that it is no easy matter to find arguments in support of those reasons. Indeed, in the first edition of this book the analysis of the problem was by no means exhaustive. One of the most patent shortcomings was, for example, the unduly brief and superficial description of one of Stravinsky's first real masterpieces, *Fireworks*.

But the analysis, brief though it was, which I made to show the mirror structure of *Fireworks*, *The Firebird*, and particularly *The Wedding*, should have been convincing evidence of a propensity on Stravinsky's part for rational and constructive thinking that was bound to predispose him towards recognizing the tremendous importance of *Pierrot Lunaire* and should have suggested an affinity between Stravinsky and Schoenberg and the possibility that their paths might converge. This adds significance to the passage in *Conversations with Igor Stravinsky*[5] concerning the impression made on him by the performance of *Pierrot Lunaire*, conducted by Schoen-

[4] ibid., p. 100.
[5] p. 69.

berg in Berlin on 8 December 1912, which Stravinsky attended with
Diaghilev. He later wrote of it: 'The instrumental substance of
Pierrot Lunaire impressed me immensely. And by saying "instrumental", I mean not simply the instrumentation of this music but
the whole contrapuntal and polyphonic structure of this brilliant
instrumental masterpiece.' Stravinsky thus makes it quite clear that
he had been particularly struck by the intrinsic structural reality of
Pierrot Lunaire, although he does not reject, but merely describes as
'not kind but correct' the statement by Boulez that he understood
Pierrot Lunaire '*d'un façon impressionniste*'.[6] With perhaps undue
modesty, but with an acute sense of historical reality, Stravinsky
wrote on the same subject: 'The real wealth of *Pierrot* – sound and
substance, for *Pierrot* is the solar plexus as well as the mind of early
twentieth-century music – was beyond me as it was beyond all of us
at that time.' On the same page of the *Dialogues*, he speaks of the
works composed by Schoenberg in the three years prior to *Pierrot
Lunaire*, namely the *Five Pieces for Orchestra*, *Ewartung*, and *Die
glückliche Hand*, as a 'body of works we now recognize as the
epicentre of the development of our musical language. (By we, I
mean a small group still, for most composers are still bumping into
each other in the dark.)' Speaking in the 1960s, Stravinsky said that
light could only come from that source which in the same context
he did not hesitate to call 'the hypostatic trinity of twentieth-century
music' – Schoenberg the Father, Berg the Son, and Webern the Holy
Ghost. It would not be unduly spiteful to attribute the tone if not
the substance of such judgements made following Stravinsky's conversion to dodecaphony, to a certain neophyte zeal – from one who,
although an old hand, had apparently renounced entirely his own
once sovereign personality and taken refuge under the wing of new
gods.[7] But to take this view would be first of all to do a grave
injustice to Stravinsky's genius; and to avoid any misunderstanding
I would like to say at once that in my opinion Stravinsky's adoption
of serial technique, far from being a sign of weakness, bears witness
to the strength and superior self-assurance of an artist who not
only did not feel the need to seek at all times to be original at all
costs in order to boost his personality, but could still be himself
even when he decided to imitate other composers. Bach and Mozart
have something to teach us on this subject. Secondly, it would be a

    [6] *Dialogues and a Diary*, p. 105.
    [7] See *Conversations with Igor Stravinsky*, p. 127: 'Webern is for me the
juste de la musique and I do not hesitate to shelter myself by the beneficent
protection of his not yet canonized art.'

distortion of the historical truth. It was not just the other day that Stravinsky described the Berlin performance of *Pierrot Lunaire* as a 'great event',[8] the 'most prescient meeting in my life'.[9] He had no sooner heard it than he recommended that it be performed in St. Petersburg; and the critic Karatygin, one of the promotors of the 'Evenings of Contemporary Music' that enlivened Leningrad's musical life, quotes the following letter[10] which Stravinsky wrote to him on 26 December 1912 from Clarens in Switzerland, where he was working on *The Rite of Spring*: 'Dear Vyacheslav Gavrilovich, I have just finished reading your review of the Siloti concert at which Schoenberg conducted his *Pelléas*. I gather from the way you wrote that you really love and understand the essence of Schoenberg – a truly remarkable contemporary artist, and I therefore feel that it might interest you to become acquainted with his latest work, which reveals most intensely the unusual character of his creative genius, namely *Pierrot Lunaire*, Op. 21, which I recently heard in Berlin. There is a work which you "contemporaries" ought to perform! Perhaps you have met Schoenberg already and he has told you (as he told me) about this work?'[11]

Stravinsky's enthusiasm was also passed on to Ravel about 1913, and he tried without success to interest Debussy too. Debussy was rather perturbed about it, and wrote to his friend Godet: 'Stravinsky is leaning dangerously *du côté de chez Schoenberg*.'[12] Less generally known, perhaps, is the interview printed in the London *Daily Mail* on 13 February 1913, in which Stravinsky, reviewing musical life in Europe during the period, writes: 'The Viennese are barbarians. Their orchestral musicians cannot play my *Petrushka*. They hardly know Debussy there, and they chased Schoenberg away to Berlin. Now Schöenberg is one of the greatest creative spirits of our era.'[13]

[8] *Expositions and Developments*, p. 67–8.
[9] *Dialogues and a Diary*, p. 105.
[10] V. G. Karatygin: *Zhizn, deyatel'nost', statii i materiali*, Leningrad, 1927, p. 232.
[11] The English translation (modified) is taken from an article entitled 'Arnold Schoenberg in Soviet Russia' by Boris Schwartz in *Perspectives on Schoenberg and Stravinsky*, ed. Benjamin Boretz and Edward T. Cone (Princeton University Press: Princeton, N.J., 1968), a collection of essays on the two composers by Robert Craft, Milton Babbitt, David Lewin, Glenn E. Watkins, Boris Schwartz, Arthur Berger, and Claudio Spies, which had appeared between 1962 and 1967 in the bi-monthly *Perspectives of New Music*: Fromm Music Foundation, Princeton University Press.
[12] *Expositions and Developments*, p. 68.
[13] Quoted by R. Craft in an article entitled 'The Rite of Spring: Genesis of a Masterpiece', in *Perspectives of New Music*, Vol. V, No. 1, New York, Autumn-Winter 1966, p. 27.

From 1920 on relations between the two composers tended to cool and there were even moments of real animosity between them. However, it is indicative of the abiding mutual esteem between Schoenberg and Stravinsky that animosity never degenerated into an open personal feud, but merely took the form of indirect contentiousness. For example, on his arrival in America for the first time in 1925, Stravinsky gave an interview to S. Roerig in which, without mentioning Schoenberg (in fact he said later that it was the quartertone merchants he had had in mind), he criticized those who presumed to be discovering the 'music of the future' instead of trying to compose the 'music of the present' as he did himself. Schoenberg assumed that the reference was to him, and wrote a reply to it, but refrained from publishing it.[14] Nor did he publish a note written in 1928 concerning *Oedipus Rex*.[15] In 1925, after hearing Stravinsky's neo-classical *Sonata for Piano* in Venice, Schoenberg wrote an ironical poem entitled *Der neue Klassizismus* which he later used as the text for the third of his *Three Satires* (op. 28) for mixed chorus. Stravinsky could not fail to recognize himself in the personage of 'little Modernsky' with a 'Papa Bach' wig, whom Schoenberg ridicules in the work.[16]

In turn, Stravinsky speaks disparagingly of *Pierrot Lunaire* : 'I do not feel the slightest enthusiasm about the aesthetics of the work which appears to me a retrogression to the out-of-date Beardsley cult. But on the other hand, I consider that the merits of the instrumentation are beyond dispute.'[17] In spite of appearances, the discrepancy between this stricture on *Pierrot Lunaire* and the statements mentioned earlier is not substantial enough to warrant accusing Stravinsky of inconsistency; the difference is merely one of emphasis. Even at the time when the gulf between Schoenberg and himself was widest, Stravinsky did not renege on his admiration for the instrumental qualities of *Pierrot*; he simply expressed his lack of sympathy for the aesthetic values implicit in the work. In fact, when he praises the qualities of *Pierrot*, he never fails to point out that it is in the instrumental structure of the work that he finds them and

---

[14] J. Rufer, *The Works of Arnold Schoenberg*, Faber & Faber, London 1962, item II. D. 104. Under item II. D. 106 Rufer quotes another of Schoenberg's writings dated 26 July 1926, entitled *The Restaurant Owner*, likewise a retort to Stravinsky's attack on 'Zukunftsmusik à la Schoenberg'.

[15] ibid., item II. D. 55.

[16] See p. 69 of *Conversations with Stravinsky* : '. . . in 1925, he [Schoenberg] wrote a very nasty verse about me (though I almost forgave him, for setting it to such a remarkable mirror canon) . . .'

[17] *Chronicle of My Life*, p. 96.

not in the vocal part, where the aesthetics he found distasteful are mainly reflected. In the 1963 *Dialogues* quoted above, again referring to the Berlin performance of 1912 in which Madame Albertine Zehme performed the *Sprechstimme* part, he notes: 'I remember that the audience was quiet and attentive and that I wanted Frau Zehme to be quiet too, so that I could hear the *music*. Diaghilev and I were equally impressed with *Pierrot*, though he dubbed it a product of the *Jugendstil* movement, from an aesthetic point of view'.

As we look back today, the points of convergence and contact between the trends represented by Schoenberg and Stravinsky loom larger and larger, while what at one time seemed irreconcilable differences seem less important. Stravinsky himself in the end stated quite rightly that 'every age is a historic unity' and no less rightly that the term 'neo-classic' has lost its connotation as the antithesis of dodecaphony, from the moment when it 'began to apply to all the between-the-war composers'. He further observes that 'The music of Schoenberg, Berg, and Webern was considered extremely icono-clastic at the time, but the composers now appear to have used musical form as I did, historically. My use of it was overt, however, and theirs elaborately disguised. We all explored and discovered new music in the twenties, of course, but we attached it to the very tradition were so busily outgrowing a decade before.'[18] And going on from this, half facetiously and half in earnest, Stravinsky draws up a table of twenty-nine points showing the differences and simi-larities between Schoenberg and himself. The differences are the more numerous – twenty of the points – but the choice is described at the end by the composer himself as 'a nice parlour game, no more'; he finds the 'parallelisms', condensed into nine points, the more interesting. Actually, even some of these points seem to me to single out quite superficial parallels, e.g. the fact that the success of two of their early works, *Transfigured Night* and *The Firebird*, was to prove an obstacle to the dissemination of their other works (point 2), or the reference to 'the common exile to the same alien culture, in which we wrote some of our best works (his *Fourth Quartet*, my *Abraham and Isaac*), and in which we are still played far less than in the Europe that exiled us' (point 4). The same is true of the statement, 'Both family men and fathers of several children, both hypochondriac, both deeply superstitious' (point 5). More sig-nificant is the statement of 'The close parallel development over the

[18] *Conversations with Igor Stravinsky*, p. 126.

span of sixty years' (point 3). The final four points seem to me of considerable interest: '6. For both of us, numbers are things. 7. Both of us were devoted to the Word, and each wrote some of his own librettos *(Moses and Aaron, Die glückliche Hand, Jacobsleiter, Les Noces, Renard)*. 8. Each of us composed for concrete sounds, unlike the later Webern, in which choice of sound is the final stage. 9. For both of us, the row is thematic and we are ultimately less interested in the construction of the row, *per se*, than is Webern.' But first and foremost among the affinities between Schoenberg and himself, according to Stravinsky, is 'the common belief in Divine Authority, the Hebrew God, and in Biblical mythology, Catholic culture.'[19]

If we try today to adjust the historical perspective, we find that in certain respects the relative positions of Schoenberg and Stravinsky are reversed. Read, for example, the commemorative article 'Stravinsky and the Century: Style or Idea?' written by Pierre Boulez in the 29 May 1971 issue of the *Saturday Review* of Philadelphia: 'Analysing Schoenberg's position has not taken us as far from Stravinsky as it may seem. For, in spite of all the labels that were attached to his production during a certain period of his life, Stravinsky's music did not reflect the neo-classical ideal I have just described nearly so much as did Schoenberg. Stravinsky's aims, when he showed his attachment to history, were not the same as those of a man of tradition such as Schoenberg. To begin with, his situation was fundamentally different. We are dealing here with a rebel.'

[19] *Dialogues and a Diary*, pp. 56-8.

Bibliography

The bibliography of works on Stravinsky and his music is far and away the most extensive that any contemporary musician can claim. The most exhaustive repertory of writings on Stravinsky and his works is probably that of Paul David Magriel: *Igor Strawinsky, A Bibliography Comprising Critical Writings on his Life, Music and Influence*, published in two issues of the Bulletin of Bibliography, F. W. Faxon Co.: Boston, January-April and May-August 1940. Subsequently the list was republished in the second edition of *Strawinsky in the theatre*, ed. Minna Lederman (see below) which contains some 600 titles.

In addition to the writings quoted in the footnotes throughout this volume, the following is a selected bibliography of books and articles in periodicals in the main European languages:

In English:

MERLE ARMITAGE: G. Schirmer: *Igor Stravinsky*, New York, 1936 (a collection of essays by Eugene Goossens, Henry Boys, Olin Downes, Merle Armitage, Emile Vuillermoz, Louis Danz, José Rodriguez, Manuel Komroff, Jean Cocteau, Erik Satie, Boris de Schloezer).

ERIC WALTER WHITE: *Stravinsky's Sacrifice to Apollo*, Hogarth Press: London, 1930.
Stravinsky: A Critical Survey, John Lehmann: London, 1947.
Stravinsky: The Composer and His Works, Faber & Faber: London, 1966 (one of the most comprehensive and valuable works on the subject to date).

FRANK ONNEN: *Stravinsky* (translated from Dutch by M. M. Kessler-Button), Continental Book Company: Stockholm; Sidgwick & Jackson: London, 1948.

EDWIN CORLE: *Igor Stravinsky*, Duell, Sloane & Pearce: New York, 1949 (with articles by Boris de Schloezer, Erik Satie, Eugene Goossens, Jean Cocteau, Henry Boys, Aaron Copland, Arthur Berger, Nicolas Nabokov, Merle Armitage, Edwin Corle, Robert Craft, Sir Osbert Sitwell, Samuel Dushkin, Cecil Smith, Lawrence Morton). Some of the material is reproduced from the Merle Armitage book (see above).

ROLLO H. MYERS: *Introduction to the Music of Stravinsky*, Dennis Dobson: London, 1950.

MINNA LEDERMAN: *Stravinsky in the Theatre*, Pelegrini & Cudahy: New York; Peter Owen: London, 1951 (with essays by Minna Lederman, Jean Cocteau, Emile Vuillermoz, Jacques Rivière, André Levinson, C. F. Ramuz, Arthur Berger, Ingolf Dahl, Georges Balanchine, Robert Craft, Nicolas Nabokov, Ernest Ansermet, Aaron Copland, Alexei Haieff, Carlos Chavez, Pierre Monteux, Walter Piston, Darius Milhaud, Leonard Bernstein, Vittorio Rieti, William Schuman, Lincoln Kirstein, Igor Stravinsky). This collection of essays, in a smaller format and without the bibliography already mentioned, was originally published as vol. VI, nos. 10-12 of the journal *Dance Index*, Ballet Caravan Inc.: New York, 1947.

PAUL HENRY LANG: *Strawinsky: a New Appraisal of His Work*, Norton Library: New York, 1963 (with articles by Paul Henry Lang, Edward T. Cone, Wilfrid Mellers, Lawrence Morton, Robert U. Nelson, Boris Schwarz, Carroll D. Wade). The individual essays collected in this volume were written for the special number of *The Musical Quarterly*: New York, 1962, dedicated to Stravinsky on the occasion of his eightieth birthday.

ARNOLD NEWMAN: *Bravo Stravinsky*, The World Publishing Company: Cleveland, Ohio. A series of photographs showing the composer at home, mostly when he was working on *Requiem Canticles*, i.e. in December 1966. Text by Robert Craft.

A. DOBRIN: *Igor Stravinsky, his Life and Time*, New York, 1970.

ROBERT SIOHAN: *Stravinsky*. Translated from the French by E. W. White, Calder & Boyars: London, 1966. A study by a conductor who more than once had occasion to conduct works by Stravinsky with the composer as soloist, and hence is able to give first-hand information and testimony concerning the way in which Stravinsky really wanted his music to be performed.

Articles in American and English periodicals:

MARC BLITZSTEIN: 'Phenomenon of Stravinsky', in *Musical Quarterly*, New York, July 1935 (an extreme left-wing anti-Stravinsky essay).

NADIA BOULANGER: 'Strawinsky', in *Lecture on Modern Music*, published under the auspices of the Rice Institute, Houston, Texas, April 1926 (a mainly analytical essay written from the 'grammatical' point of view).

BORIS DE SCHLOEZER: 'I. Strawinsky', in *The Dial*, New York, October 1928 (translated by Ezra Pound).

NICOLAS NABOKOV: 'Stravinsky Now', in *Partisan Review*, Summer 1944 (a study of Stravinsky's ideas on tempo and rhythm).

ERWIN STEIN: 'Canticum Sacrum', in *Tempo*, London, December 1956.

Special numbers of English language periodicals devoted to Stravinsky:

Tempo, London, Summer 1948 (with essays by Tamara Karsavina, Cyril W. Beaumont, Henry Boys, Eric Walter White, Charles Stuart).

The Score & I.M.A. Magazine, n.20, London, June 1957 (articles by Robert Craft, Henry Boys, Hans Keller, Roger Sessions, Roberto Gerhard, Maurice Perrin, David Dew).

Tempo, London, Spring and Summer 1962 (articles by Eric Walter White, Colin Mason, Donald Mitchell, Herbert Read, Benjamin Britten, Michael Tippett, A. Tcherepnin, Peter Wishart).

In French:

A critical work of fundamental importance for the understanding of Stravinsky's output as far as *Apollo Musagetes* is

BORIS DE SCHLOEZER: *Igor Strawinsky*, Editions Claude Aveline: Paris, 1929.

Other works in French worth mentioning are:

PAUL COLLAER: *Strawinsky*, Editions 'Equilibres': Brussels 1931 (a critical study of the works as far as *Mavra*).

C. F. RAMUZ: *Souvenir sur Igor Strawinsky*, Gallimard: Paris, 1929, republished by Mermod: Lausanne, 1946 (an account of the friendship and collaboration between Ramuz and Stravinsky).

PIERRE MEYLAN: *Une amitié célèbre*: C. F. Ramuz. On the same subject: *Igor Stravinsky*, Editions du Cervin: Lausanne, 1961.

MICHEL PHILLIPOT: *Igor Strawinsky: l'homme et son œuvre*, Paris, 1965. (Stravinsky as portrayed by a French *avant-garde* composer).

THEODORE STRAVINSKY: *Le Message d'Igor Strawinsky*, Lausanne, 1952.

With regard to articles in French periodicals, the following should be noted:

Special numbers of *La Revue Musicale* on Stravinsky: December 1923, with articles by Boris de Schloezer, Jean Cocteau, Michel Georges-Michel, André Coeuroy, André Levinson; and May-June 1939, with articles by André Schaeffner, Roland Manuel, Roger Désormière, Arthur Honegger, Alfred Cortot, Darius Milhaud, Pierre Souvtchinsky, Serge Lifar, Olivier Messiaen, Georges Auric, Charles-Albert Cingria, Arthur Hoérée, Gustavo Pittaluga, André Boll; article entitled 'Les Russes; Le sacre du printemps' by Jacques E. Blanche in the *Revue de Paris*, 1 December 1913; article by J. Rivière in the *Nouvelle Revue Française*, November 1913.

There is a study of the Nijinsky and Massine choreographic versions of *The Rite of Spring* in Michel Georges-Michel's *Ballet Russe*, Editions du monde nouveau; Paris, 1932. One of the issues of the *Cahiers de Belgique*, Brussels, December 1930, was also devoted to Stravinsky, with articles by Raymond Petit, André Schaeffner, Arthur Lourié, Paul Collaer, Franz Hellens. The March-April 1962 number of *Feuilles Musicales* devoted to Stravinsky, with essays by Yvonne Racz-Barblan, Pierre Meylan, Igor Stravinsky and Charles-Albert Cingria, and Constantin Regamey, is also of interest.

In German:

JACQUES HANDSCHIN: 'Strawinskys Weg', in *Neujahrblatt der Allgemeinen Musikgesellschaft*, No. 121, Zürich, 1933 (an examination of Stravinsky's output divided into periods, up to the Concerto for Violin and Orchestra).

HELMUTH FAUST: 'Strawinskys Gang in die Vergangenheit', in *Frankfurter Hefte*, VI/I, Frankfurt am Main, 1951.

HELMUT KIRCHMEYER: 'Untersuchungen zur Konstruktionstechnik Strawinskys', in *Diss*, Cologne, 1954; Regensburg, 1957.

K. G. FELLERER: 'Probleme neuer Kirchenmusik': Gedanken zu Igor Strawinskys Messe', in *Begegnung*, IV/I, Cologne, 1951.

WERNER BIESKE: 'Igor Strawinsky-Messe', 1948, in *Musik und Kirche*, XXI/I, Kassel, 1951.

RICHARD GOLDMAN: 'Igor Strawinsky Messe', in *Perspektiven*, III, Frankfurt am Main, 1953.

RICHARD GOLDMAN: 'Strawinsky in Amerika', *Musik der Zeit*, No. XII, Bonn, 1955 (essays by H. H. Stuckenschmidt, Jean Cocteau, Gian Francesco Malipiero, Arthur Honegger, Will Grohmann, Tamara Karsavina, Igor Markevitch, Ferdinando Ballo, Henry Boys, Gottfried von Einem, Charles Stuart, Alfred Cortot, Ernest Ansermet, Werner Egk, Eric Walter White, Ferenc Fricsay, Paul Sacher, Emilia Zanetti, Max See, W. H. Auden, Hans Mersmann).

NICOLAS NABOKOV: *Igor Strawinsky* (translated from English by Gisa Jopp). Colloquium Verlag Otto H. Hess: Berlin, 1964 (extremely valuable for the personal recollections of one of Stravinsky's closest friends).

HEINRICH STROBEL: *Igor Strawinsky*, Atlantis Verlag: Zürich, 1956.
HANS HEINZ STUCKENSCHMIDT: *Strawinsky und sein Jahrhundert*, Akademie der Künste: Berlin-Dahlem, 1957.
OTTO TOMEK: *Igor Strawinsky: Eine Sendereihe des Westdeutschen Rundfunks*, Cologne, 1963 (essays by Pierre Boulez, Jean Cocteau, Hans Curjel, Helmut Kirchmeyer, Heinrich Lindlar, Aurel von Milloss, K. H. Ruppel, Paul Sacher, Leo Schrade, Reinhold Schubert, Oscar Fritz Schuh, Pierre Souvtchinsky, Roman Vlad).

In Italian:

A. CIMBRO: 'Igor Strawinsky', in *Il Pianoforte*, Turin, March, 1922.
O. TIBY: 'Igor Strawinsky', ibid., August-September, 1924.
A. SCHAEFFNER: 'Storia e significato del "Sacre du printemps" di Strawinsky', in *La Rassegna Musicale*, November, 1929.
ENRICO GASPERONI: *Strawinsky*, UTES, Rome, 1948: Palermo, 1949.
GOFFREDO PETRASSI: 'Igor Strawinsky', in *Cosmopolita*, Rome, 12 April 1945.

In Russian:

Y. VAINKOP: *Stravinsky*, Ed .Triton: Leningrad, 1927.
IGOR GLEBOV: *Kniga o Stravinskom*, Ed. Triton: Leningrad, 1928 (Moscow, 1929).
BORIS YARUSTOVSKY: *Igor Strawinsky*, Union of Soviet Composers: Moscow, 1964 (German translation by Urte Härtwig, Henschel-Verlag: East Berlin, 1968).

In Spanish:

JUAN EDUARDO CIRLOT: *Igor Stravinsky: su tiempo, su significación, su obra*, G. Gili: Barcelona, 1949.
FEDERICO SOPENA: *Strawinsky; vida, obra y estilo*, Sociedad de Estudios y Publicaciones: Madrid, 1956.

General Index

Index of Stravinsky's Works   *(Principal references are italicized)*